Australia, New Zealand, and the United States

Australia, New Zealand, and the United States

INTERNAL CHANGE AND ALLIANCE RELATIONS IN THE ANZUS STATES

EDITED BY
Richard W. Baker

Under the auspices of the East-West Center

PRAEGER

New York
Westport, Connecticut
London

Library of Congress Cataloging-in-Publication Data

Australia, New Zealand, and the United States : internal change and alliance relations in the ANZUS states / edited by Richard W. Baker.
p. cm.
Includes revised papers from a conference held at the East-West Center, Honolulu, Aug. 1988.
Includes bibliographical references and index.
ISBN 0-275-93797-6
1. Australia—Politics and government—1945- —Congresses. 2. Australia—Social conditions—Congresses. 3. Australia—Economic conditions—1945- —Congresses. 4. New Zealand—Politics and government—Congresses. 5. New Zealand—Social conditions —Congresses. 6. New Zealand—Economic conditions—1945- —Congresses. 7. United States—Politics and government—1945- —Congresses. 8. United States—Social conditions—1945- —Congresses. 9. United States—Economic conditions—1945- —Congresses. 10. Australia—Military policy—Congresses. 11. New Zealand—Military policy—Congresses. 12. United States—Military policy—Congresses. I. Baker, Richard W.
JQ4011.A8 1991
990—dc20 90-45198

British Library Cataloguing in Publication Data is available.

Library of Congress Catalog Card Number: 90-45198
ISBN: 0-275-93797-6

First published in 1991

Praeger Publishers, One Madison Avenue, New York, NY 10010
An imprint of Greenwood Publishing Group, Inc.

Printed in the United States of America

The paper used in this book complies with the Permanent Paper Standard issued by the National Information Standards Organization (Z39.48-1984).

10 9 8 7 6 5 4 3 2 1

Contents

Tables and Figure

TABLES

FIGURE

Preface

The present volume is the product of the first phase of a multi-year study of the interrelationships between the ANZUS states being conducted by the East-West Center of Honolulu, Hawaii, in conjunction with the Australian Institute of International Affairs and the Institute of Policy Studies at Victoria University of Wellington. The project examines the evolution of the relationships among the three countries during the four decades of the ANZUS alliance, and the implications of these changing relationships for the Asia-Pacific region. Although their security alliance has been the major feature in their official relations for most of this period, the study is intended to look more broadly at the full range of interrelationships among the societies as they have evolved during the period of the alliance.

The first phase of the project, leading to this volume, focused on sociopolitical change in the three nations and changing perceptions of their national roles and relationships.

The second phase looks at economic changes in the three countries and their economic interrelationships. The final phase of the project examines the three countries' changing roles and policies in the Asia-Pacific region and the elements of commonality and difference that have emerged in their approaches to the region of which they are all a part.

The project has taken an international and interdisciplinary approach. Teams of experts from academic, government, and other backgrounds from each of the countries were assembled for each phase. Research papers were commissioned, and the team members and other resource persons were brought together in a conference to review the papers and discuss the major issues. The first project conference was held at the East-West Center in Honolulu in August 1988. The chapters in this volume are revised versions of papers presented at the Honolulu conference, and the additional material included in each section as well as the final section of the volume are based in part on the conference discussions.

All of the authors deserve profound thanks for their research and their insights which provided the indispensable building blocks for the conference and this book. The many contributions of the other conference participants are also gratefully acknowledged.

The Australia-New Zealand-U.S. Relations Project is fortunate to have the assistance of a group of senior advisers from each country who have consented to provide overall guidance to the organizers as well as to review the major findings of the project. They are: from Australia Dr. Stuart Harris, Professor Dame Leonie Kramer, Sir Russel Madigan, and Mr. Bob White; from New Zealand Mr. Noel V. Lough, CMG, Rt. Hon. Sir Wallace Rowling, KCMG, Rt. Hon. Brian Talboys, CH, and Ms. Sue Wood; and from the United States Professor Henry Albinski, Mr. Raymond F. Johnson, and Mr. James A. Kelly. All serve in their personal capacities and not as official representatives of any organizations with which they may be associated. The organizers wish to express their sincere appreciation to the advisers for their contributions to the conception and implementation of the project.

Among the many individuals who assisted with the conference and the subsequent preparation of this volume, I would particularly like to thank Mrs. Mendl Djunaidy and Ms. Sheree Groves of the East-West Center for assistance with overall project and conference arrangements; Ms. Sylvia Tonkin of the Australian Institute of International Affairs and Ms. Verna Adams of the Institute of Policy Studies for administrative support from Canberra and Wellington; and especially Mrs. Dorine McConnell and Ms. Dorothy Villasenor of the East-West Center for the painstaking work of processing multiple revisions of the manuscript in preparation for publication.

Finally, I would like to express my deep gratitude to my fellow organizers of the project: Professor Gary Hawke, director of the Institute of Policy Studies; Dr. Richard Higgott, director of the Australian Institute of International Affairs; and Dr. Charles Morrison, coordinator of the International Relations Program at the East-West Center. Without their encouragement, support, and counsel, neither the project nor this volume would have been possible.

Introduction

The ANZUS alliance, concluded in 1951, brought together in formal security cooperation three states that shared a remarkable degree of commonality in their heritages as well as a history of contact and associations between them that could be traced virtually to their founding as colonial settlements. Although the wartime partnership that evolved into the formal alliance was born of security exigencies, the common English language and cultural roots of the three societies made cooperation seem more natural and simpler to manage than would otherwise have been the case. In all three countries, there was an assumption of fundamental shared values. All three saw themselves as the representatives and repositories of the Western democratic system in the Pacific, the system they had fought to defend in World War II and thought to preserve through postwar cooperation.

The assumption of commonality was undoubtedly only partially valid even in 1951. The period of wartime cooperation showed that a common language did not erase sometimes sharp differences in national sentiments and approaches, and that a shared preference for democratic systems did not automatically translate into agreement on postwar political arrangements in the region.

Nevertheless, through the years of the Cold War, including the Korean conflict and well into the Vietnam period, the shared and relatively unquestioned assumptions of commonality generally carried the alliance relationships without serious difficulty.

However, throughout these four decades, all three societies have been evolving in individual and sometimes dramatic ways. Changes have occurred in their demographic makeups, their political agendas, and their outlooks on their international roles, security situations, and appropriate national policies. The crisis within the alliance precipitated by the 1984 election of a government in New Zealand committed to a non-nuclear security policy provided a dramatic illustration of the degree to which differences in perceptions had developed on key issues relating to mutual cooperation.

That the acuteness and intractability of the U.S.-New Zealand differences came as a surprise to most people in all three countries was testimony to the persistence of the assumption of commonality. It also showed the extent to which that presumption had distracted attention from the processes of sociopolitical change which had come to affect important aspects of the alliance consensus. At the same time, less dramatic but nevertheless troublesome problems in U.S.-Australian and Australian-New Zealand relations reinforce the case that there is a need for an improved and more sophisticated understanding within each society of the dynamics of the others and of their respective evolving conceptions of national interest.

This volume does not attempt to examine in any detail the specific controversies and issues which have been the recent preoccupation of policymakers and/or headline writers. It is not, in fact, a study of ANZUS as a security alliance per se. Rather, it attempts to trace the longer-term evolutionary trends in the three societies over the four decades of the alliance and to identify the key elements in the national experiences and outlooks that have influenced the nature and conduct of the relationships among the three partners. It also attempts to draw a balance between the elements of distinctiveness and of similarity among these experiences, and to project the implications for the future of the relationships. It is hoped in this way that this book can contribute to improved understanding in each of the societies of the others, and perhaps that it might also make some contribution to the management of relations among them.

The work is organized in four sections. The first three sections present individual country essays and integrating commentary on the changes in the societies, politics, and national self-images and attitudes respectively. The final section looks at implications for the relationships.

It should be noted that each of the individual essays in this volume presents the perspective of its author. Although each of the authors has had the full benefit of all the papers and of exchanges with the other writers, no attempt has been made to induce an artificial homogeneity of views in the final product. There are in fact significant differences on some points, and conflicting positions are described and credited in many instances.

Nevertheless, it is also true that the authors are drawn overwhelmingly from the cultural mainstreams of their societies. It is believed that the views presented here are fairly representative of informed opinion, but other perspectives—some quite different—could be asserted, and no claim is made that this range of views reflects the full possible spectrum.

SECTION I

Social Dynamics

The chapters in this section look at the major social trends in the three countries over the four decades of the ANZUS alliance. The primary interest is in identifying those changes that have had important effects on the national consciousness and politics as well as the world views of each country. Such factors as immigration and emigration flows, changing ethnic compositions and associated cultural mixes, the roles of women and minorities, rural–urban population shifts, age distributions, and education, skill, and employment patterns can all be part of this picture.

The three country chapters and the concluding commentary make clear that the relative significance of these factors has varied in the experience of each of the three countries, as all three societies have undergone major transformations over the period.

Robert Catley describes Australia's evolution from a sparsely populated, self-consciously and somewhat insecurely Anglo-Saxon nation located off the Asian continent to a much more populous, more ethnically diverse and independent-minded, but economically troubled nation now seeking—though still with some trepidation—to integrate itself into the Asia-Pacific region. He sees the period of the Whitlam Labour government of the early 1970s as a watershed in which new social and ethnic patterns, among other factors, began to be reflected in a variety of ways in national policies.

Harvey Franklin's chapter documents a series of demographic and social changes in New Zealand which have compounded the problems of a dramatic shift in government policy from the corporatist/welfare state system in place since the 1930s to the more competition-oriented approach introduced after 1984 by the Lange Labour government. Issues of unemployment, out-migration, and the search for a new accommodation with the country's Maori people and cultural heritage stand out. Franklin questions whether New Zealand society as a whole has really accepted the case for, and the associated social costs of, the changes which the leadership believes are necessary in order to regain the international economic competitiveness on which the country's economic prosperity continues to depend.

William Chafe charts the postwar evolution of U.S. society from the unprecedented affluence of the 1950s under the aegis of a "liberal consensus" on capitalism and reform, through the upheavals of the 1960s when the civil rights, women's, and student/antiwar movements challenged the prevailing structures, to the ascendancy after 1968 of a new "conservative consensus," which he sees as rejecting the need for further reform. He believes that the country has not yet come to grips with the limits to U.S. power, which became evident in the mid-1970s. Neither has it come to terms with the problems posed by a growing gap between those with a stake in the system and an increasingly entrenched and desperate underclass.

Finally, in his concluding comment Gary Hawke stresses that the numerous similarities and interconnections among the societies and their experiences over these decades should not be allowed to obscure the equally significant differences between them and their unique situations and stories. In terms of social evolution, he sees the three countries traveling broadly parallel and interrelated routes, but from different starting points and at different speeds. These are probably not, he believes, likely to lead to standardized end results.

1

Australia: Social Dynamics and International Orientation

ROBERT CATLEY

In 1945 Australia considered itself a white, Anglo-Saxon nation of seven-and-a-half million people, sparsely populated and located off the Asian continent. It was very self-conscious of that description. Almost all its politicians, business leaders, and opinion formers were Anglo-Celtic males; its aboriginal inhabitants had no place in the power structure and were not even counted in the census. A cautious, statist, economic growth-oriented Labor government had held power in Canberra since 1941. Eighty percent of the population lived in the six major cities and its annual growth rate had been slowed to less than 1 percent during the previous fifteen years through a combination of depression and war. The government determined to industrialize the country to avoid the fate of a primary producing economy falling victim to a world depression. To assist this process, for both economic and strategic reasons, it began a program of immigration to increase the population.

It was also a victorious power and a member of the empire of one of the supposed three great powers, Britain. But it had been greatly scarred by the experience of war and the first attempted invasion since European colonization. The overnight collapse of British East Asian power, for so the sinking of the *Repulse* and the *Prince of Wales* appeared, had left its strategic thinking, deeply influenced by race and ideology, receptive to—indeed impatient for—a formal alliance with Anglo-Saxon United States, though this was momentarily disguised by Minister for External Affairs Evatt's grandstanding (Renouf 1983). This alliance it achieved six years later when the ANZUS treaty was concluded. It was ill-prepared for the decolonization of Asia and the collapse of the long-standing European hegemony on that continent.

By 1988 the Australian population had more than doubled to over sixteen million and its ethnic composition was greatly altered in the process. Its diversity, which now reflected the injection of over four million migrants and their offspring, was recognized in its official policy of multiculturalism. It was even more urbanized. Australia's cautious, deregulatory, growth-oriented Labor government was firmly committed to improving the social and political standing of its women, aboriginals, and ethnic communities, whose votes it by and large received. It attempted to revise the effects of industrialization based on state regulation and protection by making its economy more efficient and more closely integrated with the Asia-Pacific region, the fastest growing regional component of the world economy. But it remained heavily dependent on primary products for export earnings and the 1980s decline in their terms of trade had created severe balance-of-payments problems and left a foreign debt legacy of over 30 percent of the country's gross domestic product (GDP). It was a regional power of some but declining standing, as the growth rate in its indices of national power was lower than those of many of the states in the region to its north. It remained linked to Britain only by diminished flows of culture, capital, migrants, and constitutional forms. It was firmly committed to its alliance with the United States but in a form modified by its simultaneous embrace of the doctrine of self-reliant self-defense. It faced its new status as what the minister for foreign affairs had called an Asian country with great trepidation. Those few of its population who seriously considered that prospect mused periodically on whether its status might be Argentinian, "banana republic," or "the poor white trash of Asia."

These changes were brought about by a combination of social processes and political action, and it is the interaction of the two that deserves our attention. In the political sphere the life of the ANZUS alliance has witnessed four main periods. The first involved the era of Liberal-Country Party rule, which lasted from 1949 to 1972. It was a period of great political stability, but one marked by considerable underlying social and economic change, growth, and dislocation. Some of the negative aspects of these changes were united into the political alliance which the Labor Party put into a voting bloc to win the December 1972 election. The second period witnessed a Labor government led by Gough Whitlam, which marked a turning point in Australian history. During the third period of Liberal-Country (then National) Party rule under Malcolm Fraser from 1975–83, the clock was not turned back. Indeed on many issues—multiculturalism, China, the Third World, southern Africa, human rights, immigration—one is struck by the policy continuities between two administrations that were, for different reasons, desperate to assert their dissimilarities. The fourth period has seen a Labor government led by Bob Hawke, of quite different ideological complexion from that of its social democratic predecessor, though on many foreign policy issues continuities again abound.

This periodization attributable to political processes reflects other changes of a demographic and social nature that deserve attention. It would be cause for surprise if the doubling of the population, over half of which may be attributed to migration from countries of quite diverse cultures and strategic concerns, did not produce some change in national perspective. Further, the increased demands for greater political power for both women and aboriginals, which have been met in part, may have also had their impact on national consciousness and politics. Finally, the same period has witnessed a massive expansion of the tertiary education sector and the communications industry, whose twin development has expanded the politically attentive public and intellegentsia broadly defined. It is around these themes of social and intellectual processes and political power that the diplomatic and strategic orientation of Australia during the four periods of ANZUS may be examined.

THE 1950S AND 1960S: MIGRATION, WHITE AUSTRALIA, AND CONSERVATISM

The period of Liberal-Country Party rule, 1949–72, coincided with the bipolar world of the Cold War and ended almost precisely with the formal outbreak of detente, Nixon's visits to Beijing and Moscow, and SALT I. The Australian alignment with the West was represented by a series of agreements with the major Western powers. Some—like the Australia, New Zealand, and (the British in) Malaya agreement (ANZAM)—were concluded by the postwar Labor government in 1948; others—like ANZUS and the South-East Asia Collective Defense Treaty (SEATO)—were concluded by the coalition (Richelson and Ball 1985). But it would be wrong to see in this the bones of a wholly bipartisan policy. It is true that Labor was anxious to gain a U.S. alliance and supported the ANZUS treaty when it was concluded in 1951. But Labor was not united on this issue and in the mid-1950s it split, partly as a result.

The division of the Labor Party into an ALP (Australian Labor Party) led by moderate leftist Evatt (and then after 1960 by Arthur Calwell), and a smaller, vociferously anti-Communist Democratic Labor Party (DLP) was one of the key reasons that the coalition held power until 1972. The DLP was essentially a Catholic party that in Europe would be readily recognized as a Christian socialist or Christian democrat party. Heavily represented in its ranks were Irish Australians who had effectively formed the ALP in the late nineteenth century and then split it over the issue of conscription in World War I. The party also received support from the Catholic Church and Catholic immigrants who were arriving in the country in great numbers through the 1950s and 1960s, and from East Europeans. East European refugees had been recruited by Labor Immigration Minister Calwell, despite the electorate's reluctance to accept migrants, but out of passionate anti-Communist sentiments they proceeded to vote overwhelmingly not for Labor but for the coalition or the DLP.

This is not to say that settlement policies for the migrants of the 1945–72 period were benign. Immigrants were clearly expected to integrate, and little deference was paid to their native cultures. They formed a critical part of the working class that was concentrated in the least attractive occupations but underrepresented in labor councils. They received few settlement services other than temporary accommodation in unattractive migrant hostels. They contributed greatly to the stock of entrepreneurs and over-achievers in the Australian population. But, at least until 1972, they voted less, and voted less for Labor, than otherwise might have been the case for a working-class constituency of that kind (Collins 1975). When Labor returned to office in 1972, however, it did so with "ethnic Australians," as they had become known, as a key constituent in the Whitlam voting bloc.

The largest source of migrants, however, remained the British Isles. There is some evidence of a tendency for them to vote Liberal, probably in accord with the upwardly mobile aspirations that usually accompany the act of migration. They also confirmed that migrants could and would assimilate into white Australia. The non-English speakers would take only a little longer. Migration has never been popular in Australia. British migration is least unpopular and the percentages expressing opposition merely rise as the country of origin becomes more exotic. The trick for any migration minister is to overcome that resentment, which is easiest when the economy is most buoyant. During the long boom of 1951–72 this was the situation, such that as many as 150,000 annually entered the country in the late 1960s. But they did so without disturbing Australia's ideological or racial view of itself.

Until 1966, Australia maintained an official "White Australia" policy. This description ignored the aboriginals and other races who had entered earlier, or those few who circumvented the rules. Essentially the influx was ethnically European and did little to disturb Australia's view of itself as a white nation located near Asia. Much of the intense support for the U.S. alliance, indeed much of the fear of Asian Communism, can be ascribed to motives as racial as they were ideological. China, the nineteenth-century source of unwanted migrants and epitome of the "Asian hordes" demonology, had assumed a Red guise by the time Australia sent troops to Vietnam to stop "the downward thrust of Asian communism between the Indian and Pacific Oceans."[1]

This ethnic dimension of Australian perceptions of the outside world not only politically consolidated the myriad agreements and treaties that bound Australia to the other major "Anglo-Saxon powers." It also ensured that in the long process of decolonization Australia was a singularly insensitive observer and participant. It generally supported the colonial presence in Asia, arguing against independence movements unless led by impeccably conservative politicians. Australia's early Indochina policy was formed in some measure by a desire to delay the departure of the French and later by a more concerted attempt to ensure they were replaced by the Americans. Relations with Indonesia were soured throughout much of the Sukarno period, despite a promising beginning, by Australia's support for the Dutch presence in West New Guinea.

But perhaps the most visible symbol of Australia's desire to cling to a world now passing was its intention, it seemed, to be among the last great colonial powers with Papua New Guinea, and the last supporter of the South African contention that apartheid was a domestic issue. Australia permitted the white-minority Smith regime of Rhodesia to set up an information office in Sydney after its Unilateral Declaration of Independence. The British were not alone in having a "kith and kin" dimension to their strategic thinking.

In 1966 the "White Australia" policy was officially abandoned. This was to a degree disingenuous. While there was an increase in migration from Asia, it was restricted largely to educated, skilled, professional, or business persons and even then allowed only on a small scale, in contrast to the mass migration from Europe for the following six years. As a result, Asian migrants were encountered by the general population mainly in occupations of high socioeconomic status.

It should finally be observed of this period that the political elite who conducted Australia's strategic business were singularly British in style. Again, a heavy representation of Irish-British had to be acknowledged, but the observation remains true. Prime Minister Menzies's allegiance to the

British Crown has been widely documented; many of his ministers, senior public servants, and military personnel were attached to Britain by training, education, past residence, or imperial honors. This was not incompatible with a strong strategic connection with the United States, since the British had themselves adopted the same strategic posture in the 1940s and were bound to the United States in all manner of ways. Indeed, as the British determined to withdraw from east of Suez and join the European Economic Community (EEC) it perhaps seemed only natural that British Australia should align with Britain's successor in East Asia, the United States.

The decisive turning point for the strategic posture built on a "White Australia" was the defeat in Indochina. In 1965 Australia sent forces to Vietnam to encourage the U.S. government into a major military presence, interspersing (mostly) white U.S. soldiers between Australia and the source of the trouble, China (Sexton 1981). At the subsequent election in 1966 the ALP was decisively rejected by a bellicose electorate. As it became clearer that the war was being lost, however, opposition mounted. By 1969 there was nearly a Labor election victory and polls by 1970 were showing a majority against the war. The troops started coming home in accord with electoral considerations and the Nixon Doctrine. In the ensuing disenchantment a Labor victory was won in December 1972.

THE WHITLAM WATERSHED: NEW COALITION, NEW POLICY ORIENTATIONS

Many of the social forces unleashed by the victorious voting bloc constructed by the Labor party would never go back in their box. In the last four years of coalition rule the government had outlived its utility and its opponents' checklist of reform was formidable indeed. But many had been bred by the coalition itself. Its rigid commitment to the Indochina war, where it was more militant than the United States, and its non-recognition of China alienated a generation of the intelligentsia. Much of the opposition to the war originated, particularly in the early years, within a tertiary education system which the coalition parties had generously funded. The universities bred a generation hostile to the "White Australia" posture in a post-colonial world and sympathetic to Third World aspirations in general. From 1970 onward, almost any Third World political movement espousing radical language could be sure of an Australian constituency and access to the ALP.

This became even more pronounced as the migration program widened its sources and integration was abandoned as official policy. By the late

1960s articulate ethnic Australians, first- or second-generation migrants, were emerging on the political landscape with a catalogue of complaints that ranged from settlement services (or lack of them) to lack of political representation. Whitlam and other Labor figures were able to fill halls with ethnic audiences and promises of a new deal.

But the Whitlam coalition was wider than ethnicity. Here a number of points need to be made about its social, ethnic, and ideological components (Lloyd and Reid 1974). Sociologically, the dominant component in the Labor coalition remained the working class. This class is notoriously difficult to define, particularly when it is acknowledged that there is an extremely high correlation between voting Liberal and a white-collar or clerical occupation, which might otherwise be defined as working class. Nonetheless, Whitlam gained a high proportion of working-class votes partly because of the erosion of the DLP, partly because his party's policy program became more pragmatic in its appeal to workers of whatever status, and partly because it was designed to attract working women and ethnics who saw themselves as disadvantaged, rather than upwardly mobile workers. It also incorporated the increasingly vocal movement in support of aboriginal emancipation.

In this context some mention should also be made of the political Left. Historically, Australia has usually contained a disproportionately large radical movement. At the height of the Grand Alliance in 1944, it is estimated that the Communist Party of Australia (CPA) had 23,000 members and was probably proportionately the most influential Communist party in the English-speaking world. By the early 1970s the party had, despite some rejuvenation during the Vietnam War, sunk into the obscurity its continuing splits and ideological gyrations deserved. Nonetheless, the radical tradition was maintained by the emergence from the antiwar movement of a New Left, similar to that in the United States but with an Australian agenda. While this movement had little influence in Australian society as a whole, it was (and remains) extremely influential in some sectors of Australian political life, notably the ALP, the trade unions, the intelligentsia broadly defined, and the Uniting Church. This reorganized Left, with its traditional industrial component subsumed into a larger coalition, remains influential in Australian foreign policy formulation. This is particularly true during periods of Labor government, when its influence usually extends to cabinet level.

The Whitlam years faced four serious changes in the international environment: the culmination of the U.S. defeat in Indochina; the high water mark of detente; the consolidation of the Third World solidarity movement; and the great economic dislocation associated with OPEC. Its responses involved a combination of the dynamic interplay between the component parts of the Labor coalition and the relevant ministerial personalities.

The U.S. government had accepted by about 1970 that it was unlikely to achieve victory in Vietnam. This was not so obvious in Australia, although the government withdrew Australian forces at a somewhat more rapid pace than the Americans. The first serious crisis in Washington-Canberra relations during the Whitlam years occurred in Christmas 1972, when members of the Cabinet, including Jim Cairns of the Left, publicly denounced U.S. bombing of Hanoi. The government could hardly have acted otherwise in view of the status of the peace movement within its political coalition. But that was not the end of the matter. The Left argued for the government to adopt a more militant position in Indochina and within the U.S. alliance as a whole. The government was reluctant to go any further than it had for fear of alienating the United States and the overwhelming majority of Australians who wished to remain in the alliance, and out of the conviction of many senior ministers that the alliance should be retained.

The Whitlam government welcomed detente in both its East Asian and European manifestations and adopted what it termed an even-handed approach to the superpowers. Detente coincided remarkably well with the political ascendency of the anti-Cold War coalition represented by the Whitlam government.

The same could be said for the emergence of the ideologically triumphant Third World in the international political system. The increasing number of postwar, post-colonial states in Asia and Africa aligned with others who had been decolonized earlier, particularly in Latin America, around a program of political and economic demands on the advanced industrial countries, many of whom had a colonialist past, for a realignment of world wealth to the Third World's benefit. The Whitlam coalition was fertile ground for this propaganda, which combined a general redistributive program with an antiracism that pro-Aboriginal and ethnic activists could associate with, anti-imperialist policies the national liberation solidarity groups viewed as important, and the generally anti-exploitative policies demanded by the women's action groups.

The results of this pro-Third World sentiment from within the ranks of government supporters were not always simple. In the case of the decolonization process as a whole, it was clear which direction it took the government. Canberra for the first time became a leading critic of South

Africa, both for its apartheid regime and for its hegemony across southern Africa in general. It moved very quickly to eliminate its own status as a colonial power, and Papua New Guinea became independent in 1975. When the Portuguese radical military regime came to power in 1974 on a platform of evacuating its empire, Canberra quickly expressed some sympathy, a posture it maintained toward Portugal's African colonies. East Timor, however, proved more complex.

Since the 1965 coup and counter-coup the Indonesian regime, though pro-Western, received a decidedly bad coverage in Australian Left and intellectual circles. In 1975 this situation was greatly worsened when Indonesia invaded, pacified, and annexed East Timor. In the process five Australian journalists were killed, probably by the Indonesian army. The intense dislike for the Indonesian regime current in the Left intelligentsia spilt immediately into a media industry previously receptive but now incensed at the death of its own. This coalition of anti-Indonesian sentiment was buttressed over the next few years by refugees arriving from East Timor, either directly or through Portugal. This legacy of hostility was to survive.

In the Middle East, the period 1967–74 was one in which a fundamental realignment took place. Israel, for long the darling of the Left, was displaced by the Palestinians as the focus of Left attention in Australia. Israel became a pariah to the Left by the time of the 1973 Yom Kippur War.[2] First, it had won the 1967 war; in so doing and by occupying captured Arab territory it became both a dominant and a colonial state. Second, the Palestinians had worked assiduously within the Third World to gain majority support for their case. This was effective by 1974 in getting Third World states to equate Israeli Zionism with imperialism and racism. Finally, within Australia growing Left support for the Palestine Liberation Organization (PLO) was buttressed by an infusion of Arab money into the Left and by Arab immigration.

The Whitlam government was in office during a commodity price boom closely associated with the oil price rise orchestrated by OPEC. Whereas for two decades Australia had aligned with the First World for reasons of culture and ideology, it became clear that there might be good economic reasons for Australia to associate with Third World groupings on issues of the exchange of commodities and manufactured goods. Indeed, it became part of Australian policy to pursue "minerals diplomacy."

In short, the Whitlam government marked the end of Australia as a British or white country on the edge of Asia but linked economically and strategically to the Western, Anglo-Saxon alliance. Its status had become more ambivalent. For good economic, some social, and understandable ethnic reasons, a constituency that linked Australian interests with the fortunes of the Third World had come into existence. For understandable political reasons concerning the disaster in Vietnam, the alliance with the United States had come into question. The detente with China and the Soviet bloc initiated by the United States received enthusiastic support from that majority of Australians who had become disillusioned by the military opposition to Communism in Vietnam.

This new diversity in external orientation was only enhanced by the new Labor policy of multiculturalism. The policy came into existence at the time of Whitlam but it has been the official policy of all federal and most state Liberal and Labor governments since. What is multiculturalism? The idea has been the subject of various definitional wrangles that will not greatly assist an understanding of its impact on policy (Phillips and Houston 1984). In one sense it consists of a policy of enabling the great diversity of cultures brought to Australia by migrants from over 100 countries to coexist alongside one another. Successive governments have established ministers for ethnic affairs at state and federal levels and various ethnic bodies, usually known as the Ethnic Affairs Commission, at state level. Public funding has been provided for a wide diversity of activities undertaken by ethnic communities ranging from trade union liaison officers to nursing homes and cultural festivals. These activities have steadily grown since 1973, partly as a byproduct of the different parties' efforts to win the ethnic vote or, more accurately, the votes of different ethnic communities. But another process is also at work.

The multiculturalism industry has very little impact on non-ethnic Australians, who comprise about 80 percent of the population. True, they are affected by ethnic festivals, restaurants, shops, and so on. But the wide variety of media communications in foreign languages, ethnic community associations, and even soccer clubs has a limited impact on the community at large. Similarly, the government also provides a wide range of services to ethnic groups which have the effect of producing integration rather than multiculturalism, including English-language teaching and compulsory schooling for ethnic children conducted in English. And of course all applications for resources from public funding need to be made by ethnic communities to governmental agencies through well-established political processes.

The longer-term effect of the policy of multiculturalism on ethnic communities is in fact the same as that of the policy of neglect which preceded it—integration. Most ethnic communities have become integrated into Australian society by the second generation, exhibiting social behaviour in terms of unemployment, birth and marriage rates, criminality, and so on very similar to that of long-settled Australians (aboriginals excepted). Multiculturalism indeed may assist integration by enabling non-English-speaking communities to relate quickly to the existing power and social structure and helping their offspring to become part of it. There is also some limited evidence that the era of multiculturalism has eroded the segmented labor market, which had witnessed the migrants of the 1940s, 1950s, and 1960s entering low-skilled, low-paid occupations in greatly disproportionate numbers. But this may be as much the result of more careful migrant recruiting on a skills basis in the post-1973 period (Chapman and Miller 1985).[3]

But this should not gainsay the fact that, notwithstanding the ready integration of millions of non-British migrants into Australian society, that society itself also changed in the process. It became increasingly difficult to automatically view Australia as an unqualified member of a white man's club. For while the Whitlam Labor government cut back heavily on immigration, as part of an economic program designed to upgrade Australian industry with more skilled labor rather than imported unskilled migrant labor, it sought to ensure that those who did enter were not selected by racist criteria. This became even more apparent during the term of the government led by Malcolm Fraser, in which mass Asian immigration became a reality.

THE FRASER YEARS: CONSERVATISM AND CONTINUITY

The return of the coalition parties to government in November 1975 until their defeat in March 1983 did not mean that the clock was turned back to the 1960s. True, on certain issues the coalition quickly reaffirmed its previous policy. This was perhaps most notable on the question of the alliance with the United States, for which both the prime minister and the foreign minister, Andrew Peacock, restated their unequivocal commitment and renewed for long periods the agreements relating to U.S. strategic installations in Australia (Ball 1980). In other areas, however, the situation had changed and the coalition parties continued some of Whitlam's initiatives, though in modified form.

The Liberal Party in particular took up and continued the policy of multiculturalism. Some ethnic communities, notably those from Eastern Europe, had long been closer to the Liberals. As the period of settlement of other communities lengthened, so their upwardly mobile members found themselves rubbing shoulders with Liberals in business and society. The Greek community was deeply divided, with one section leftist and the other more conservative in orientation. Italian names started to crop up in Liberal pre-selection ballots with greater regularity. It was becoming apparent that while many ethnic communities had voted Labor, this vote was not locked in, and that as these communities became more integrated into Australian society they increasingly voted on the same basis as did other Australians: class, occupation, personality, special issues, and so on.

During the late 1970s, Australia hosted a large number of political refugees for the first time since the 1940s. They came from two principal sources: Indochina and the Middle East. They were to form the two most vocal, new ethnic communities in Australia by the 1980s.

The Indochinese community in Australia is predominantly Vietnamese, although there are also both Cambodians and Laotians, who tend to be much less politically active. The history of recent Vietnamese migration to Australia has been related elsewhere and may be briefly recapitulated (Grant 1983; Viviani 1984). The conquest of South Vietnam by the National Liberation Front (NLF) in 1975 was quickly followed by unification. By 1976 large numbers of Vietnamese were leaving Vietnam, mostly by boat to first-destination refuges in Southeast Asia and Hong Kong. Some of the "boat people" arrived directly in Australia, usually at Darwin. Most, however, were rechannelled from host refuges in Thailand, Malaysia, or elsewhere in Asia to Australia. The international community became sufficiently alarmed at the number of boat people and their treatment on the high seas (and on arrival in some countries) to convene a special conference on the subject in Geneva. As a result, Vietnam agreed to orderly departure routines and Australia, together with the United States and other countries, agreed to receive a designated annual number of these refugees. Since Australian immigration regulations permit very extensive family reunion rights, the Vietnamese community has been greatly augmented by orderly departure of immigrants to Australia.

By 1980, a similar problem had arisen with respect to Kampuchean refugees who had fled to Thailand from the Pol Pot regime, in front of the invading Vietnamese army, or later. They formed a refugee community of perhaps half a million people who initially had some hope of returning to a post-Vietnam-occupation Kampuchea. Again third countries, including Australia, agreed to take numbers of refugees.

During the period of the Fraser government, these Vietnamese were in little political evidence in Australia. They did periodically demonstrate against visiting officials from Hanoi, got into scuffles with leftist demonstrators, and formed forlorn societies dedicated to overthrowing Communist rule in their native land. They had little direct effect on government diplomacy, however, since they very much approved the government's policy, which was broadly hostile to Hanoi and the Soviet Union. In 1979 the government cut off its small aid program to Vietnam following its occupation of Kampuchea. It is generally thought that, as with the East European political refugees in the 1950s, the Vietnamese voted overwhelmingly for the Liberal Party until 1984.

The Lebanese refugee question arose when that country collapsed into a collection of warring tribes in 1976–77. About 40,000 people were to flee to Australia as a result of its refugee program and the attendant family reunion provisions. While there had long been Muslims in Australia—Afghan camel drivers had been widespread in the nineteenth century and Turks had been trickling into the country since the 1960s—this was the first large Muslim community to settle in Australia. Again, during the Fraser period they presented no problems for national diplomacy. Australian policy was to adopt an even-handed approach toward the Middle East conflict, a policy which in fact amounted to supporting the state of Israel while periodically criticizing some aspects of its behavior. In 1979 the government agreed to contribute a force to help implement the Camp David accords. While this policy was pursued, and while the Lebanese Muslim community was newly settled and not familiar with Australian political processes, it remained quiescent. This was to change in the 1980s.

The Indochinese and Lebanese communities were part of the growing constituency of Australians who had originated from the Third World, though it is doubtful that they have yet had any great impact on Australia's Third World diplomacy. Indeed, it is frequently surmised that the Fraser government's policies in this regard were primarily driven by the personality of the prime minister himself (Harries 1979).

Fraser's southern African diplomacy (Higgott 1983) may be, however, more directly related to domestic considerations. The coalition had returned to power as the aboriginal community was becoming better organized and more vociferous in its demands for access to political power in general and to land rights in particular. This coincided with the rise of Third World power in the United Nations and elsewhere, branding Israel with South Africa (and Taiwan) as "pariah states." This was a condition that Australia could ill afford but to which the dreadful conditions of the aboriginal people could readily propel it. The Fraser government actively pursued the anti-apartheid cause in South Africa, Fraser made an immense personal contribution to the evolution of a black government in Zimbabwe, and Canberra aligned itself very much with the black frontline states. Certainly there was a degree of grandstanding in this performance, and until the 1980s there was no certainty that the post-Fraser coalition parties would maintain this posture, but it was a deliberate course. Australia could not again afford to be linked into a white man's club.

But if the Fraser government took over many of the initiatives of the Whitlam government (albeit in modified form), on two counts the differences were very striking: relations between the superpowers and multinational investment in Australia.

Fraser was not a supporter of detente, which he regarded as providing the Soviet Union with the opportunity to expand its strength and sphere of influence. For the most part his reservations fell on deaf ears until the Soviet invasion of Afghanistan in December 1979 led to a turnabout in U.S. policy. Nonetheless, the effect within Australia was surprisingly limited and although Fraser talked at one stage of the danger of war in three days, defense hardly figured in the 1980 federal election. The coalition won narrowly by focusing on the capital gains tax proposal of the ALP.

The question of foreign investment involved more domestic controversy. During the 1970s much of the Australian Left had come to regard multinational corporations as entities capable of supplanting the powers of the democratic state (Wheelwright and Crough, 1982). The Fraser government was to relax many of these restrictions, including those on foreign ownership, exports, and price negotiations. The Left, the ALP, and many unions were hostile to this process in part for ideological reasons, but the conflict also had a geographic dimension.

The minerals and energy sectors had grown strongly since the mid-1960s, chiefly by servicing the growing East Asian economies, notably Japan. They received an additional fillip during the OPEC-initiated commodity price boom of the mid-1970s. By 1980 the coalition parties were anticipating a new mining boom and borrowed heavily internationally to provide the infrastructure. The government also increased the immigration intake to supply labor. The industry was chiefly located in the outer states of Queensland and Western Australia, and the Northern Territory, and it was from these areas that the political lobbying for free trade originated. The heartland of the ALP, the Left, and of organized labor (that is, New South Wales, Victoria, and South Australia) stood to benefit less from these changes and feared a drain of resources away from the population centers of the southeast of the country. Even the Liberal Party in these regions showed signs of apprehension about a minerals boom. For some time there was a distinct geographic component to the political spectrum in Australia which came to an end with the collapse of the minerals boom in 1981 and the onset of the global economic recession of 1982–83.

THE HAWKE GOVERNMENT: LABOR TAKES THE CENTER

As in the world recession of 1974–75, so in the world recession of 1982–83 almost no government in a democratic country was reelected. The major exception was Britain's Thatcher government, which had just won a war. The Fraser government followed the rule and was beaten by the ALP, led by Bob Hawke, in March 1983. Hawke had taken over as leader only in February 1983, replacing Bill Hayden, who bitterly observed that Fraser could have been beaten by a "drover's dog" in such an economic recession. The Hawke government was to stand in sharp contrast to its Whitlam-led predecessor.

In order to consider the effect of social and demographic factors on Australia's current international orientation, it is necessary first to discuss the structure of government under the Labor Party during the 1980s. Within a year of the Labor federal victory the ALP formally resolved itself into three factions: Right, Centre Left and Left. In the federal caucus of Labor parliamentarians the numerical proportions have been, roughly, the Right with just under half, and the Left and Centre Left around a quarter each. In the area of external relations the Left has had almost no say in Labor government policy. With the exception of getting the government to reverse its offer to assist the United States in testing the MX missile, it might be argued that the Left has been irrelevant to Australia's international orientation under Labor.

Why has the political influence of the Left been so weak, particularly in such stark contrast to the Whitlam years? The Hawke/Right leadership promised to do one thing for Labor: put it in office. Once in office it made economic growth and the creation of 500,000 new jobs its chief objective. Both the Left and Centre concurred with these objectives. The Right then sought to take international policy out of domestic political debate by making the key foreign and defense policy issues bipartisan. The key issues that Labor took off the political agenda were relations with the British crown, the alliance with the United States, the hosting of joint U.S.-Australian defense facilities, and the commitment to an effective defense policy. The Left could do nothing about this since it lacked the numerical capacity, but it was given domestic portfolios where it could exercise some authority, such as housing and social security. The Centre expressed occasional doubts about policy, but these rarely amounted to much. In addition, the extra-parliamentary or non-Labor Left suffered an extraordinary collapse during the mid-1980s and after decades of decline, temporarily arrested by the anti-Vietnam War upsurge, split into half a dozen groupings of little influence. The Left had been domesticated and decimated.

This is not to say there is no Left sentiment in the country. Two senators have been elected solely on an antinuclear platform, while the Australian Democrats, who regularly return 6 to 8 senators and get 10–15 percent of the popular vote, have a strong peace plank in their platform. It might even be argued that during the Hawke government period the Democrats have become the effective Left party. The antinuclear demonstrations in 1984–85 were the biggest ever mounted, though they evaporated with Gorbachev and detente. But opinion polls have made it clear that a less demonstrative public majority favors Australia's participation in a nuclear-armed, Western alliance system. While that is the case Labor will pursue such policies. It has developed a highly effective system of committees and factions within which almost all policy decisions are cleared behind closed doors by faction managers before seeing the light of day. This approach minimizes public acrimony and squabbling and also locks the official Left leadership into government policy. One price extracted for their gaining access to limited power ministries has been compliance with the Right's foreign strategy. There is little sign of this system breaking down. But it would be the coalition parties, not the Left, who would benefit from its breakdown.

An examination of the membership of this party's power structure makes it clear very quickly that ethnic Australians and women politicians are not greatly interested in the foreign policy/defense areas. This is true despite the fact that the capable Ms. Ros Kelly became the minister assisting the minister for defense. Ethnic politicians are chiefly concerned with the immigration and ethnic affairs portfolio, while women tend to concentrate on social services, community welfare, health, and education. This is quite understandable since they are expected to nurture the ethnic and women's vote and these are the issues that chiefly concern these constituencies at large. This does not mean that ethnic communities or women as separate groups have had no influence on Australia's international orientation, but that influence has been limited or mediated by other considerations.

During the term of the Hawke Labor government, the ethnic communities as such have been overwhelmingly concerned with the issue of immigration, and to a lesser extent with multiculturalism. The immigration portfolio has been one of high profile and pressure and had five ministers in five years. It was the subject of great controversy in 1984. During the 1982–83 recession the government cut back on immigration levels, a traditional Australian response based on the argument that there were not enough jobs to go around. But the political refugee intake, of which Australia takes proportionately the largest number in the world, was little reduced and family reunion immigration rights and programs were not affected. As a result, the most recent ethnic communities to arrive formed a larger percentage of the reduced intake and these were mostly from Asia, particularly Vietnam. As a consequence, Asian immigrants briefly formed the largest source of migrants for one period in 1984. Professor Geoffrey Blainey, a widely respected historian, observed that this might endanger race relations within Australia, and a widespread public brawl ensued on the ethnic question.

The debate over Asian immigration had the potential to endanger Australia's regional status. Clearly it would be difficult to become a good neighbor integrated into the region's burgeoning economy while retaining the reputation for European racism so much associated with the colonial era and the "White Australia" policy. What made it more difficult was that opinion polls make it clear that a majority of Australians still oppose Asian immigration. The Liberals briefly flirted with support for this position and so shocked ethnic Australians that it is widely believed that despite their ideological position, Vietnamese Australians voted Labor in 1984. The issue was then defused somewhat. The Liberals adopted a policy of supporting Asian immigration; the government increased the global immigration intake and stepped up the economic skills testing component, a combination of which (together with some statistical realignment) reduced the Asian percentage of immigrants below figures that would excite alarm.[4]

But the issue of Asian immigration remains a delicate one. On the one side is the consideration that economically Australia needs increased population; of necessity many of the new people will come from Asia. In any case they may be expected to enhance Australia's chances of taking advantage of regional economic dynamism. On the other side, opponents of mass Asian migration range across the political spectrum and have widespread support. The issue requires delicate fine-tuning if it is not to upset Australia's regional aspirations.

Aside from these general considerations, ethnic issues only currently intrude seriously on external policy in three areas: the Middle East, Indochina, and South Africa. The influx of Lebanese political refugees in the 1970s has formed the basis for a domestic support group for the Palestinians. Some of the initial intake were likely Palestinians and many of the subsequent inflow, some entering under the family reunion program, were of similar origin. By the mid-1980s it was claimed that there were 250,000 Muslims in Australia. This is almost certainly an exaggeration, and 100,000 is a more plausible figure. This would make Muslims about equal in number to Jews. By the mid-1980s they had formed a PLO Information Office in Melbourne and comprised a significant proportion of the electorate in perhaps three Sydney federal seats and one in Melbourne. This served to offset somewhat the received wisdom that the Jewish community was important for electoral considerations in two Melbourne seats and one in Sydney. In terms of domestic support, therefore, Australian governments would in future be faced with a finely balanced domestic position concerning the Middle East. During the Hawke government a fairly even-handed position was adopted in which the foreign minister would meet Palestinians and criticize Israeli behavior but would not recognise the PLO. The prime minister was well known to have very strong pro-Israeli sympathies. The Socialist Left, on the other hand, had taken up the Arab cause in general and the PLO cause in particular, partly for ideological and partly for financial reasons. The ALP was balanced between these forces. The coalition parties were faced with similar electoral considerations but also had a pro-Arab component in the form of a National Party whose rural constituents were exporting in increasing numbers to a growing Middle East Arab market.

The case of Indochina was similarly complicated. The ALP had come into office with a pro-Vietnam platform to restore aid to that country, a plank inserted by the Socialist Left at the 1979 national conference. The foreign minister was faced with U.S. pressure not to implement this plank and obtained agreement from Hanoi that both would prefer Hayden to use his good offices with China and the Association of Southeast Asian Nations (ASEAN) to get a diplomatic settlement to the Kampuchean dispute and that the aid issue could be shelved. The wishes of the Australian Vietnamese community received scant attention at that stage. Then in 1984–85 two events changed the political landscape somewhat. First, Hanoi gravely embarrassed Hayden while he was in Vietnam by assuring him that its forces were not in action on the Thai border and having him make a statement to that effect; this was subsequently proved to be wrong. Second, the Vietnamese community in Australia swung heavily toward Labor at the 1984 poll when the Liberals vacillated on the "Blainey debate." The combination of these two events eliminated the mildly pro-Vietnam diplomatic position of the government. While it is difficult to be sure, census figures suggest that Vietnamese may comprise 3–5 percent of the electorate in three federal seats—one in Melbourne and two in Sydney. This, together with Hanoi's behavior, ensured that the Australian government would not do much for Vietnam.

The issue of South Africa was much clearer. The Whitlam government had shifted Australian diplomacy away from support for the white regimes of southern Africa, a posture that the Fraser government maintained. The Hawke government continued what had become a bipartisan policy throughout a long series of issues involving sporting contact, migration, and the domestic upheavals and violence that erupted in South Africa during the mid-1980s. Indeed, a special foreign affairs program of sponsoring visits by South Africans critical of South Africa was instigated. On South Africa, sentiment and self-interest coexisted to ensure that Australia was always on the militant side of the demand for sanctions in international forums. On the one side the Labor Party, the anti-racist dominant wing of the coalition parties, and all Australian ethnic communities could unite in a demand for strong action to assist the ending of apartheid. On the other hand such a policy disassociated modern Australia from the White Australia of the past, fudged the aboriginal issue in the world at large, and helped reduce the viability of an economic competitor whose exported products were almost identical to Australia's. There is little like a combination of self-interest and the convert's ideology to produce a zealot, and on the apartheid issue so did Australia and its media become.

A NEW AUSTRALIA

Australia had long ceased to be a white dominion. During the life of the ANZUS treaty it shifted irrevocably from being a self-styled European nation on the edge of Asia to a hesitantly multicultural society seeking to integrate into the Asia-Pacific region. It retained ties with its Anglo-Saxon great and powerful friends, but these were being constantly revised. These changes came in part from the unavoidable changes in the international environment, and in part from changes in the demography, society, and ideology of Australia itself. It was no longer a white man's country in a white man's world. Australia would be on its own.

NOTES

1. This is the phrase Menzies used when announcing the commitment of Australian forces to Vietnam.

2. This subject has been widely researched and canvassed by Dr. W. D. Rubinstein and Dr. R. Gouttman. Their findings can be traced in the *Australia/Israel Review* (Melbourne) over the last six years. I am grateful to Rodney Gouttman for access to his filing system.

3. Chapman and Miller, like other economists, suggest that the critical variable is duration of residence rather than prejudice.

4. See the statement by C. J. Hurford, minister for Immigration and Ethnic Affairs, Parliamentary Debates, House of Representatives, April 6, 1986.

2

New Zealand Social Dynamics: Changing Models

S. HARVEY FRANKLIN

> The smallness of New Zealand deserves a mention of its own . . . for in the national psychology of the Dominion the desire to continue small has become a dogma as sanctified as free trade to late nineteenth century Englishmen. . . . Being prosperous on the whole, and flourishing in a material sense, the few inhabitants of the Dominion have preferred to maintain their relatively high living standard by skimming the cream off a rich little country.
>
> (Leslie Lipson 1948: 495)

The facts of New Zealand's social dynamics are very much the facts of any developed country's social dynamics: the postwar baby boom, urbanization and suburbanization of the population, establishment of alternative family arrangements, emergence of minority and women's rights movements, and prospects of an aging population. In New Zealand's case, however, these changes have occurred in a total population that elsewhere amounts to the equivalent of a fair-sized metropolitan city. If New Zealand doesn't differ greatly from other countries in terms of its social dynamics, it does pose a particular problem of social scale. It also poses a problem of interpretation.

DYNAMICS AND MODELS

To understand New Zealand in the postwar era one has to appreciate that for a large proportion of the New Zealand electorate all these dynamics constitute at best a diminution of, and at worst a detraction from, a superb and unique achievement of which the New Zealanders had convinced themselves by the end of World War II: the creation of a society that, on the basis of an efficient export sector, had achieved a degree of social welfare and security, racial harmony, and social equality unparalleled elsewhere in the world; the creation of a model (I shall call it the quest model)[1] to which other nations might and in fact should aspire, and against which all developments, changes, and innovations were to be assessed. As Walter Nash, then minister of state in Washington, informed the world, and in particular the Americans in 1943, New Zealand was a working democracy, "a practical example of the kind of social organization that may well become typical of most democracies" (Nash 1943: 211). Michael Savage had earlier voiced a deep-felt, if impossible, aspiration: "The standard of living . . . should not be influenced by any external force whatever" (Brown 1962: 167).

Social dynamics—the term itself implies movement and change. But what need for change is there in a perfect society? Of course there has been change, but New Zealanders seem to have expected any change would be incorporated by the model without necessarily changing the model or the achievement it represented.

These convictions have been regularly strengthened by an array of visitors who have spoken and written in support of these achievements. I remember listening in the mid-1960s to one notable American making his first and only acquaintance with the country, telling his Auckland audience how sensible New Zealand was not to pursue the illusion of economic growth, with its inevitable outcome of private affluence amidst public squalor. How sensible it was, he said, to use the powers of government intervention to fashion a better society. It was a popular message with many New Zealanders at that time because it raised no difficulties. They had been schooled in the belief that their country had one of the highest per capita incomes in the world.[2] The fact was asserted in one of the standard histories of the time. There was almost no acknowledgement of the increasingly illusory nature of this belief.

However, as the outside world changed, as New Zealand's export industries had to face changing consumer preferences, the byproduct of affluence itself, the country's standing in the per capita stakes slipped badly. It became apparent that the country lacked the resources to accommodate the consequences of these postwar dynamics. To combat the underlying deficiencies, a different model—the deregulated model—has been introduced by the present Labour regime. In comparison with the quest model, it runs a very poor second with a considerable portion of the electorate, as the voluminous report of the Royal Commission on Social Policy makes clear. The Commission's recommendations are little more than a reaffirmation of the country's support for the old beliefs that were embodied in the quest model.

THE BABY BOOM

New Zealand experienced a postwar baby boom and the subsequent decline in family size, thus setting in motion a wave-like phenomenon that affected every aspect of economic, social, and cultural life. A long-term decline in the total fertility rate, a feature of New Zealand's social history since at least the beginning of the century, was reversed after 1935. From a low point of 2.5 births per woman, the rate rose through the war years to reach a peak of almost 4.5 births per woman in 1960. By that time total births were running at a rate of 60,000 to 65,000 per annum (currently the figure is around 50,000) and New Zealand's total fertility rate was some 20 percent above the corresponding Australian and U.S. rates. Thus the image of New Zealand as the place to bring up children, with its stereotypical nuclear family of three kids and their parents, was made manifest.

Unkind critics of those times, like Clement Freud, who said he had tried to visit New Zealand but found it closed for the weekend, missed the point. No one had bothered to take them out to the suburbs where it was all happening, and happening the way the majority wanted it to happen. There, secure in their welfare state, people were raising their children, doing up their homes and gardens, cleaning their cars, caravans, and boats in preparation for the run with the family—acting out the New Zealand dream. Between 1951 and 1971 the number of private dwellings increased 1.6-fold for the country as a whole; for Auckland the number increased two-fold. It was the era in which the suburbs, particularly those of the major metropolitan centers, expanded.

Since the high point of the 1960s, the total fertility rate has progressively declined. The long-term prospect now is of the population failing to reproduce itself and a decline in the total population during the next century, the result of a remarkable decision on the part of the baby boom generation to reject the dream that has so conditioned the events of the past few decades.

The task of finding jobs for the postwar generation was complicated somewhat by the peculiar structure of the economy, which had been fashioned under the aegis of the welfare state. The prosperity of the farming sector rested on a massive application of capital and technology to the land and the steady elimination of the inefficient farm. Few additional jobs were to be found there, though there were many opportunities in the supporting industries. The highly protected manufacturing sector chose capital-intensive methods and capital-expensive technology as the basis for its expansion. And while many jobs were created, the bulk of the new employment was found in the tertiary sector, as was to be expected in a modern economy whose definition was the expansion of service industries. Between 1951 and 1971, the tertiary sector supplied 268,000 new jobs, manufacturing supplied 168,500 new jobs, and agriculture returned a decline. However, the New Zealand structure provided full employment. The numbers of registered unemployed were derisory.

Most of the new jobs were concerned with supplying goods and services to the home market. This fact meant that the manufacturing firms chose to locate near the biggest markets, the metropolitan centers, especially Auckland. With few jobs being created in the rural sectors, the rural proportion of the population dropped from 32 percent in 1951 to 17 percent in 1976. The proportion of Auckland's population residing in the outer suburbs rose from 21 percent in 1951 to 61 percent in 1976; the other centers displayed similar trends. And the burgeoning Maori population urbanized. During 1961–66, for the twenty-four main urban centers the natural increase of the Maori population was estimated as 10,700, while the increase due to migration amounted to 24,400. Migration exceeded natural increase by 38 percent during the next intercensal period 1966–71. But in 1971–77, natural increase had become the principal source of growth. The Maoris from then on were to be city dwellers.

Everything—full employment, rising living standards, the expansion of the suburbs—however, depended in the last resort on the performance of the export industries: agriculture and forestry. The rest of the economy, more than 80 percent of the labor force, was completely sheltered from external economic forces, which is a nice way of saying it was internationally uncompetitive. From the early 1960s it had been clear to some people that New Zealand must widen the base of its export industries. The architect of the quest model, Walter Nash, in 1960 had said: "It is time to shift the emphasis from security and stability . . . and to direct our efforts towards growth; [it is] time to shape our policy less in terms of the past and to look more to the future." But successive governments found the transition difficult to accomplish. When finally the transformation could no longer be avoided—a necessity that explains the final replacement of the quest model with the deregulated model—the employment of postwar generations could no longer be secured. For a country whose development had rested on immigration, whose principal achievement was recognized to be full employment, emigration and unemployment suddenly became prominent issues.

UNEMPLOYMENT AND MIGRATION

Since 1977, male full-time employment has failed to grow. It reached a figure of 589,000 at that date, as compared with a figure of 307,000 in 1947. In an uneven manner the total declined to 550,000 in 1987, representing a decade of no growth. Female full-time employment, which amounted to 118,000 in 1947, reached a peak of 302,000 in 1980, fell below that number in subsequent years, but surpassed it to reach 332,000 in 1987. Part-time female employment rose from 6,000 in 1947 to 147,000 in 1987. New Zealand has followed other countries with respect to the increase in working women. Male part-time employment has increased also, but amounts to only 45,000 persons.

1968 was the first year of the postwar era in which the country experienced significant unemployment. As compared with previous years, when the unemployed had been numbered in the hundreds, the total of registered unemployed hit 6,556. Ten years later it had risen sharply to almost 20,000, and then rose progressively to reach 78,000 in 1987. When one includes persons employed on various work schemes the total is over 100,000. As a proportion of the labor force, the figure (5.3 percent in June 1988) is somewhat below the figures prevailing in other countries of the Organization for Economic Cooperation and Development (OECD). But as in those countries, unemployment has hit hardest the young (18 percent for males of 15–19 in 1986), the least skilled, and the minorities among the general population (12.3 percent for Maoris, 11.8 percent for Pacific Islanders). One of the reasons the figures are not greater is that many New Zealanders have chosen to emigrate.

Since the European colonization of Aotearoa, long-term and permanent immigration, rather than emigration, has been a constant if at times minor feature of New Zealand life. There have been some notable periods in which net immigration has exceeded 10,000 per annum—during the 1860s, the 1870s, the 1900s, the 1920s, and especially during the 1950s through 1970s. These migrations were largely from the British Isles (the Dutch migration postwar is the only other major source of European settlers). What distinguishes the last decade from the previous ones is the appearance of large-scale permanent emigration. In 1976 a net loss through migration of 1,000 actively engaged persons was recorded. The next year the figure had risen to almost 16,000. By 1979 it had reached 28,000; and it was not until 1984 that the exodus was over. It has since been resumed.

Is this permanent migration? It is still to be determined. The New Zealanders as a nation are great travellers and they enjoy their overseas experience, which has contributed in many positive ways to making life more interesting and more varied. But everyone knows of many New Zealanders who will spend the whole of their working lives overseas and whose talents have been permanently lost to this very small nation. The great fear is that the country's reputation for driving away its most talented citizens may still be true. Only an expanded and restructured economy will keep the brains and the talent at home. This country is one of the few nations in the world where the chance of permanent migration represents a real alternative for a significant section of the labor force.

Australia is of course the most immediate labor market for these migrants, and some 200,000 New Zealanders reside there, an equivalent of 6 percent of the total New Zealand population. No one knows how many other New Zealanders reside permanently abroad as members of another country's labor force.

Strikingly, and exceptionally, the indigenous population of New Zealand, the Maoris, share in this experience—a rare occurrence for a people who were recently tribal in their form of social organization, and a mark of the degree to which they have assimilated. So large is the Maori population of Sydney that Labour politicians once thought it worthwhile to visit and drum up votes for an election taking place at home. Maoris have achieved permanent migrant status in the United States and Britain. Over the period 1981–86 natural increase added some 25,700 to the Maori population. Emigration removed 8,100 persons, the equivalent of 31 percent of the natural increase, resulting in a total intercensal increase of around 17,600. These figures set them apart from the indigenous peoples of North America and Australia.

But if the figures for migration are an indication of the degree to which the Maoris have assimilated into European society, nevertheless the discontinuities and discrepancies between the Maori and European populations constitute the gravest element of New Zealand's social dynamics today.

THE MAORI PEOPLES

When the Europeans arrived, the Maoris, a tribal and aristocratic people, numbered about 250,000, some 50,000 less than they number today.

Intertribal warfare following the adoption of the European musket, but particularly European diseases, reduced their numbers to a mere 42,000 at the turn of the century. But since reaching that nadir, a demographic revival has occurred. By 1936 their numbers had doubled and by 1961 doubled again to 167,000; since then they have increased further to reach the present figure of around 300,000. They now constitute a young, urbanized, and suburbanized population, occupying the less skilled jobs, and displaying an acute condition of youthful unemployment. A mark of their assimilation of Western and urbanized standards is the trend for their total fertility rate to match that of the rest of the population. In 1971 this rate was five children per woman, as compared with the non-Maori rate of three per woman. By 1983 the Maori rate was 2.1—just above the replacement level. The non-Maori rate was just below it. But since the bulk of the Maori population is young, they are likely to return at least a 50 percent increase of population in the period 1981–2011, thus raising their numbers to somewhere between 430,000 and 450,000, and with it their share of the total population from 12 percent now to 15–19 percent (Pool and Pole 1987: 13–14, 31).

Unquestionably the Maori people are in transition. Their demographic history has posed for them both a problem of leadership at such a critical time as well as the issue of cultural identity. It is in matters like this that the issue of social scale comes to the fore in New Zealand. There were in 1985 only 570 males of sixty years of age who were classified as Maoris. This figure has to be compared with the 14,000 males of sixty years of age reported for the European population. And even in an age in which political leadership in New Zealand has descended to the forty-year-olds, there were only 1,240 Maori males of forty years of age as compared with 20,000 European males of that age. Over the past twenty years the senior cohorts from which the Maori leadership can have been drawn have numbered little more than 10,000 males, many of whom would have completed their education before the end of World War II. This same demographic experience has meant that the memories of the majority cover only the last two decades. Is there any wonder they are desperately seeking their language, history, culture, and a sense of national identity? Is there any wonder a fairly rigid educational system has been unable to meet the extraordinary requirements placed on it?

If there is a major division between the European and the Maori communities, where does that division occur? And how great is that division? According to a survey of values and attitudes undertaken for the Royal Commission on Social Policy, satisfaction, not dissatisfaction, prevails in the suburbs.[3] Eighty-five percent of the European population and 79 percent of the Maori population reported they were very satisfied or fairly satisfied with their standard of living. The very dissatisfied amounted to only 3 percent of the Europeans and 5 percent of the Maoris.

Over a wide range of issues the two races display a remarkable degree of accord, separated from one another by no more than six or fewer percentage points. For example, close agreement was recorded on issues such as the quality and fairness of the health and educational services. A high percentage were satisfied with their housing conditions and both races preferred to own their homes. In short, there was widespread and general support for many of the fundamental middle-class values espoused by the creators of the quest model. But on five matters the races were far apart. The Europeans were far less favorable than the Maoris regarding the important Maori issues of language, a bicultural society, fishing rights, the return of Maori land, and adherence to the Treaty of Waitangi. Table 2.1 summarizes the differences.

Race relations in New Zealand are not as good today as they were planned to be in the 1960s when the Hunn Report assumed—as did most New Zealanders at the time—an accepted model of New Zealand society to which the Maoris could assimilate over time. That model—the quest model—no longer holds, for New Zealanders of either European or Maori descent. The new model, the deregulated model, puts some sections of the European society at a disadvantage, for example, the manual workers in the import-dependent manufacturing sector who must bear the immediate consequences of less protected home markets, and government employees in the new state-owned enterprises. The new model makes it difficult for the less qualified school leavers to find employment, while the current labor market is making parents very conscious of the need for good educational standards. Consequently unemployment, redundancies, and early retirement are hurting sections of the working class and the lower middle class.

Table 2.1. Comparative Views of Maoris and Europeans

	In favor of policy (%)	
Policy	Maoris	Europeans
All students taught Maori	43	11
Government should spend more on bi-cultural society	46	15
Protection of Maori Fishing Rights	80	24
Return of Maori Land	64	20
Treaty of Waitangi be honoured	78	44

Source: Royal Commission on Social Policy.

Sections of the young population are finding it difficult to get attractive jobs, or any job at all in some cases. Housing and accommodation is becoming a problem for some people. And parents are worried by the poor prospects of the 32 percent of boys and the 25 percent of girls who leave secondary school with no qualifications whatsoever. The quest model, with its promise of full employment, security, and equality, no longer operates.

But in every instance the conditions of the Maori working classes are worse than those of the European working classes. They are more likely to be hit by unemployment, youth unemployment, by housing and accommodation difficulties, and by poorer educational prospects than their European equivalents. Furthermore, they are more likely to go to prison. Sixty-eight percent of Maori boys and 65 percent of Maori girls leave secondary school with no qualifications at all. Only 7 percent of Maori boys, as compared with 30 percent of European boys, leave secondary school with higher qualifications. Maori males who receive the same rate of pay for comparable work as European males are likely to have to support larger families, where health and housing conditions are likely to be poorer than for the European equivalents. They are likely to live in state rental accommodation and thus to lose out on the benefits of equity ownership during a time of rising house and land prices.

In short, the benefits that may or may not arise from the introduction of the deregulated model are more likely to fall into the hands of the European middle and working classes, while the costs of the model are more likely to hit the Maori working classes even harder than some sections of the European working classes.

Rising living standards brought progressive changes in attitudes toward the state and its delivery of services, as well as demands for more specifically targeted and often more costly programs. The Maori people became correspondingly less and less certain that the state was in fact paying sufficient attention to their needs. When it did, the methods adopted sometimes smacked of paternalism. A turning point was reached when the Crown tried to sell off a prime piece of real estate—Bastion Point—in Auckland, which the local tribe claimed to be theirs, as indeed it was eventually recognized to be. The "Think Big" schemes of the Muldoon administration had the effect of suddenly valorizing natural resources: iron sands, fishing and water rights, strategic and therefore valuable pieces of land. In the race for exploitation the Maori people saw their interests overruled, disregarded, or neglected. Also symptomatic was the outcome of free university education. Available to all, nevertheless only 8 percent of the students at Auckland University had fathers who were classed as semi-skilled or unskilled, where the Maori labor force is heavily represented, even though these categories constitute 30 percent of the male work force. The Maori Land Movement, the Maori Rights Movement, and the Waitangi Treaty issues arose from the inadequacies, insufficiences, and uncritical assumptions of the quest model. These matters now have to be accommodated within the framework of the deregulated model.

A REVIVAL OF IMMIGRATION?

Some advocates of the deregulated model include a resumption of programs to encourage immigration as a factor influencing the success of the model. One has to assume the migrants would be suited to the advanced technological, scientific, and managerial requirements of the restructured, market-led economy that the model is designed to call forth. In addition, the immigrants would have levels of training, levels of rewards, and aspirations above the average. Past evidence indicates immigrants prefer to settle in the three main centers, and the structural trends in the economy suggest Auckland above all other centers would be the most attractive place. In general these immigrants would swell the better educated, highly professional, and managerial middle classes or the well paid, highly skilled sections of the working class. It would not be surprising, given the immigrants' preferred locations, if the emerging Maori middle class and the Maori urban dwellers as a whole viewed these newcomers as direct competitors for jobs and favorable residential sites.

Auckland is sometimes publicized as the largest Polynesian city in the world. The claim rests on two facts. First, it contains a major concentration of Maori people, who are located in two particular subdivisions of the metropolis. Of the 400,000 people with some degree of Maori ancestry, 90,000 are located in Auckland, half of them being in the southern zone and a further 25,000 in the central zone. Second, of the 90,000 Pacific Island immigrant population living in New Zealand, two-thirds are concentrated in Auckland, and in particular in the same southern and central zones. A second major concentration exists in the Wellington region.

A diverse group of peoples themselves, these Polynesians are separated from the Maoris and the Europeans by many facets. Some, like the Cook Islanders (24,000), the Niueans (8,500), and the Tokelauans (2,300), are New Zealand citizens, and there are as many of their people resident in New Zealand as in their home territories. However, the Samoans (50,000), the Tongans (9,200), and the Fijians (2,000) are not citizens and hence have been the object of the illegal immigrant or overstayers controversy.

However, as a group these peoples have been integrated into the economy, particularly in the manufacturing and service sectors. Therefore to all intents and purposes they must be considered permanent residents, especially the New Zealand-born offspring who now account for almost half of the total group. As immigrants they have displayed the customary drive to achieve upward social mobility—not without a measure of success—and thereby appear as competitors to the Maoris. A recent report cites 739 Pacific Islanders attending Auckland University as compared with a Maori total of 495 (Legat 1988: 70).

These peoples are in the process of working out for each of their own communities their needs and aspirations in a world economy that offers minimal prospects for the microeconomies they have left behind and in a society that has still to determine the terms of the inevitable debate concerning multiculturalism and biculturalism. The issues that concern the Pacific Island people cannot be addressed simply as a subset of the issues that concern the Maori people, though there is much in common. The Maori class them as immigrants. In turn, some of the Pacific Islanders are concerned that Maori radicals will create a European backlash against them and fear that intra-Polynesian tension and prejudice will be aggravated. Some of their leaders "believe that bicultural initiatives will stifle the needs of their own peoples; that the country must proceed directly to multiculturalism" (Legat 1988: 78). A common thread running through many of the Pacific Islanders' submissions to the Royal Commission on Social Policy was: "We are unique. We are different. We are not a minority in this our mother region—the Pacific" (Royal Commission on Social Policy 1988: vol. 4, 578).

THE AGED

The demographic waves arising from the fluctuations in fertility have created an aging phenomenon within the population. By 2011, however, those over 65 will constitute only 13 percent of the total. The emergence of the aged as a social problem does not set aside the need to find employment for the 26 percent increase in the labor force that is about to occur. According to the logic of the deregulated model, market forces will solve this matter. It doesn't appear, however, that market forces will be given much opportunity to deal with the aging issue because of its very sensitive and acute political aspects, which are a direct outcome of the quest model.

In the 1970s Sir Robert Muldoon bought the electorate's support by introducing a superannuation (pension) scheme paid for directly out of government revenue, a system which has proved to be fiscally unsustainable. National superannuation expenditure has already ballooned from $366 million in 1975 to $3,650 million in 1987, representing 66 percent of total cash benefits paid out by the government and 56 percent of gross spending on social welfare. The cost of the scheme for each member of the labor force is now $1,900. In constant terms that cost will rise by 2041 to $4,033, unless the scheme is amended. Ninety percent of the population agree that the elderly should be supported from taxation, but 60 percent regard reform as inevitable if the scheme is to be maintained. The Royal Commission on Social Policy, given the gravity of the matter, recommended that the whole issue be removed from electoral manipulation by the adoption of a bipartisan stance—a remarkable display of faith in the statesmanlike quality of politicians elected on a three-year basis.

SINGLE MOTHERS AND ALTERNATIVE LIFE STYLES

It would be interesting to discover if New Zealand is alone in enshrining the three-child family in legislation. Under the quest model this happened. Section 3 paragraph 5 of the Industrial Conciliation and Arbitration Amendment Act of 1936 required the Arbitration Court to fix basic wage rates for males at a level that would ensure a reasonable living standard for a married couple with three children. As we have seen, most married couples appear to have listened to this piece of bureaucratic advice. The three-child family became a way of life in the postwar era. Consequently large sections of the population were not prepared for the emergence of the single-parent family. Neither were they convinced of their responsibility as taxpayers to maintain the living standards of the less conventional members of society. Along with the freedom of abortion issue, debate has raged over the ethics and proprieties of new life styles.

By 1987 there were 31,600 women living apart from their spouses, 14,000 women living apart from their de facto husbands, and 14,000 unmarried women all receiving the Domestic Purposes Benefit. They had in their care a total of 110,000 children. The single-parent household and the childless couple are two of the more conspicuous trends away from the three-child nuclear family arrangement. In 1966, 47 percent of the households whose head was between the ages of 25–44 had three children; only 10 percent had none. By 1981 the proportion with no children had increased to 15 percent and families with three children had fallen to 32 percent.

Those who objected to the state's support of the less conventional were not arguing that the state's welfare function should be abolished; merely that it should be restricted to what was ethically conventional. But in the last decades of the quest model these conservative spirits were swimming against the tide. The popular thrust of argument regarding the future of the welfare state (which disregarded totally the emerging fiscal and economic crisis) was that it should functionally encompass everything. That groundswell has not been dissipated.

THE DISTRIBUTION OF INCOME

Of course it was the single-parent households that tended to show up in the lower-income brackets and in those categories with less than adequate housing conditions, along with the elderly and Maori households with larger families. Brian Easton's investigation of income distribution in the 1970s concluded that all the evidence before 1974 pointed to increasing equality in wealth, factor income, and personal income distribution, and to a more equal distribution of wealth and personal income than is the case in most other countries. Nevertheless, even in these favorable circumstances he estimated that 18 percent of the total population suffered relative poverty (Easton 1983).

The redistribution of income was a central objective of the quest model. Obtaining that objective led to the creation of budget deficits which in turn led to the demise of the quest model and its replacement by the deregulated model. That model in turn implies for most of the electorate increasing inequalities, a perception that its advocates have had little success in dispelling, particularly following the emergence of the new plutocracy. The recent work of Susan Snivelly has consolidated our knowledge of the redistributive processes and raised some new questions; it hasn't dispelled the fears of the egalitarians.

In the early 1980s the top decile of households commanded 27 percent of total market income. The top four deciles commanded 71 percent of total market income. The bottom two deciles commanded only 0.8 percent. The effect of governmental redistribution policies—taxation, benefits, grants and subsidies, not all of them working in the same direction—was to raise that proportion to 8.7 percent and to reduce the top decile's share by 6.7 percent percentage points while reducing the top four deciles' share to 59 percent of total income. The results can be looked at in two ways. First, regarding the impact government policies have on household incomes there has been a ten-fold effect on the income of the two lowest deciles. Second, concerning the considerable differences of income that persist despite the redistributive efforts, there is still no agreement on the amount of inequality the society is prepared to accept. I doubt if one will ever be forthcoming. However, 47 percent of the community supported the idea that incomes should be more equitable. Those with administrative and managerial occupations were the principal dissenters; only 29 percent of them favored more equality of income.

Snivelly's report contained some rather surprising results, which drew attention away from the different levels of income within the population and toward the shifts in resources that occur between different elements of the society as a consequence of government intervention. Overall that intervention has favored the elderly and single parents. Income and resources have been distributed away from the central concern of the quest model—families with children, and particularly families with one or two children. Families with three or more children and large households have done rather better.

How this came about is readily discernible. The national superannuant household is largely the beneficiary of government expenditure on social welfare: 12.9 percent of the population consumes 57.7 percent of social welfare expenditure and 30.2 percent of health spending. Households with three or more children, 37.7 percent of the total, consume 55.9 percent of education expenditure, whereas the households of two adults with one or two children, 24.8 percent of all households, consume 24.9 percent of the education vote. The suggestion is that households with three or more children tend to be wealthier households; being wealthier, they consume more of the tertiary education expenditure and the expenditure on the later years at secondary school. This may be true, but disguised among these larger families is a category of poorer families.

Just who constitutes the poor in New Zealand remains a matter of debate. An initial analysis reveals what one would expect. The aged, the single-parent families, and the unemployed make up the bulk of the poor. But when household disposable income is adjusted for the effects of government intervention, 64 percent of the poor are made up of people in the workforce. Poverty in New Zealand may be, as elsewhere, a matter of access, but it is also a matter of participation in low productivity occupations, a matter for serious concern.

EDUCATION AND WEALTH

The New Zealanders are great believers in the value of education. They should be. Education has been a great engine of upward social mobility in the postwar era. Most of the better paid and more prestigious jobs, however, have been located in the sheltered and protected sectors of the economy. The future of education is a matter of intense debate at the moment. Inevitably, the impotency of the quest model has cast doubt on the potency of one of its great supporting arches. Indicative of the importance attached by the electorate to the education issue was the prime minister's assumption of the education portfolio in 1987, and his establishment of a task force on educational administration headed by a private sector millionaire—as was the case with the review of hospital and health administration. In addition to these Picot and Gibb reports, Treasury provided the Cabinet with its own 294-page analysis, and the universities produced their own bland report on the future of tertiary education.

One thing seems certain: Education will continue to be funded by the state. After that there is doubt and confusion. In the prime minister's own words, "the community is split on [educational] issues" ("What does David Lange really believe. . ." 1988). He acknowledged a fundamental conflict between Maori aspirations for their young and the Pakeha (European) people centered on the bilingual education issue, as we have already highlighted. "There is," he continued, "a degree of unease about secondary schools. . . . We have a real conflict between those who have a vision for their child of being academically excellent and literate and able to move into a world of high technology and skill, and the simple reality of some people who are going through the school so that they can be good waiters." Significantly, it was the administrative and managerial occupations (29 percent), the professional and technical (20 percent), and the service occupations (23 percent) that perceived the quality of education in the secondary schools to be bad, as compared with the average of 14 percent for all respondents (Royal Commission on Social Policy 1988: vol. 1, 463).

The supposed relationship between education and economic growth is currently the cornerstone of every speech delivered by educational enthusiasts. No one dares to raise the point that recent experience in New Zealand hardly supports the existence of the relationship when expressed in its more simplistic forms. What is overlooked is the structural element that determines if there is a place in which the educational input may be absorbed and whether the educational preparation is relevant or not. The prime minister concluded that the school-to-work issue is the critical issue of our time. Regrettably, the problem of dead-end jobs and the need for flexible educational and managerial systems to meet the new international trading conditions, both of which have been so ably publicized in the United States by Robert Reich, have produced little response in New Zealand.

New Zealand, of course, displays the same close relationship between income and education as do the United States and Australia. With such a fortunate history of full employment, education's function as a sorting mechanism, and education's role as a positional good have not been so apparent in New Zealand as elsewhere, though they are likely to become more evident following the emergence of a class of wealthy and influential families.

As a country New Zealand has fallen behind other countries in its investigations of wealth—never an easy matter—as opposed to income. The wealthy in New Zealand are conspicuously the beneficiaries of the sheltered economy or the deregulation of the financial sector, in some instances the beneficiaries of both. Surprisingly, with this schooling they have been called on by the Labour administration to help steer the ship of state through the narrow channels that lead to the ocean of competition. The metaphor is chosen not without reason.

I have nothing better to work with than a sample of twenty-five very rich families, and seventy-five very rich men. The wealth of fourteen of the families has been derived from the sheltered sectors of the economy. Seven families have accumulated wealth because they have been protected against competing imports for half a century. Only four of the families derive their wealth from the export sectors, and the traditional ones at that.

Of the rich men, 34 percent derived their wealth from the financial and sharebroking sectors, which have recently benefitted from deregulation. As a group they are young: 48 percent were born after 1940 and 76 percent were born since 1930. Three-quarters of them are self-made men; the other quarter had the advantage of family fortune. Only a third of them have any tertiary qualifications. Twelve percent are immigrants. If they did not make their money in the financial sector, then 37 percent of them made it in the construction and property sector when inflation and a regulated financial sector left them with no other sensible place to put other people's money. Only 13 percent of these entrepreneurs are connected with the production of goods. Some of them have come to ruin following the share market crash, but the majority have been able to secure their wealth and its advantages. Some are planning to transfer their business overseas. The combination of regulation and deregulation has produced a plutocracy—one of the most novel social developments since the original European settlement of the country produced a squirearchy.

The privileged classes created by the quest model—workers, capitalists, and managers alike—once safely harbored by the sheltered private and public sectors of the economy, now see their privileges threatened, and in some instances withdrawn. Some elements in society have more easily safeguarded the fruits of their privileges than others, and have in fact transferred their wealth overseas. As David Calleo put it, "Market freedom is all too often a euphemism for radical devaluation of one kind of power at the expense of another" (Calleo 1982: 189). The injustices of this devaluation are likely to fuel the social dynamics of New Zealand in the coming decade, unless the authors of change can ameliorate the consequences.

INTERPRETATIONS

If one stands back from the events and social dynamics of the past four decades, one can see perhaps a little more clearly what has been happening in New Zealand. Considerable changes have been underway and the consequences of these changes have been building up to create pressures and the inevitability of more change. Quite basic to the whole process was the shift in fertility behavior that produced the baby boom and then the rapid decline to the bare replacement levels of the present era. The demographic swells induced by this behavior were accompanied by rising living standards and marked shifts in the location of the population, both geographically and occupationally, with a differential impact on the European and Maori communities. Finally, they were associated with a change in *Zeitgeist*, itself an expression of affluence and the desire to exert greater choice in all aspects of the individual's life that accompanies affluence. The conformity so characteristic of New Zealand life has been steadily eroded except in one important and astonishing instance: the retention of the quest model as the test of all social and economic policy.

The dramatic replacement of that model, so very different in its philosophical origins, institutions, and objectives, without any warning or preparation of the electorate, in fact without the electorate's consent, was a long delayed and therefore all the more convulsive adjustment to the external trading conditions underlying New Zealand's prosperity. The pressures and problems that have built up over the last few decades, the novel modes of life, the newer aspirations and attitudes now have to be dealt with or accomplished not within the security of the old welfare state but within a less certain and more competitive environment in which outside factors will exert greater influence than in the past.

The men who dismantled the quest model are preeminently the beneficiaries of that model. Their fathers had constructed the welfare state to ensure that no future generation would suffer the indignities their fathers had suffered as a result of laissez-faire capitalism. The quest model contained one huge deficiency, never apparent to those who believed in it. The quest model contained no prescription for dealing with change, for what change can be necessary in a society that is deemed to be perfect? The model did contain a prescription for conformity. Everything that was undertaken had to be undertaken in conformity with its aims and objectives: security, equality, and social justice. This point allows me to deal, and deal very briefly, with the effect of all these dynamics on New Zealand's world view and international orientations.

Quite simply, the effect was introversive. Only a small elite has been capable of understanding that a changing world has created a set of different priorities for this intensely introverted society; being an elite has meant its message has been lost on most of the population. If this were not true, how could one explain that in an era that is certain to be the Pacific Basin era, when the region's newly industrializing economies are rampant, the Royal Commission on Social Policy could make full employment a prime objective of the state's economic agenda? In an affluent, technologically advanced world, an economy and a labor force capable of facing the task of constant restructuring would have been a more realistic objective (Franklin 1985: 116).

Where there has been some recognition of this changing world, emphasis has been placed on the political changes associated with postcolonialism in the South Pacific rather than the changed trading circumstances that now dominate the world economy. It is now fashionable to refer to New Zealand as a Pacific nation—more specifically, a South Pacific nation. New Zealand is in the Pacific, but its trade is not of the Pacific and particularly not of the South Pacific. Instead of sending 80 percent or more of its exports to Britain as it did until the 1950s, despite a remarkable diversification of its trading partners, the country now sends 80 percent of its exports to the rich OECD economies, particularly Australia, Japan, the United States and Canada—who may be said to be grouped around the Pacific—and the EEC. An even larger percentage of the country's imports is drawn from these same trading partners. In many parts of the rest of the world the country trades at the margin in those commodities that are in excess supply. New Zealand's trade has always been with the rich, the technologically advancing, and the powerful nations of the world—never with the poor, the weak, the desperate.

The fulfillment of every aspiration touched on in this analysis—whether it be Maori, European, Pacific Islander (or those of the smaller minorities), young, middle-aged, old, rich or poor, yuppie or alternative life-styler—

depends in the last resort on success as an exporting nation. New Zealand may be in the Pacific, but it is *of* the Pacific only in part. Location is here being confused with commercial geography. The structure of New Zealand's trade is fundamental to its prosperity. A major shift in trading patterns will be a long-term process, the pace of change being set by the emergence of additional wealthy trading partners. Some New Zealanders may see the role of Moral Utopia as befitting their country. But all past prescriptions for utopias—as well as dystopias—have been based on autarkic, never open economies. Open economies inhibit the degree of social control utopias and dystopias require.

The leadership of the Labour government—those beneficiaries of the welfare state—found the institutions and philosophies of their fathers' generation an impediment to their finding a place in this new world. They are prepared to compete for a place and believe the country itself is capable of competing.

Let us hope they are right.

However, in the minds and hearts of the people the objectives of the quest model are still revered. As the Royal Commission on Social Policy pointed out,

> A number of submissions looked back to the good old days particularly in relation to the welfare state. For many people the security offered by the welfare state after the depression of the 1930s is no longer there. People are once again worried about the future, often indeed about the present. The previous system's predictability gave a security which is not given today now that people are exposed to the vagaries of market economic forces.

NOTES

1. The term "quest model" is derived from the title of W.B. Sutch's famous book, *The Quest for Security* (1966). Indicative of the universal acceptance of this model in postwar New Zealand, it never required a designation until the introduction of the deregulated model. Before then it was widely regarded as the only possible basis for an economy and a society.

2. Like all articles of faith, this one helped to maintain an illusion long past the point that it bore much relation to reality. The illusion served to deflect the electorate's interest from any inquiry as to the fundamental causes behind the steady erosion of the country's world standing. By 1965, New Zealand had fallen from third to eighth place in the world per capita stakes. By 1975 it had fallen to nineteenth place; by 1978 to twenty-second place.

3. Pages 608 to 700 of the 1988 April Report contain an exhaustive statistical analysis of the Royal Commission's survey of attitudes and values, from which these figures have been derived. The survey results, if anything, are slightly weighted toward the majority who occupy the middle ground, but they are the only figures one has to work with apart from the earlier results of the Social Indicators Survey 1980–81. This, like similar surveys carried out elsewhere in the world, displays a high degree of satisfaction with and acceptance of living conditions and circumstances.

3

Social Dynamics and Political Consciousness: The United States Since 1945

WILLIAM H. CHAFE

In many respects, the history of the United States since World War II is self-contained, coherent, and distinctive. It was a time marked by unparalleled social change, profound challenge to traditional barriers of gender and race discrimination, and a significantly new posture toward the rest of the world. Rooted in the fundamental experience of fighting a world war, each of these trends shaped America's modern history in a different way. Postwar economic growth coincided with massive changes in educational achievement, the explosion of suburbia, creation of a postindustrial, affluent society, and emergence of a "liberal consensus" (actually quite conservative) in politics. Other changes initiated during the war, meanwhile, eventually challenged this consensus. With the civil rights movement as a primary catalyst, social activists questioned existing patterns of power and privilege, including the prevailing economic system and traditional definitions of men's and women's roles. All of this occurred within the context of the Cold War, with a constant dialectic taking place between social and economic developments at home, and America's sense of itself in the larger world. Each of these three themes requires separate analysis, yet in the end, none can be understood fully without attention to the others.

POSTWAR AMERICA—THE AFFLUENT SOCIETY

When World War II ended, most Americans feared a resumption of hard times. Fewer than 40 percent believed that their children would have better opportunities than they had enjoyed. Yet fifteen years later a new world had come into being. The gross national product (GNP) had increased by 250 percent; per capita income was 35 percent higher in 1960 than the boom year of 1945; 75 percent of the American people owned their own washing machine, 87 percent their own TV, and 75 percent their own car. Nearly 60 percent had achieved a "middle-class" standard of living, double the percentage of 1928. "The remarkable capacity of the U.S. economy in 1960," observed one economic historian, "represents the crossing of a great divide in the history of humanity" (Leuchtenburg 1983; Chafe 1986; Galbraith 1958).

Much of this prosperity could be traced back to war-related developments. In the full employment economy of wartime, the proportion of the population earning less than $3,000 (in 1968 dollars) had been cut in half. Spending capacity soared as savings mounted due to wartime rationing. Liquid assets increased three-fold to $140 billion, helping to fuel the massive consumer binge that resulted when wartime plants were reconverted to production of cars, appliances, and other household goods. In the meantime, the GI Bill helped to ensure that veterans would be able to secure the decent education, jobs, and housing that made possible a continuation of postwar prosperity. Tuition benefits gave former GIs the wherewithal to find training for decent jobs; housing loans from the Veterans Administration (VA) spurred a substantial growth in home ownership; and small business loans helped aspiring entrepreneurs to start their own companies. War-related scientific breakthroughs also helped create the new industries where veterans could seek jobs. Chemical plants, electronics, plastics—all benefited enormously from wartime growth and innovation.

As a result, a new service-oriented, consumer economy took off during the 1950s and 1960s. Technology generated labor-saving devices and productivity increases. Research and development offices became the most important departments of many large corporations. And "automation" became a byword for expanded efficiency. In 1956 the United States crossed the dividing line between an industrial and a postindustrial economy, with white-collar workers outnumbering blue-collar workers for the first time. The new jobs were in occupations that served the consumer—salespeople in automobile showrooms, investment counselors, advertising executives, bank tellers. Between 1947 and 1957 the ranks of salaried middle-class workers grew by 61 percent, and William Whyte's "organization man" became the symbol of the huge corporation that came to dominate the nation's economy (Whyte 1959; Leuchtenburg 1983; Chafe 1986; Galbraith 1958; Blum 1975).

Needless to say, the new jobs required far more education and skill than those associated with blue-collar labor, spurring an unprecedented expansion of "the knowledge industry," as Daniel Bell (1968) called it. In 1940, approximately 15 percent of 18- to 22-year-olds attended a college or university. A quarter century later the figure had skyrocketed to 44 percent. The "multiversity" became a new term describing huge educational complexes like Berkeley and Michigan where classrooms with 500 students were commonplace. Between 1940 and 1965 the number of universities with more than 20,000 students increased from two to thirty-nine, with at least some students wondering whether they were anything more than a faceless number in an educational wonderland. Yet the emergence of such massive universities was essential to the maintenance of an equally massive economy that required millions of college-educated employees (Bell 1968).

The growth of a highly educated, technologically sophisticated workforce went hand in hand with the gradual levelling of regional differences in economic development. Silicone Valley in California and Route 128 in Boston were most associated with high-tech industries, but by the early 1960s, states like North Carolina, Arizona, and Texas also had their research parks. The Sunbelt—a series of states including the old Confederacy and the newer states of the Southwest—had become a magnet attracting industry and population from the Rustbelt of older Northern industrial cities.

Not surprisingly, this new economy coincided with the growing dominance of a new living space, suburbia. Not since the great floodtide of European immigration at the turn of the century had there been such a massive shift of population. In the early 1900s, more than 1.2 million people per year came to the United States from Eastern and Southern Europe. Now, the same number each year moved to the suburbs. Between 1950 and 1960 alone, 18 million people took the trek to suburbia. During the same years the total population increase was only 28 million.

Although suburbs first appeared in the late nineteenth and early twentieth century, this phenomenon was different in character and quality from its precursors. Huge tracts sprang up overnight, concentric circles of houses and backyards proliferating endlessly. Yet the new suburbs met a critical social need with a life style and set of varied opportunities that meshed perfectly with the new era of growth and prosperity. Millions of people were searching for housing after the war. The number of marriages doubled in 1946, and by 1948 over 2 million couples were living with relatives. Ambitious developers negotiated with county governments desiring new settlers and purchased large plots of empty land where they could build houses that could then be sold to families using VA and Federal Housing Administration (FHA) loans to buy their own home for the first time. Each suburb had its own economic level, and in an era of mass mobility (approximately 25 percent of the population changed their home address each year), families could move from one suburb to the other as their circumstances improved. As a consequence, millions of people found a new niche, the initial cost largely defrayed by government loans. It was a perfect formula for giving young families a sense of optimism and growth, while continuing to fuel the major engine of the postwar economy, consumer spending. By 1960, one-quarter of the population was living in suburbia, and the number of home owners in America had increased from 40 percent of the population in 1940 to 62 percent in 1960 (Jackson 1984; Donaldson 1969; Gans 1957).

With some justification, we can look back to the period of suburban expansion and economic growth during the fifteen years after World War II as a halcyon time that shaped significantly the parameters of America's distinctive postwar society. Rarely before had so many people seen such great improvements in the actual conditions of their lives. Whether it be a new home, the first college degree in a family's history, a second automobile, the first cross-country jet airplane ride, a new boat, or a trip to Disneyland, these were years full of excitement and discovery for millions of families. America was a land of opportunity. When Richard Nixon debated Nikita Khruschev in the model kitchen at the American exhibit in Moscow in 1958, he appropriately boasted of America's access to consumer goods as the hallmark of its national achievement. Russia may have had Sputnik, but the United States had kitchen gadgetry and appliances that were the envy of the world. The typical American family, Nixon could argue, actually owned its free-standing five-room house with trees and a lawn, a picnic table and a barbecue, a self-cleaning oven, and a new car. The children of that family could grow up breathing clean air, go to new schools, and have a realistic hope of winning a college degree and securing a well-paying job with a national corporation that boasted ample opportunity for advancement. It was the age of the baby boom, when a near doubling of the birth rate (up to 27.2 births per 100,000 population in 1957) seemed commensurate with the jump in the GNP, and when nothing seemed impossible to achieve. Some might cavil at the enforced conformity of the suburban lifestyle ("the bland leading the bland," as Arthur Schlesinger, Jr. said), or the "ticky-tac" houses of the developer's tract. But in fact, Nixon had every reason to celebrate the glitter and gleam of America's model home and kitchen. They symbolized a remarkable achievement that would have been difficult to imagine just a generation earlier.

POSTWAR AMERICA—THE CHALLENGE TO COMPLACENCY

Relatively unnoticed during the late 1940s and early 1950s, but burning steadily like an underground fire preparing to explode, the civil rights movement gathered its forces in these same years to raise a different set of questions about the direction America should be taking. While most beneficiaries of prosperity saw primarily the positive side of America's postwar story, black Americans, grass-roots citizens as well as national leaders, persisted in focusing on America's oldest and deepest shame.

Like the economic good news of the postwar years, the energy of the civil rights movement also found its roots in the war itself. More than two million blacks had migrated from the rural south to the industrial north and west during the war. Mobilized by civil rights groups who emphasized the absurdity of fighting racism abroad while condoning it at home, these and other blacks joined the protest movement in record numbers. The ranks of the National Association for the Advancement of Colored People (NAACP) swelled by 900 percent; blacks in the north registered to vote in record numbers; and a new determination to secure first-class citizenship spread throughout the black population. Returning veterans organized throughout the south around issues of voter registration and better schools. When their efforts were repelled by local law enforcement agencies and vigilantes, they turned to the litigation process championed by the NAACP. But throughout, it was local teachers, parents, and ministers who put their lives on the line to demand change. Eventually their efforts would result in an effort to transform a whole society, spreading to include issues of gender and class as well as that of race (Sitkoff 1975).

The struggle for racial progress highlights both the "hidden" history of the affluent 1950s and the extent to which established political processes, by themselves, offered little prospect for far-reaching social reform. Following the strategy of litigation, the NAACP had successfully argued before the Supreme Court that segregation was inherently unconstitutional. But despite the court's unanimous decision in *Brown v. Board of Education* (1954), little progress in school integration actually took place. President Eisenhower refused to implement the court's decision with any vigor, and Southern politicians took that indifference as a cue to mount their own campaign of massive resistance. When it became clear that strong leadership would not be forthcoming from Washington, the civil rights movement entered a new phase of direct action protest, spearheaded by ordinary citizens. In Montgomery in 1955, middle-aged seamstress Rosa Parks joined with union leader E. D. Nixon and women's club organizer JoAnn Robinson to spark a boycott of the city's segregated buses that lasted 381 days, attracted international attention, and brought to prominence a young minister named Martin Luther King, Jr. After Montgomery, it was hard for white Southerners to argue any longer that "our Negroes are happy" (Sitkoff 1983; Marable 1984; Kluger 1976).

Four years later in Greensboro, North Carolina, young college students carried black protest to a new plateau, using a new language—that of the "sit-in." Thirteen years old when the Supreme Court outlawed segregation, they grew to maturity with the expectation that the shameful indignities of second-hand books and balcony theater seats would soon disappear. The NAACP youth group to which they belonged talked about the need to challenge segregation. So when they became college students and talked at night about how little had changed, they concluded that it was now up to them to rebel. They determined to expose the absurdity of racism by buying supplies—as equals—in the local Woolworth's, and then proceeding to the lunch counter in the same store and insisting on equal treatment there as well. When they were refused service, they sat down and started to study. They stayed until the store closed. The next day, the four became twenty-three, the day after that sixty-six, and on the fifth day, 1,000. Word of their protest spread across land, and within two months similar demonstrations had broken out in fifty-four cities in nine different states. The 1960s direct action civil rights struggle had begun (Chafe 1980).

Initially, the civil rights movement was a classic manifestation of American reform spirit. Accepting the basic structure of the society and its values, civil rights activists simply asked for inclusion as equals so that they too might share in the benefits of a booming economy and a growing suburbia. "The Negro dream," Martin Luther King, Jr. told the March on Washington in 1963, "is rooted in the American Dream." Civil rights demonstrators sought "freedom now" and believed that with the abolition of discriminatory laws, blacks could achieve the goal of equal opportunity.

But as time passed, a significant portion of the movement became radicalized, persuaded by bitter experience that integration into the existing system offered no solution because the system itself was the problem. When young civil rights workers saw first-hand the impoverishment of sharecroppers in Mississippi, witnessed FBI officials standing by as

Southern sheriffs wantonly beat blacks trying to register to vote, and endured repeated betrayals of promises from white officials, they began to attack the entire social and economic structure, no longer believing that equality could be won with the vote. Instead, even as the movement won its greatest legal victories with the Civil Rights Act of 1964 and the Voting Rights Act of 1965, these more radical activists were denouncing the system and insisting that true change required a substantial redistribution of power and wealth, away from white junior executives living in Westchester suburbs, and toward the poor and powerless. The ghetto uprisings in Harlem, Detroit, and other cities in the mid-1960s dramatically underscored this new anger. Led by people like Stokely Carmichael in the South and Malcolm X in the North, more radical blacks questioned the whole value of seeking assimilation. Why should blacks seek integration, Black Power advocate Stokely Carmichael asked, when white society was dominated by values and institutions that were profoundly alien to black interests (Sitkoff 1983; Chafe 1986; Marable 1984; Forman 1975)?

Eventually, the same kind of challenge emerged from a revitalized women's movement as well. No area of American life had shown quite as much underlying behavioral change—though paradoxically very little attitudinal change—as that of gender roles. Again, the war proved a pivotal event. In 1940 the average woman worker was young, single, and poor. It was thought to be unnatural and inappropriate for a woman to have a career and be married. Throughout the Depression, government, business, and labor had all waged campaigns against married women's employment. But when the war started, all that suddenly changed. Women workers became the key to victory as men went off to fight. More than six million joined the work force, 75 percent of them married, 60 percent over thirty, and many the mothers of young children. The female labor force increased, temporarily at least, by 57 percent. When women first took these war jobs, the expectation was that they would gladly return home as soon as the fighting ended. But by 1945, it turned out that more than 75 percent wanted to remain on the job. They enjoyed their work, appreciated receiving a paycheck for their efforts, and welcomed the camaraderie of the factory or office.

During the next twenty years, a remarkable cultural schizophrenia occurred in the history of gender relations as these two conflicting forces interacted. As soon as the war ended, the campaign resumed to force women back to the home. "The independent woman," one prominent bestseller pronounced, "is a contradiction in terms." Any woman who wanted a job outside the home, a popular psychiatrist said, must be neurotic, victimized by masculine tendencies. What Betty Friedan later dubbed "the feminine mystique" had begun to assert its cultural hegemony. Yet simultaneously, many of the same women who were supposed to find new fulfillment and happiness in their careers as housewives and mothers were returning to the workforce. Although few women war workers held on to jobs at the same level of skill and pay that they enjoyed during the war, large numbers went back to work as saleswomen, office and clerical workers, and as factory operatives. Indeed, much of the economic expansion of the postwar years took place in precisely those service areas in which women were most likely to be hired. Throughout the 1950s, women's employment rate grew at a rate four times faster than men's, and although the jobs in no way meant progress toward equality, they did suggest a change of enormous significance.

Perhaps most important, the women going to work were the same middle-aged, married, and increasingly middle-class women who had first gone to work during the war. By 1960, 30 percent of married women were employed as compared with 15 percent in 1940, and the greatest increase had occurred among women whose husbands earned from $7,000–10,000 a year (from 7 percent in 1950 to 25 percent in 1960). All of these figures pale beside subsequent increases in the 1960s through 1980s, but they do indicate the extent to which a quiet revolution was in process even in the midst of the triumph of domesticity. By the 1960s, it was the norm, not the exception, for a woman worker to be middle-class, middle-aged, and married, whereas in 1940, it had been virtually unheard of (Anderson 1981; Hartmann 1980; Banner 1975; Chafe 1972).

The explanation for the schizophrenia is two-fold. First, the expansion of women's economic activity could be tolerated because in many instances it was the indispensable prerequisite to achieving a middle-class life style. In the 1960s, the census bureau reported that the number of households earning $15,000 a year or more would be cut in half if women's incomes were excluded. Many families could afford an addition to the house, a second car, or a vacation at Disneyland only because they were two-income households. Second, and even more important, this change could occur because in no way did it appear to be a challenge to traditional definitions of women's "proper" role. Women workers were seeking jobs, not careers. They did not present themselves as feminists demanding equality. Since they said they were working in order to "help the family," their activities outside the home did not seem inconsistent with traditional family norms. Moreover, the fact that most of these workers were over thirty-five, with children already well along in school, conferred a certain cultural logic on their employment. They were not, in fact, leaving behind what the society said was their primary role.

Still, these changes helped to create the foundation for a far more serious challenge to traditional ideas about gender roles because the prevailing norm that "a woman's place is in the home" no longer had a basis in reality. As women's employment steadily spread, expanding to younger married women in their childbearing years, more and more women had the first-hand experience of being underpaid and undervalued. Thus, when a new feminist movement was born, focusing attention on the massive inequities of women's lives, a large constituency existed with a background that prepared them to respond.

That movement, in turn, grew directly from the civil rights struggle. A natural symmetry existed between the demand that race be abolished as a criterion for discrimination and the demand that gender also cease to be a justification for discrimination. Both represented visible, physical characteristics that had historically served as a basis for denial of citizenship rights, property rights, educational rights, and equal economic opportunity. In the 1830s the anti-slavery movement had given rise to the first women's movement, and now, the civil rights movement gave rise to women's liberation. Ironically, for at least some of the women involved, the precipitating issue was the second-class treatment that women received within the civil rights struggle, with some of the white women in the student civil rights movement becoming the chief organizers of a separate feminist struggle.

In reality, the women's movement of the 1960s and 1970s had two parts. One, represented in the National Organization for Women (NOW), was primarily middle class and reformist in approach, working like the NAACP to change laws and policies in order to facilitate women's acceptance as complete equals within the existing social and economic structure. The other, more associated with the term "women's liberation," grew out of the student and civil rights movements and attacked the entire framework of beliefs and institutions that perpetuated a hierarchical structure of power, sex roles, and attitudes. For these more radical women, as for the more radical students in the civil rights movement, there was no point in becoming part of a mainstream dominated by values of competition and aggression. Although divisions persisted between the two parts of the movement, by the 1970s both had become radicalized to the point that many people who embraced traditional values and participated in the benefits of middle-class affluence felt under attack and threatened by the feminist challenge (Evans 1978; Freeman 1975; Chafe 1977).

A final movement that grew quietly during the prosperous and happy 1950s and eventually challenged the complacency of that era involved the college students who were among the chief beneficiaries of postwar prosperity. This was the generation, as the organizers of the Students for a Democratic Society (SDS) said in 1962, that was "bred in at least modest comfort," but was now questioning "the world we have inherited." At first dubbed the "quiet generation," some of these students began to take seriously the critiques of the new affluent society. When the civil rights movement came along and gave an ethical focus to their concerns, a number of them journeyed to Mississippi and Alabama to act on their commitment to create a better society. Eventually that experience generated protest movements on campus and, once the war in Vietnam became a major national issue, led to a mass movement that in at least some of its manifestations also began to challenge the very structure of the society and its most powerful institutions. Some of these students also became part of what was known as the "counterculture," a vague label for young people who embraced greater sexual liberation, acid rock music, indulgence in mind-altering drugs, and contempt for bourgeois manners and morals. For millions of older people who had grown up believing in the traditional values of hard work, monogamy, patriotism, and respect for law and order, these tendencies—like those embodied in Black Power and women's liberation—seemed a fundamental assault on middle-class institutions and all the gains that had been achieved in the postwar years toward a prosperous and healthy society.

THE POLITICS OF POSTWAR AMERICA—THE LIBERAL CONSENSUS

One way to understand the politics of postwar America is to see them as a response to the social dynamics discussed thus far. As the nation emerged from World War II, there were two concerns that dwarfed all others: maintaining the peace, and restoring domestic vitality through a healthy economy. The second, as we have seen, became a dominant reality within a relatively brief time, partly due to the legacy of the war itself, and partly due to government-assisted policies, most notably exemplified in the GI Bill. The first concern, in the meantime, became inextricably connected to the Cold War and America's policy of containment toward the Soviet Union. Beginning even before the war ended, but certainly dominant from 1948 to the present, the politics of anti-Communism became the *sine qua non* for all discourse about public affairs. No one dared criticize the Cold War or question America's responsibility as leader of "the free world" lest they be pilloried as "soft on Communism" and chased out of public life.

In the end, not surprisingly, the two concerns of the postwar years defined the parameters of American politics, constituting the twin pillars of what Godfrey Hodgson has called America's "liberal consensus." Beginning with a faith that "capitalism works" and that economic growth is the engine that can drive society to perfection, the liberal consensus affirmed a commitment to reform where problems existed, but abjured all notions of irreducible class conflict. Social unity at home, according to the liberal consensus, was a prerequisite to developing a non-partisan foreign policy of anti-Communism. Hence, it was wrong—and self-defeating—to emphasize domestic problems as either insoluble or chronic. Rather, there were no inherent flaws in America's social and economic structure, and any problems that did exist could be resolved incrementally, largely through the gains made possible by economic growth.

Whatever the differences associated with personality and political rhetoric, the presidential administrations of Harry Truman, Dwight Eisenhower, and John Kennedy all reflected this liberal consensus. Truman and Eisenhower both operated within the social welfare framework established during the New Deal, made the Cold War the cornerstone of their foreign policies, and encouraged continued expansion of the economy through housing and highway legislation, and their monetary and fiscal policies. Ironically, the man usually associated in the public mind with a rejection of 1950s quietism—John F. Kennedy—was as much a part of this liberal consensus as anyone. Kennedy believed fully in the organic health of the American economic system. His major criticism of Eisenhower was that he had not let the economy grow fast enough. Instead of far-reaching reform, Kennedy embraced the idea that economic growth would solve most social problems ("a rising tide lifts all boats") and committed his administration to the primary task of fine-tuning the economy so that it would perform better. No one—until perhaps Ronald Reagan—was more a cold warrior than Kennedy, and he took office exhorting the American people to be ready "to pay any price, bear any burden" in defending freedom during its hour of maximum peril (Leuchtenburg 1983; Chafe 1986; Hodgson 1975; Hamby 1984).

The politics of the years between the late 1940s and the early 1960s thus seem appropriate to the confidence and optimism reflected in the nation's unprecedented economic growth. The country was strong militarily, dominant in the world, and its dominance there appeared to be a direct outgrowth of the health of capitalism at home. If there were problems, they would be solved in due course, with no need for radical change or challenge. Ideology no longer had a role to play in America, the sociologist Daniel Bell wrote, because the nation had reached a position of maturity and affluence in which political factions were unnecessary. The liberal consensus seemed unassailable.

It was the civil rights movement that initially challenged and later shattered the liberal consensus. Although John Kennedy had promised moral leadership on issues of race, he had done little of substance to deliver on his promises, counting instead on prosperity, good times, and gradual, incremental reform to solve the problem. By 1963, however, that posture proved inadequate, and when street demonstrations exploded in Birmingham, Alabama in 1963—with millions of Americans watching on television the brutalization of black women and children by police dogs and fire hoses—Kennedy was forced to abandon his noncommittal stance. For the first time identifying his own presidency with the movement, Kennedy told the nation that civil rights was "above all a moral issue, . . . as old as the Scriptures and as clear as the Constitution." Proposing a broad range of reforms, from equal access to public accommodations, to abolition of economic discrimination based on race, Kennedy expended vast resources of time and political credit to correct a fundamental flaw in American society.

Within days, he took two other actions, each in its own way an implicit recognition that the liberal consensus had problems. In the first, he ordered his staff to draft legislation to wage war on poverty, acknowledging that economic growth by itself was not adequate to "lift all boats." In the second, Kennedy rejected most of the shibboleths of the Cold War, telling an American University audience that it was time for both Russia and the United States to reexamine their assumptions. No system of government, he declared, was totally evil or good. Negotiation for peace offered the only intelligent path to follow given the fact that in the end, "our most basic common link is that we all inhabit this small planet. We all breathe the same air. We all cherish our children's future and we are all mortal." Two months later, Russia and the United States signed a treaty banning nuclear weapons-testing in the atmosphere. These three different actions each testified to a willingness to reexamine some of the pivotal assumptions of the liberal consensus—that the Cold War and anti-Communism should never be questioned, that American society was without basic flaws, and that economic growth was adequate to solve all problems.

When Kennedy was assassinated, it became Lyndon Johnson's responsibility to pursue the agenda of reform. With brilliance and skill, Johnson identified himself with Kennedy's domestic vision, broadened it over time, and eventually implemented it, passing a legislative program unmatched in scope since the height of the New Deal. But Johnson was himself a devoted believer in the liberal consensus, especially its centerpiece of Communist containment, and when the time came to decide what to do about Vietnam, Johnson could not disengage. Traumatized by the fear that appearing "soft on Communism" would endanger his domestic program, Johnson made the war his own, quickly becoming entrapped by a vicious cycle of escalation, defeat, then greater escalation. In the process, Johnson lied about the extent of his military build-up and eventually became a prisoner of his own fortress in the White House, unable to overcome or dissuade the growing army of critics, who by 1967 and 1968 insisted that the war was stupid and immoral (Kearns 1977; Dugger 1984; Caro 1982; Herring 1981).

As the civil rights movement became radicalized by Black Power, as students denounced the "system," and advocates of sex equality questioned the basic tenets of bourgeois society, the stage was set for a decisive battle between those defending established order, and those demanding radical change. To a degree unmatched in American history except by the election of 1860, the presidential campaign of 1968 became the battleground, each political candidate and platform reflecting underlying social and cultural tensions as well as traditional political divisions. For those who still held out some hope for change within the system, Robert Kennedy and Eugene McCarthy acted as spokesmen, both pledging an immediate end to the war in Vietnam and far-reaching domestic change. On the other side, Alabama's Governor George Wallace and former Vice President Richard Nixon spoke for those fed up with activism. "If any demonstrator ever lays down in front of my car," Wallace told one audience, "it will be the last car he will ever lay down in front of." Nixon, in turn, sought to identify with the "forgotten Americans, the non-shouters, the non-demonstrators, . . . those who do not break the law, . . . who love this country [and] cry out, 'That is enough, let's get some new leadership.' " Rarely had political rhetoric so accurately reflected fundamental social and cultural divisions.

Ultimately, it was the roller-coaster traumas of 1968 that determined the outcome. The TET offensive in January, McCarthy's apparent victory against Johnson in the New Hampshire primary in February, Robert Kennedy's entry into the race in March, Johnson's withdrawal as a candidate, King's assassination in April, the mass outbreak of urban violence that then ensued, Kennedy's assassination on June 4, then the riots in the streets of Chicago in August during the Democratic National Convention—each event was magnified and brought into every living room in the land by television. It all seemed too much. The only surprise in November was that the candidate promising to speak out for stability and law-abiding, patriotic Americans won by such a narrow margin.

With the election of 1968, the threat to the liberal consensus was thrown back, and a new "conservative consensus" became ascendant. Similar in virtually every respect to the liberal consensus, the conservative consensus was notable primarily for its reluctance to endorse reform—even incremental reform—as a positive responsibility of government. Instead, with the social issues of law and order, busing, and judicial "permissiveness" as rallying cries, Nixon and his allies urged a retreat from government-sponsored attempts to promote desegregation, wage war against poverty, or actively intervene on behalf of disadvantaged groups such as Chicanos or Native Americans. Government's primary role was to lower taxes, get out of people's lives, and force every individual to take responsibility for his or her own well-being. Convinced that he could forge a new and permanent Republican majority by appealing to the conservatism of the Old South and the new Sunbelt, Nixon thus allied himself with the forces of traditionalism on race and poverty, portrayed the Northeast and the media as deviant, and set out to use regional pride and cultural nationalism as vehicles for solidifying his power. Had it not been for Watergate, he might well have become one of the most politically successful presidents of the twentieth century (Leuchtenburg 1983; Chafe 1986; Witcover 1970; McGinnis 1969; Phillips 1969).

Notwithstanding the intervention of political scandal, however, Nixon inaugurated an era of conservative politics that reigned supreme for two decades. With the election of 1968 and the resurgence of a cultural and social politics based on traditional social values, most of the insurgent movements of the 1960s were repulsed, or at least contained. Even the Democratic exception to Republican rule during these years largely fit the new mold. A Southerner who boasted of being business-like in his administrative style and opposed to big government, Jimmy Carter cultivated the same values of traditional morality that Republicans had appealed to in 1968. With moralistic intensity, he preached the importance of restoring truth, integrity, and decency to government, boasted of being a "born-again" Christian, and had the intuitive genius to run "against Washington" at a time when the nation's capital symbolized corruption and confusion.

Although Carter in the end fell victim to a series of social, economic, and political crises that reflected problems unprecedented in America's postwar experience, his own political appeal drew on many of the same conservative values that were first introduced by Nixon and then brought to triumph by Ronald Reagan.

THE CULTURAL AND SOCIAL POLITICS OF THE 1970S AND 1980S

Ironically, the ascendancy of conservatism coincided with, and in some ways provided a response to, the first significant erosion of confidence Americans experienced about their own ability to control and dominate the world. From World War II onward, the American economy had expanded steadily, with the country's technological expertise and business acumen offering a model for the rest of the world. In the 1970s, the nations that America had put back on their feet after World War II suddenly started to outperform and outsell the United States. Countries like Germany, Japan, and even Korea started to challenge American dominance. Starting in 1973, the real income of America's workers began to fall as inflation soared, productivity fell, and jobs moved to Third World affiliates of multinational corporations. "Stagflation" (high inflation and high unemployment simultaneously) became a byword of 1970s economics, and by the end of the decade as many as 75 percent of Americans said that they expected their fortunes to decline rather than improve in the future.

All of this was simply reinforced by a series of events that called into question America's place in the world. The Arab oil embargo of 1973 highlighted not only America's dependence on foreign sources of energy, but also the helplessness of a once mighty world power. The nation's inability to provide its own energy meant it could no longer, in the most fundamental way, shape its own destiny. That message became even clearer as Americans watched television footage of the helicopter evacuation of the U.S. embassy in Saigon in 1975. In effect, when the Ayatollah Khomeni sanctioned the captivity of more than fifty Americans for over 400 days in 1979–80, he confirmed in the most galling manner possible the new sense of dependency and impotence that had overtaken the American people (Yankelovich 1982).

Ronald Reagan's triumph was to persuade the American people that these new realities were an illusion. Although he preached very much the same message of traditional values and morality that Jimmy Carter had offered four years earlier, Reagan added to it answers that insecure and troubled Americans wanted: they *were* strong, freedom *could* triumph over Communist tyranny, the United States *would* regain military and economic dominance in the world.

And to a remarkable extent, Reagan proved able to follow through on his promises—at least for six years—partly due to simple good luck, partly because of extraordinary political skill. Bringing to fruition many of the programs and ideas first associated with Nixon, Reagan succeeded in cutting back welfare programs, deregulating the economy (which Carter had started), rescinding government involvement in civil rights issues. At the same time, he cut taxes while dramatically expanding military spending, thereby pumping money into the economy and increasing the country's international power, albeit at a cost in deficit spending that promised eventually to paralyze the government's ability to pursue any new programs at home. Throughout, Reagan held on to his conservative constituency, massaged those on the "new right" who waged war against feminism, gay rights, busing, or abortion, and persuaded the average voter that through his presidency, America had once again learned to stand tall. By the 1984 election, Reagan had come to personify America itself, so that any attack on his presidency seemed an effort to downgrade the country and its newly recovered pride (Wills 1984; see also "Letters from Washington" in *The New Yorker*, periodic).

In the midst of this conservative ascendancy, at least some of the changes associated with the civil rights movement and women's movement continued. The new opportunities made possible by civil rights legislation and court decisions led to better jobs, more upward mobility, and greater economic and educational fulfillment for many. The number of blacks attending college, for example, increased from 250,000 in 1960 to more than 1.2 million by the mid-1970s. Black married couples graduating from college in the late 1970s were earning as much as whites with a similar background. With legislation outlawing discrimination in housing and employment, more and more black families were able to move into the middle class—as many as 40 percent by some estimates. Voting rights laws, in turn, resulted in black registration and voting that quickly came close (proportionately) to white figures, and led to increased representation of blacks in virtually all elected offices, but especially as mayors of large cities.

Changes for women were even more pronounced. By the end of the 1970s, nearly 65 percent of married women were employed, more than half of all mothers of children under six held jobs, and the fastest increase in the female labor force was occurring among women in their twenties.

Women seeking careers saw perhaps the greatest change, as college graduates crossed historical barriers to women participating in traditionally male-dominated professions. As late as 1970, barely 5 percent of those entering law school or medical school classes consisted of women. Today the figure is more than 40 percent.

Partly as a consequence of these changes, the composition of the typical American family also altered dramatically. As late as the 1950s, more than 70 percent of all American families consisted of a father who worked, and a mother who stayed at home to take care of the children. By 1980 that description applied only to 15 percent of all families. During the same years, birth rates declined precipitously. At the height of the baby boom, the average family had more than three children. By 1980 the figure had fallen to less than 1.6 children, achieving the reproduction level required for zero population growth. During the same period as well, the divorce rate climbed dramatically—more than 100 percent in the twenty years after 1960—and by 1980 more than two out of five marriages were expected to end in divorce (Yankelovich 1982).

For at least some blacks and women, these changes meant a significantly better life than had seemed possible just a generation earlier. Those individuals who started from a place of economic security and educational opportunity were especially able to take advantage of civil rights victories and transcend traditional barriers of race and gender.

Yet one of the consequences of the conservative ascendancy was to ignore the plight of those who were not economically well situated or educationally prepared to take advantage of these new rights. Class became an increasingly central reality for millions of blacks, women, Hispanics, and other minorities who were condemned to low-income housing, inadequate schooling, poor health care, deadend or nonexistent jobs, and a welfare system that offered little if any opportunity to escape. America seemed increasingly to be moving toward a two-tiered social structure, even among blacks, women, and Hispanics, in which less-fortunate members of minority groups were left behind, unable to take advantage of the opportunities seized upon by their better-off brothers and sisters. The proportion of black Americans living in poverty grew from 31.1 percent in 1986 to 33.1 percent two years later, while poverty among Hispanics moved from 27.3 to 28.2 percent. At the same time, the jobs that were available tended to be concentrated at the low-wage level, with half of the new positions since 1980 paying less than the poverty level for a family of four. The richest one-fifth of the nation increased its share of the national income, while the lowest one-fifth saw its share decline.

Such social trends as the newly discovered "underclass" went hand in hand with a high-tech economy requiring more education for decent jobs, an escalating drop-out rate among inner city youth, and the growing "feminization of poverty," by which adult women and their children, disproportionately black and Hispanic, would comprise the overwhelming majority of poor people by the twenty-first century. Even women who worked, for example, often headed households with incomes beneath the poverty level, largely because 80 percent of all women's jobs were clustered in the 5 percent of occupations that were predominantly low-paying service positions.

Symptomatic of all these problems was the growing phenomenon of female-headed households, highlighting the intersection of race, class, and gender as sources of inequality. While the number of white families headed by women increased from 9.4 percent in 1970 to 14 percent in 1980, the number of black families headed by women skyrocketed to 47 percent, and of Hispanic families to 41 percent. Minority women also experienced most severely the debilitating consequence of new sexual mores. One out of every three black children was born to a teen-age mother, and 55 percent of all black babies were born out of wedlock. All of this, in turn, correlated directly with poverty. A child born into a family with no father present had a one in three chance of being poor; if the family were headed by a man alone, the chances improved to one in ten; and if both parents were present, the chances were only one in nineteen (Auletta 1981).

Thus positive change for some did not necessarily bring progress for others, and while discrimination based on race and gender had certainly become less significant for those well-positioned to take advantage of new civil rights, the burdens of class, gender, and race had become greater for millions of others. Threatening to add to the problem even further was the influx of millions of new immigrants—up to six million per year, the overwhelming majority of them illegal entrants. With nearly two-thirds of the new immigrants coming from Hispanic nations, especially Mexico, or from Asian nations, there was the ever-present danger of class tensions becoming conflated with ethnic hostility. While Asian immigrants fared better economically than others, and an ever-expanding economy in Southern California absorbed many Hispanics, the two-tier problem remained. The new economic position of America in the world, with U.S. customers more dependent on foreign production of basic commodities such as clothing and automobiles, meant fewer and fewer decent economic opportunities for those without a college education. As class differences became more entrenched, there also seemed less likelihood of mobilizing a political constituency able to chart a program to address such issues, especially when low voter turnout correlated directly with poverty (Muller 1985; Glazer 1985).

Thus the new conservative consensus, whatever appeal it had to those already possessing a stake in the society, offered little hope for those who were already left out. If the liberal consensus seemed inadequate to those who perceived the need for structural change in order to secure equality, it at least acknowledged the need for incremental reform. The conservative consensus essentially argued that all had been accomplished that needed to be accomplished, with all citizens now left to take care of themselves. As the chasm widened between rich and poor, inner-city dweller and suburbanite, college graduate and high school dropout, there seemed less and less likelihood that the nation could regain the sense of common values and shared self-interest that had marked the optimistic era of the 1950s and early 1960s.

TURNING POINTS

The story of the United States during the years since World War II thus presents a mixed message. On the one hand, there were all the positive changes that occurred—almost miraculously—in the postwar years. The extraordinary increase in education, consumerism, homeownership, and economic prosperity constituted a breakthrough in living standards almost unheard of in human history. Consistent with such changes, the nation evolved a political viewpoint, embodied in the liberal consensus, that exuded optimism, faith in perfectibility, and confidence in national strength.

Yet positive changes also highlighted eventually the inequities that remained, and the extent to which whole groups of citizens were left out of the American dream. Especially visible were black Americans, the rapidly growing number of Hispanic-Americans, and ultimately women as well. The positive story of white migration to suburbia had, as its negative counterpart, the growing ghettoization of the nation's inner cities. For a brief period of time in the 1960s, there seemed reason to hope that the basic inequalities in American society could be addressed, even including the inequality of income and impoverishment. But in the end that hope dissolved, a victim on the one hand of the evolving radicalism of those who saw the need for a thorough restructuring of American society in order for equality to be achieved, and on the other, by the insistence of those in power on devoting resources to a war against Communism that might otherwise have been spent in a war against poverty. Ultimately the strain became too great for the existing political arrangement to withstand, resulting in the confrontations of the late 1960s.

Two turning points stand out in this story. The first is the election of 1968, which in effect became a referendum on the amount of fundamental change that would be acceptable within the traditional framework of America's values and institutions. In that referendum, those who sought to bolster the status quo and defend traditional values prevailed. The second turning point occurred in 1973, when Americans discovered for the first time in postwar history that they were not in control of the world, that there were limits to the U.S. economic machine as well as to the nation's ability to dictate its own fate.

In many ways, the country has not yet come to grips, socially or politically, with the second turning point. Instead, the prevalence of a conservative consensus, modulated and reinforced by the rhetorical brilliance of a Ronald Reagan, has allowed many Americans to deceive themselves into thinking that the good old days are still here, and that nothing fundamental has changed. The 1988 presidential campaign did little to redress the problem. One candidate attempted to wrap himself in the flag and denounce his opponent as soft on crime, and the other, for the most part, sought to flee from any association with the "L" word—liberalism. Such exercises in self-deception managed to ignore the social reality of internal fragmentation, the growth of ethnic tension between blacks, Chicanos, and other inner-city minorities and the white-dominated culture that remains in power in the world outside, and the economic bad news that increasingly we live in a world in which it will be difficult for the average American citizen to buy a house, or live a life like those we associate with the generation of the 1950s and 1960s. The fact that by the year 2020 we will be an aging population, with fewer and fewer young people being asked to support more and more senior citizens—the product of the baby boom—has yet to even enter our national consciousness.

Comment

GARY R. HAWKE

The chapters by Bob Catley, Harvey Franklin, and Bill Chafe illustrate the general theme that the three societies of Australia, New Zealand, and the United States have a great deal in common, but that too ready an acceptance of these similarities can hide significant differences and generate misunderstanding. In the 1950s and 1960s, the three societies experienced economic growth, population growth and urbanization, and a continuation of historical traditions directed toward progress. In the 1970s and 1980s, conventional attitudes and policies toward encompassing these trends within continued social cohesion came under more pressure. But there were also national pecularities within these similarities, and their extent has often been underestimated.

Even the similarities should not be taken to mean that the three societies of Australia, New Zealand, and the United States formed any kind of unit; to some extent, their experiences were similar because they all participated in wider international processes. So it was with economic growth. In the years after World War II, ways were found to use resources of all kinds to produce more of the goods and services that people wanted and most countries experienced economic growth. The availability of income and an optimistic stance toward the future engendered population growth through higher fertility in many countries. The goods and services that people wanted were more readily available in urban than in rural settings so that cities grew, and they grew through spreading suburbs into the surrounding countryside. Australia, New Zealand, and the United States shared in these trends.

They shared them in different ways. The United States grew economically mostly as a major unit in its own right, so rich and populous that it was a significant force in world trade but able to achieve so much efficient production and consumption within its own boundaries that international trade was a relatively minor component of its economy. Australia and New Zealand were much more directed toward international trade, protecting their industries from international competition in order to provide high levels of employment and opportunities to develop talents and skills needed for new and exciting forms of employment. Fortunately for the maintenance of common interests, the security concerns of the U.S. leadership, and pressures from its wheat farmers, led the country to assume leadership of moves toward freer international trade, so that Australia and New Zealand regarded it as an ally in what they saw as most important to their continuing economic growth.

Similarly, one of the major international trends of the postwar world was decolonization and increasing recognition that world affairs were not all centered in Europe. From the independence of India, through decolonization in Africa and Asia, and the creation of the "Non-Aligned Movement," international gatherings became much more varied in the peoples and cultures found in prominent roles. The United States had a major role as it tried to reconcile support for independence and self-determination with maintenance of alliances against the Soviet Union. Australians and New Zealanders probably saw the international trend most clearly in the changed composition of gatherings of Commonwealth leaders, and both were directly involved as decolonization encompassed Papua New Guinea and Western Samoa. But again, while the countries disagreed about precisely how decolonization should proceed in particular cases, they could see a common interest within a much wider process.

Within this wider international community, the United States occupied a much more prominent place than Australia or New Zealand. The United States was most often the place where the agenda of social life was set.

This was true of the way in which economic growth was diffused into social life. Comparisons of levels of real income are notoriously difficult and as economic growth and standards of living became matters of national policy, Australia and New Zealand had some basis for the belief that their standards of living were higher than those of the United States. But such calculations rested on definitions of living standards that reflected conditions in Australia and New Zealand; they emphasized things like space and homeownership, which were relatively readily available, and not artistic innovation, which was much more likely to occur in the United States.

When high resource levels were shared among few people in the nineteenth century, Australia and New Zealand probably did have very high levels of average real incomes in an international perspective. This was probably true briefly during the Korean War commodity boom in the early 1950s too, but the common beliefs in Australia and New Zealand were more myth than reality. The better generalization is that all three countries were rich in an international perspective, the United States more so than Australia and New Zealand. Furthermore, all three shared the experience in the 1960s and 1970s of seeing Japan and European and newly industrializing countries rapidly achieving at least comparable levels of real incomes.

The more obvious leadership of the United States in the context of the link between economic growth and social dynamics was in the composition of consumers' expenditure. The United States led in the shift toward services, in the accumulation of household durable items, in higher expectations of the level of comfort provided by homes, and in the extent to which social life was dependent on access to motor vehicles for personal travel. New Zealand and Australia had developed British ideas of social security and put their independent development of them into a British terminology; they could easily adopt such terms as "welfare state" but it was the United States that was first seen as the "affluent society," the place which had first reached "the age of mass consumption" and where the "welfare society" was most discussed.

All three countries saw themselves not only as societies that were successful in using resources to produce high standards of living but as guardians of a tradition of reform, of building "good societies," of concern for the less fortunate. Each also tended to exaggerate its uniqueness. The United States talked a lot of its international role, and its foreign aid program was in part a genuinely altruistic effort to help others secure material comfort of the kind available in the United States while it also contributed to its worldwide security interests. As Bill Chafe points out, governments of the 1950s and 1960s accepted the changes of the "New Deal" and the "Fair Deal." Australians talked of the "lucky country," where resources made it possible for even the relatively poor not to be severely disadvantaged in social life and unions ensured that wage-earners shared in increasing prosperity through government-provided wage-setting systems. New Zealanders put even more emphasis on security in political and public rhetoric, achieved the elimination of unemployment to a greater extent than most countries, and often thought of their welfare state as unique.

There were differences among the countries. Americans sometimes thought that the willingness of Australia and New Zealand to use state institutions was too close to socialism for comfort. New Zealand, especially, with its absence of federal-state constraints, used central government decision making more than the other countries. George McGovern, who was widely regarded in the United States as an extremist in his willingness to use government action in pursuit of the reform tradition of the United States at the expense of its capitalist one, would not have been out of place in the more conservative political party of New Zealand. New Zealanders who thought that unions had secured too strong a place in determining business decisions were unaware of what had developed in Australia. Yet all three countries could see that in some senses, they shared common attitudes and responses.

The reform traditions of the three countries were kept alive by centers of activism. These were fed from the United States both in their content and in their tactics. Perhaps the clearest example of this is the increased prominence of women in all aspects of social life and in the consequent challenges posed to existing social and political institutions. Many influences are important in this—the availability of contraceptive methods, the development of mechanical aids for domestic work, and so on—but the most important is simply the inequity of excluding half of society from positions of most influence. The process is a long one: parity in the "rate for the job" whether it is held by a man or a woman; the current debate in all three countries about fair relative rewards for occupations that are held predominantly by one gender; nondiscrimination against women in recruitment and promotion policies; policies that ensure that women have fair career prospects despite their greater contribution to childrearing; representation of women in significant decision-making bodies; recognition that women may define the important issues in ways different from men.

In all three countries, and in others, women chose various tactics from radical feminism to backroom advocacy within established institutions. They encountered opposition, especially from people committed to the traditional organization of family life and from religious groups opposed to contraception or abortion. This certainly differed among the three countries but there was a common core of similar experience. Tactics varied depending on whether wages and salaries were mostly set in negotiations among employers and employees or through central arbitration bodies, and on whether abortion was controlled by a constitution, the courts, or parliament.

Another center of activism was concerned with race issues. The United States was again in the lead. It also drew on a basic issue of fairness, but it was assisted by recognition that the country could hardly play a leading role in a world that was increasingly non-European while not paying attention to race issues within its own boundaries. The U.S. Constitution has always had the great strength of being capable of reinterpretation in line with changing social attitudes. Thus a constitution that had initially been compatible with slavery, and that had remained compatible with markedly different civil rights depending on race, came in the 1950s and 1960s to be incompatible with unequal access to education. Legislation redefined what constituted fair voting districts and fair access to registers of voters. Blacks were assisted toward a more equal participation in all aspects of U.S. life. Attention turned to the way that the Indian community was treated. Their original dispossession was reconsidered in the light of current attitudes toward justice rather than what had been considered fair at the time. New means were sought of enabling Indians to participate in mainstream U.S. life while preserving their own culture.

The rhetoric and tactics of black activists were observed in New Zealand. The Maori people had preserved much of their culture, especially its tribal or *iwi* basis, while government policy had followed a well-meaning but patronizing effort to incorporate Maori into New Zealand life with pan-tribal advisory structures and non-Maori control. During World War II, the Maori community had been allowed to control its own contribution to the war effort, but thereafter old patterns had been reasserted. The Maori community waited, and despite sharing in the universal movement to cities and a rapid loss of facility in the Maori language, it preserved its cultural strength. It always argued for recognition of past wrongs and sufficient control of resources to manage its own development.

Change was later in Australia. The Commonwealth had been formed on the basis of a "White Australia." This was changed first in the context of immigration, but Australia too could not accommodate a population of increasingly varied ethnic background and secure a position of influence on the rim of Asia without recognizing the disadvantaged status of its own aboriginal population. Australian aborigines had been less able to thrive in mainstream society than had the Maori in New Zealand. In New Zealand a person of mixed ancestry but always known as a Maori was acting premier in the 1890s and some Maori had reached high levels in every profession. The problem was one of proportions and of recognition of the validity of Maori ways rather than exclusion.

In contrast, Australia deliberately developed multiculturalism through immigration. For a mixture of reasons—filling open spaces to preempt uncontrolled invasion from the north, the traditional importance of development or use of natural resources, and the belief that Australia would gain economically from a larger population able to provide a larger market for its own manufacturing industries—Australia promoted immigration. It was willing to do so by recruiting from non-traditional areas of South and Southeast Europe, from Lebanon and increasingly from Asia as well. Immigrants were expected to assimilate—they were "New Australians"—and with the suspicion of governments and anti-Communist sentiments that were strong among them, they were widely expected to bolster conservatism in the community. But while they did assimilate, their cultures were preserved to some extent. Australian political and social leaders found that they had to reexamine the belief that Australians looked to Britain for their roots and consider what it meant to be a multicultural society. They knew that the United States had faced the same issue much earlier. There was not a great deal in common between the United States and Australia in immigration policy from 1950 to the present day, and yet there was a basis for the belief that the two countries shared a common experience.

New Zealand's experience was rather different. The pressure for population growth was less strong than in Australia. The populations nevertheless grew at about the same rate, but immigration provided fewer, and natural increase more people than in Australia. The traditional sources of migrants in Western Europe provided the level of immigration deemed desirable, especially as official opinion ran ahead of popular opinion in doubting whether the economic gains of immigration were substantial. Ethnic issues were much less prominent in New Zealand than in Australia. New Zealand did, however, accept immigrants from the South Pacific. Some Polynesians, such as those of the Cook Islands, were New Zealand citizens and had a right of entry. For others, New Zealand governments accepted responsibility as their own islands did not provide for modern living. Furthermore, in the years of low unemployment, employers were often glad of labor drawn from Samoa, Tonga, and other Pacific islands. New Zealand's experience of immigration was therefore different from that of both Australia and the United States, but immigration issues were another aspect of race relations. Again New Zealand's opinion leaders thought they were meeting issues similar to those of the United States, moving in the same direction, and improving on the U.S. record.

Professor Chafe has argued cogently for activism provoking a reaction so that the liberal consensus of capitalism and reform gave way to a conservative consensus, with the 1968 presidential election marking the turning point. The discussions of Australia and New Zealand by Dr. Catley and Professor Franklin seem to me right in describing a rather different path. The Vietnam experience did provide something in common, although it was less searing than in the United States in both Australia and New Zealand, especially in the latter, from which all who served in Vietnam were volunteers. The end of intervention in Vietnam was presided over in both countries by Labour governments. Both governments fell because of the oil crisis of 1973–74, which enforced a substantial transfer of income from countries like Australia and New Zealand to oil producers. The subsequent governments of the more conservative parties in both countries continued to be managers of economic and social trends rather than vigorous pursuers of traditional values, and wanted to rein in activists who tried to continue the pursuit of reform.

The swing of the political pendulum returned Labour governments in 1983 and 1984 respectively and official support for social change became more vigorous. It was from 1984 that the Waitangi Tribunal in New Zealand was empowered to reconsider all Maori grievances about the past and to recommend to the government means of acknowledging wrongs and providing a basis for *iwi* development. The Australian government has maintained its commitment to developing multiculturalism. It is hard to see in these areas any conservative consensus's rejection of reform.

There are, however, some parallels. In Australia, and even more in New Zealand, there was increasing dissatisfaction during the 1970s and early 1980s with the rate of economic growth being achieved. The Labour governments elected in 1983 and 1984 responded with an increased emphasis on the efficiency with which resources are used. The emphasis on efficiency surprised some of their traditional supporters. In New Zealand, especially, many people think that the economic policy of the Labour government resembles that of the Reagan administration in the United States (and the Thatcher government in Britain) rather than the welfare policies of earlier Labour governments. Certainly, the economic policy of the government has attracted unusually strong support in business circles, although some have been surprised to find that they were travelling along parallel paths rather than seeing the diminished role of government in general sought by supporters of a conservative consensus.

More efficient resource use includes greater decentralization and reliance on individual endeavour—but the Australian and New Zealand Labour governments have not espoused conservative doctrines of support for traditional family structures or valued diminished government activity for its own sake. They have attempted to adapt social policies to social trends, recognizing that the emancipation of women has led to more two-income families and made families with young children more likely to experience relatively low household incomes. They have attempted to reconcile the claims of public health and education systems with the imperative of efficient use of all resources. They have continued to seek to address the consequences of social and political changes that have created pockets of society excluded from increased living standards and positions of influence. The extent to which they have succeeded in maintaining the tradition of reform is a matter of legitimate political and social debate.

Recent experience always appears to have divergent currents compared with earlier periods. It is easy to look back to the liberal consensus of the 1950s and 1960s and see a period of quiescence in which the main social trends are readily apparent. That wasn't how it seemed at the time. Thus the divergence of the present might come to seem more ordered as we look back on it with hindsight. But my conjecture is that we shall then see some similarities among the three societies, but continued differences as well.

SECTION II

Political Evolution

In this section we look at the changing political processes and agendas of the three countries. We are interested in their political systems—the structures through which decisions are made, the strength of the key institutional actors, interest group alignments, and so on—and the issues that have dominated their political debates and decision making during this time. We also look at the degree to which there is now consensus or division over the basic national political agenda in each case.

Each of the political systems, of course, has historical roots well before the period on which this volume focuses, and all the authors have drawn on this history to some degree in setting the context of postwar events and evolution. Each also documents significant changes over the four decades of this study.

Hugh Collins tracks the progressive centralization of the Australian political system. He cites the growing power of the Commonwealth government in the postwar period, though with important constraints imposed by the federal structure and by the power of the Senate in the bicameral national legislature. These two features distinguish Australia from both of the other countries. He also argues that competition for the middle ground in national electoral politics has produced a dominant ethos of pragmatic utilitarianism in government policy, citing the present Labor government's adoption of a cooperative government-business-union approach to economic management as the latest example. He worries, however, that the power of the representative organs of government has not kept pace with the growth of executive capability, and that the politics of the middle ground, with its focus on familiar issues, does not necessarily ensure that the right issues are being placed on the national agenda.

Roberto Rabel characterizes the changes in New Zealand politics following the election of 1984 as a revolution, in which the previous "mold" of New Zealand politics was definitively broken and a fifty-year tradition of pragmatic welfarism and corporatist democracy was replaced by an approach based on market liberalism. He comments that the nature of the new mold remains uncertain, with significant internal divisions within both major parties over policy directions. He suggests that the future of New Zealand's politics may be more characterized by diversity and fragmentation than by the development of a new consensus.

Donald Stokes identifies three key elements in America's postwar political history: the central role of presidential leadership; the breakdown of the Roosevelt-era political party alignment; and the function of presidential elections as barometers of overall public satisfaction rather than as referenda on specific policy positions. He points out that these factors have motivated a degree of improvisation in presidential policymaking, with the Reagan tax cuts and resulting legacy of major budget deficits a recent prime example. He also concludes that in such a political process, the issues of most concern to America's ANZUS partners, even those that are contentious in Australia and New Zealand, are extremely unlikely to achieve high public visibility in the United States.

In his concluding comment, Charles Morrison discusses some of the common factors and trends that underly these otherwise disparate processes of political change, as well as some of the common questions the three systems face for the future. He speculates that, reflecting the parallel forces at work, the future evolution of the three systems is likely to continue to reflect more broadly similar than distinctive trends.

4

Central Power in the Australian Commonwealth: The Postwar Polity

HUGH N. COLLINS

The subject of this section poses an analytical task that is both extensive and restrictive. It is extensive simply because the sweep of events, issues, personalities and processes covered is so broad. We are talking about half of Australia's federal history: The period since World War II is now longer than the span of the Commonwealth's existence from its inauguration on January 1, 1901, to the declaration of war announced by R. G. Menzies on September 3, 1939.

Consider some of the features of Australia's postwar politics. Since the war, there have been eighteen elections for the House of Representatives in the Commonwealth Parliament, with changes of government occurring at four. Of the nine prime ministers during this period, three (Chifley, Whitlam, and Hawke) have come from the Australian Labor Party, which has had six parliamentary leaders in this time; five (Menzies, Holt, Gorton, McMahon, and Fraser) have been drawn from the Liberal Party of Australia, which has had eight parliamentary leaders; one (McEwen) has been supplied by the Liberals' coalition partner in government, the Australian Country Party (now the National Party of Australia), which has had four parliamentary leaders. The terms served by these prime ministers have varied from more than sixteen years (Menzies, December 19, 1949 to January 26, 1966) to less than one month (McEwen, December 19, 1967 to January 10, 1968). The turbulence of the period is reflected in the variety of ways in which these terms ended. Of the eight who have left office, only three did so at the hands of the electorate (Chifley, McMahon, Fraser); one is presumed to have died in office (Holt); one resigned, effectively retiring after a long career in parliamentary politics (Menzies); one was dismissed by the governor-general (Whitlam); and one was deposed by his party (Gorton); one was a stopgap appointee serving only until his coalition partner had selected a new leader (McEwen). The electorate has been required to consider twenty-three proposals to alter the constitution by referendum, of which only five have achieved the majority both of the overall vote and of the number of states that is required for passage. The federal electoral system has undergone several changes, of which the most significant are the introduction (in 1948) of proportional representation in voting for the Senate and the extension of the franchise (in 1973) to eighteen-year-olds.

The task of this chapter is restrictive because—even if it could be accomplished within the compass of a single essay—a complete analysis would seek to relate these changes in politics to social evolution and economic history. The brief accepted here is an assessment of the polity in a rather narrow sense. This chapter is concerned chiefly with those developments in Australia's structure of governance that may be of particular importance for understanding the trilateral relationship between Australia, New Zealand, and the United States.

But how are the changes in institutions, roles, and powers to be related to changes in ideas, styles, and issues? To impose some order on a disparate set of problems, I have turned to the phrase employed by Sir Robert Menzies as the title for a set of lectures that he delivered at the University of Virginia shortly after his retirement from parliamentary politics in 1966.

Sir Robert's theme was the growth of the Commonwealth's power within the Australian federation. His choice of topic was characteristically deliberate. Menzies considered an exposition of the constitutional development of a federation to be appropriate for a U.S. audience—especially an audience on Jefferson's campus. But in what proved to be his only published reflections on government, he was signalling the major phenomenon in Australian politics during his long experience.

That the dominant change in the Australian political system since 1901 has been the shift in the federal balance by which the Commonwealth has achieved supremacy over the six states may be a common judgment, but it is surely also an incontestable one. As this has been largely a postwar change, much of this chapter is concerned with the sources and significance of the growth of central power.

As well as its plain, institutional meaning, however, I intend a twist to the title which was certainly not present in Menzies's Virginian exposition, but which joins his political statecraft to his constitutional analysis. For "central power in the Australian Commonwealth" may also be used to signify the power of the center in Australian politics—the electoral significance of capturing and holding the middle ground. The politics of getting to the center is the key to electoral success in Australian postwar politics. What constitutes the middle ground in Australian politics? Who defines it? How has it shifted? The second part of the chapter explores these issues.

Finally, a concluding section attempts an evaluation. Does the current agenda accurately reflect the nation's needs? Can the institutions analyzed in the first part translate into effective policies the issues and agendas surveyed in the second? What are the political and intellectual resources for meeting political challenges? Do Australia's specific problems relate to generic dilemmas for liberal democracies evident also in American and New Zealand politics?

CENTRAL POWER IN THE AUSTRALIAN COMMONWEALTH: GOVERNANCE

Australia's political system is federal in structure. The constitution, which created the national polity and which delimits the powers of the central government, has stood very largely unchanged since receiving Queen Victoria's assent on July 9, 1900, as the Commonwealth of Australia Constitution Act of the British Parliament. Yet despite the fact that the text of the constitution remains relatively unchanged, the operation of the Australian political system in 1988 is very different from the form envisaged in 1898 or the experience of the nation by 1938.

A fundamental shift in the balance of power within the federation has occurred, by which the Commonwealth has assumed a political supremacy over the six states. This shift has been largely a postwar phenomenon, in which the central power has grown both in resources and in legislative domain. Some figures may illustrate the trend. Take the increase in size of the Commonwealth government alone. The national parliament has grown from the original seventy-five members of the House of Representatives to 121 in 1949 and 148 in 1984; the Senate has increased from thirty-six to sixty to seventy-six over the same period. (The proportionality between these leaps and bounds is a consequence of the so-called "nexus" clause: Section 24 of the constitution provides that the number of members of the House of Representatives "shall be, as nearly as practicable, twice the number of the senators." Offered an opportunity to break this nexus through a referendum in 1967, the electorate rejected change and committed the nation to a surge in the Senate whenever demographic pressure requires an increase in the lower house.) Within this enlarged legislature, the number of ministers has increased from nineteen after the war to thirty in the third Hawke ministry. The number of full-time staff employed under the Public Service Act has grown from 154,992 in 1950 to 173,014 in 1986, having reached 277,455 in 1975. Thus the apparatus of government, elected and official, is larger.

This bigger government machine operates across a progressively wider range of issues. The broadened scope of Australian national government is not simply a response to the increased demands for social provision in the age of the welfare state and the exigencies of economic management in an era of global interdependence, which are evident in all postwar liberal democracies. In a federal system that accords specific powers to the center, this growth is possible only if the broader powers are implicit in the original distribution or conferred in subsequent changes. The powers by which the Commonwealth has extended its legislative and executive reach have been owed chiefly to judicial decision. Through a series of landmark judgments in the postwar period, the High Court has interpreted the constitution to permit the growth of central power.

In the 1980s, for example, through cases such as *Koowarta* and the *Tasmanian Dam*, in which states challenged the authority of the Commonwealth (in the former, over the extent of Commonwealth powers to prevent racial discrimination under the Racial Discrimination Act 1975; in the latter, over the Commonwealth's ability to enforce specific environmental protection legislation against the developmental policies of a state), the court upheld the validity of the Commonwealth's powers through its interpretation of the "external affairs power" (Section 51 (29)) of the constitution. In each case, a majority on the court maintained that action to which a state objected as an illegitimate intrusion into its sphere was a valid consequence of the Commonwealth's legitimate obligations under international law. Such decisions produce major changes in the federal balance without formal alteration to the constitution. So it may fairly be held that the growth of central power has been achieved largely through judicial decision rather than by popular approval through referendum. Indeed, the formal process of amending the constitution through referendum has demonstrated electoral resistance to change, particularly change enlarging the scope of Commonwealth powers.

An expanded financial base has also been a prerequisite for the growth in central power. This has again been an essentially postwar achievement, buttressed by judicial interpretation. Uniform taxation powers assumed by the Commonwealth during World War II were entrenched thereafter by the Chifley government in legislation upheld by the High Court. Driven from the field of income tax, the states have become supplicants for their shares of revenue to which the Commonwealth holds the purse strings. An annual ritual of Australian politics is the Premiers' Conference, at which the state premiers convene in Canberra with the prime minister and treasurer to negotiate federal allocations and loans policies. These are negotiations within margins effectively set by the Commonwealth government. Their rhetoric, in which the periphery's protest against the center must equally reflect the nuances of partisan alignment, provides the script of contemporary Australian federalism.

The growth of central power in the Australian Commonwealth has been essentially an expansion of the executive government. To be sure, the legislative powers of the Commonwealth have increased. Federal parliamentarians have more issues to examine, to debate, to represent, and to pursue. But the growth of Commonwealth powers has not seen the legislature more powerfully armed against the executive. Rather, an already powerful executive has largely maintained its sway. The party organization of parliamentary politics has ensured the domination of the back benches by their front bench leaders on each side of the house. The governing party's executive—the cabinet—continues its dominant influence over the conduct of parliamentary business and the funding of Parliament itself.

The burgeoning of executive power is reflected in the growth of the Commonwealth bureaucracy. The increase in the number of departments and officials noted earlier relates to growth in the central and coordinating departments as well as to expansion in the functional agencies. The growth in size, influence, and initiative of the Department of Prime Minister and Cabinet is the clearest example of the need of leaders of Labor and non-Labor governments alike for more active policy support.

Some of the postwar changes in the bureaucracy have immediate consequences for the relationships between the ANZUS allies. Thus, following the U.S. model, the Department of Defence has pulled together the once relatively independent service departments into a more cohesive structure intended to produce policies within a consistent strategic design. The reorientation of Australian defense policy under the present government is premised not only on the intellectual contribution of an expert review (the "Dibb" Report of 1986) and a skillful ministerial approach (Beazley's *White Paper* of 1987), but also on the bureaucratic machinery to implement the changed direction. In political and economic diplomacy, the amalgamation of former rivals into a single Department of Foreign Affairs and Trade is the culmination of a long struggle by the Department of Foreign Affairs (until 1970, External Affairs) to assert its bureaucratic preeminence in the conduct of relations with other countries and international organizations. The intelligence area has undergone a series of changes, reflecting political and administrative uncertainty about the best method of linking intelligence gathering and analysis to policy- and decision-making.

The product of this bureaucratic growth and change is a better-articulated government machine that should be better able to advise government and implement policy. Not until the mid-1970s, for example, did Foreign Affairs have a section specifically designated to analyze U.S. domestic politics; there were significant gaps in official and governmental information and perception to be plugged. Were the intelligence agencies not as differentiated and as independent as they now are, it would have been much more difficult for the Australian government to walk the tightrope between maintaining the confidentiality of U.S. communications while sustaining the bilateral links with New Zealand in areas unaffected by the U.S. embargo on the provision of U.S.-origin intelligence to New Zealand following the nuclear ship-access blowup. Both Washington and Wellington have needed this capacity in Canberra. Twenty and thirty years ago, it would have been difficult to achieve.

The architectural transformation of the national capital attests to the growth of central power in the symbols as well as sinews of government. It has not been considered insignificant that the High Court achieved its massive permanent home before the Parliament. The legislature, which did not move to its now familiar temporary home in Canberra until 1927, had to wait until 1988 to occupy its permanent quarters. Those quarters accommodate the executive as amply as they do the legislature. The provision of an executive wing literally sets in concrete the power relations of Australian national government. The edifice on Capital Hill in Canberra stands in marked contrast to the Capitol's proclamation of the separation of powers in Washington as well as to the more muted but nevertheless discernible distinction between Westminster and Whitehall nurtured by the British Parliament.

The symbolic prominence achieved by the national institutions of government in Canberra is mirrored in the growing number of organizations and interest groups now focused on the capital. Influence is its own industry, and lobbyists have pitched their tents around the perimeter of Parliament and among the encampments of the bureaucracy. Federalism's social impact is evident as the headquarters of voluntary and professional associations are moved to, or created in, the national capital. The same dynamics are evident in the major political parties, whose central secretariats are now firmly established in Canberra rather than continuing a tug-of-war between Sydney and Melbourne.

Despite the massive increase in the scope and salience of central power, the structure of the Australian political system remains federal. It is a mistake to interpret Australian politics as if it were a unitary system like New Zealand. This is an important point to register with American observers, because federalism is more insistent, immediate, and intractable in Australia than in the United States.

While it has suited some in the states to present the growth in central power as a zero-sum game conducted at their expense, in fact all levels of government in Australia have grown since the war, whether in size, in share of GDP, or in their intrusive and regulatory activities. In 1986, of Australians in government employment, 65 percent were on the payrolls of the states and the Northern Territory. (A further 9 percent were employed by local government, which comes within the ambit of state jurisdiction.) The political parties continue to be state-based, with significant variations in their regional complexions. Australia is a federal nation socially as well as politically. Much voluntary activity is organized federally, with equal representation by state on a national council. Such structures reinforce the identity of, and identification with, the state of residence. These are ties equally fostered by the media: The press remains essentially a set of metropolitan papers (a national newspaper did not emerge until 1963, and has nowhere supplanted the major local daily), while television still combines strong local identity, especially in news presentation, with national networking.

Politically, federalism provides opposition parties with opportunities to exercise leverage against a government in Canberra. State premiers can be powerful allies or formidable adversaries of the party in national power. These dynamics are evident in a comparison between the Whitlam and Hawke administrations. Certainly, there are important and deliberate differences in style and policy between these two ALP governments. But with Labor premiers in all mainland states except Queensland for most of its life, the Hawke government has enjoyed a smoother passage than the Whitlam government, whose only experience of Labor premiers was in Tasmania and South Australia.

The political complications produced by federalism extended to the international sphere. The juristic link between international treaties and the domestic division of powers has already been noted. But states are active in external representation, in tourism, investment, and transnational exchange, complicating the life of the federal government. Even where the legal division of power is clear, a complex web of administrative interdependence is necessary. When citizens march in protest to the U.S.–Australian "joint defense facility" at North West Cape, it may be a set of policies and arrangements conducted under the Commonwealth's powers that draws their attention, but the responsibility for the protection of peace and order will fall primarily on the state's police force. And if the Commonwealth has been able to assert its authority in external security (against, for example, the attempt by the Cain government in 1982 to prevent the entry of nuclear ships into Victorian harbors), it has been less successful in imposing its will over foreign trade in raw materials (where, for example, the Bjelke-Petersen government in Queensland undercut the Wran government in New South Wales in setting a price for coal exports to Japan). These are complexities which neither the United States nor the New Zealand government had to face. They are a constant constraint on the reality of central power in the Australian Commonwealth.

The other major constraint on central power lies at the center itself, in the bicameral structure of the national legislature. The constitution's provision for two chambers—the House of Representatives, with representation roughly proportional to population by constituency or district, and the Senate, with equal representation by state—is conventionally understood to be the adoption of an American form by Australia's founding fathers. (They did so, it should be noted, relying on a British interpreter; what they knew of the United States was owed chiefly to Bryce's *The American Commonwealth.*) The Senate was given powers equal to those of the House, except that money bills cannot be initiated or amended by the upper chamber. These powers and their significance lay dormant for much of the nation's history, but have assumed dramatic political significance in recent decades. Indeed, in the multiple political and constitutional crisis of November 1975, when the conflict between the two chambers of the parliament had become the arena for the contest between the Labor government and Liberal/National opposition, the explosive potential of this issue was fully demonstrated.

The trigger for the Senate's power becoming so acute has been the political transformation in that chamber since the introduction of proportional representation as its electoral system. Ironically, this system was intended by Labor to improve its position, but it has ensured the participation in the Senate of minor parties and independents, largely frustrating the ability of either the ALP or the non-Labor coalition to control both houses. The parliamentary pattern in which the House of Representatives divides on essentially two-party lines, Labor and non-Labor, while the Senate sees a balance of power held by a minor party, was first evident in the 1960s. At that time (from 1967 to 1974) the Senate balance was held by the Democratic Labor Party (DLP), a splinter group from within the ALP. The DLP's dedication to keeping Labor out of office made this not altogether inconvenient for the Liberal/Country Party coalition. However, it made the task of the Whitlam government much more difficult. Since the 1970s the significant minor party has been the Australian Democrats, which began as a Liberal splinter. Less prone to obstructive tactics than the DLP, and mindful of the 1975 crisis, the Democrats have promised not to wield the ultimate power of joining with an opposition to refuse supply. Nevertheless, they are still able to modify legislation and to participate in the scrutiny of executive action which the Senate's extensive committee system enables. Recent Senates have also included a representative of the Nuclear Disarmament Party and an Independent Senator for Peace. Thus the electoral system places groups and parties that cannot expect to attain government in positions of parliamentary access and influence.

The implications of this structure for foreign and defense policies are clear. The presence of senators committed to non-nuclear strategies and a critique of the alliance, and unconfined by the discipline of the two major parties, has broadened the defense debate beyond the bipartisan assumptions that had previously prevailed. The opportunity provided by proportional representation has affected the significance of public opinion in this area. In the early stages of the New Zealand nuclear ships controversy, much was made of the difference between public opinion in Australia and New Zealand on this issue. The markedly different positions adopted by the two Labor governments were not unrelated to the significant majorities opposed to the nuclear aspects of alliance policies in New Zealand and supporting those aspects in Australia. It is possible that some of the American response to the New Zealand policy was intended to keep the majority firm in Australia, where the U.S. stakes are higher. But as well as watching the majority opinion that will affect the government party in the House of Representatives, an eye must also be kept on the minority opinion that may have political effect in the Senate.

The brake placed on government by the Senate is an obstacle no New Zealand administration faces in that unicameral system. For an administration to be vexed by a hostile Senate is hardly novel in American experience, but there it occurs within a separation of powers between distinct branches of government. The opportunities for obstruction and challenge by the U.S. Senate are part of the constitutional design of the American republic. By contrast, the current position of the Australian Senate is not related to the constitutional provision for a states' house, but—as 1975 demonstrated—to the operation of party politics.

The combination of proportional representation and strong Senate powers has given minor parties in Australia access to influence far beyond any of the classical assumptions of majoritarian party government in Westminster systems. This might be celebrated as a radical innovation in democracy, were the electoral system more satisfactory. The race to the wire for the final Senate seat, on which minor parties will usually be dependent for election, is typically between candidates of very different political positions separated by very few votes which are a complicated amalgam of transfer values from other candidates' surpluses. The 1987 election provides an example. The twelfth Senate seat in New South Wales was won narrowly by a candidate from the Nuclear Disarmament Party who was subsequently declared by the High Court to be ineligible for office because he lacked Australian citizenship at the time of the election. Had that place then gone, not to the second candidate for that party, but to the next party in order of preferences, it would have been taken by a representative of the Call to Australia—a party of diametrically opposite views. Similarly, by a hair's breadth Senator for Peace Vallentine achieved the twelfth place for Western Australia, edging out a National Party candidate whose views were very different and whose votes were scarcely fewer.

To summarize, the growth in central power means that the Commonwealth government with which the allies deal in the 1980s is constitutionally more powerful and bureaucratically better supported than the government with which the ANZUS treaty was concluded in 1951. It is a larger, wealthier, more confident machine. Yet it faces constraints that its predecessors did not. The impact of federalism has increased as the competition for resources to meet a wider range of public demands occurs within the volatile environment of modern media publicity. The force of bicameralism also sets limits to executive power which were not unknown to earlier governments, but which were more manageable. (Menzies secured a double dissolution in 1951 to overcome the frustration of an ALP-controlled Senate.) In both the growth in central power and the constraints on power, the political system has increasingly departed from its constitutional design. At moments of domestic political crisis, such as 1975, that lack of fit is discovered anew.

CENTRAL POWER IN THE AUSTRALIAN COMMONWEALTH: ALIGNMENTS

Labor has governed for fifteen and the Liberals (in coalition with the Country Party, now National Party) for thirty of Australia's forty-five years of postwar experience. Ten of Labor's fifteen years in office were within the last eighteen years, so the long term of coalition supremacy appears to dominate the postwar period. Yet the margin of electoral victory and defeat was relatively small and at times very close. The underlying feature is the constant contest between the two major contenders. As its principal analyst never ceases to remind us, the Australian party system in uniquely stable. The shares of votes between the two major sides have been remarkably consistent: in House of Representatives elections since the war the Liberal Party and the ALP have regularly accounted for at least four-fifths of the total vote. With the balance roughly even, what explains shifts from one side to the other?

The key to electoral success in Australia has been to capture and hold the middle ground of public opinion. This interpretation conforms to some well-known theorems in economics and political science about the dynamics of oligopolistic competition; majoritarian politics in two-party systems is generally supposed to drive the rival parties toward the center rather than the extremes. But this is only possible if the parties are not so tied by ideology and interest to particular groups or positions that a generalized appeal is implausible or impossible. This is not to say that ideology is irrelevant, but that it must be sufficiently malleable to appear compatible with the rhetoric and interests of the middle ground.

Australian politicians who have led their party into office have typically based their appeal on such a strategy. Thus Menzies's return to office in 1949 relied on an ability to promise the same social and political agenda without the restrictions that the Chifley government appeared to be imposing. Individualism, with its implications for private capital, was a theme, but so too was national development, with its commitment to public spending. The "It's Time" campaign by Whitlam in 1972 was able to play on the sense of an opposition in tune with a populace eager for changes that a government trapped within its policies and too exhausted to innovate could not achieve. Women's policies and politics are an instance of that success. In 1983 Hawke's call for consensus succeeded in presenting the Fraser government as having deserted the middle ground, which the ALP moved swiftly to occupy.

Even if they prefer the fruits of victory to the bitterness of defeat, the political parties have not always been happy with this means of achieving success. For each contender, the identification with the middle ground is a compromise with some aspects of declared party policy. This is especially the case for the ALP, which has traditionally sought to impose greater discipline over its elected representatives than have the non-Labor parties. It is not surprising, therefore, that Hawke's popularity has generally been greater as prime minister within the country than as leader within his party. Judging the balance between party and people becomes the art of political leadership. At times the calculation can go astray: witness the 1985 episode concerning Australian support for U.S. testing of the MX missile, in which, with U.S. assistance, the prime minister had to reverse a policy his party caucus would not accept.

Pragmatism of this kind is possible because the differences between the major parties are not ordinarily as great as either would like the electorate to believe. The appeal to the center is possible because the spectrum of opinion on each side of the party contest contains a significant overlap. Those in the center are likely to have more in common across the party divide than with elements of their own machine. Within each of the major parties there is discernible conflict about the extent of compromise with the party's principles. The debate between the pragmatic "wets" and the more ideological "drys" in the Liberal Party after 1983 reflected this tension. Much of the factional dispute within the ALP turns on the same theme. The minor parties that have done best are those that have achieved similar appeal. The DLP combined a traditional welfare-oriented social program with its conservative defense policies, while the Australian Democrats, in policies, style, and membership, are a party of the extreme center.

What constitutes the middle ground in Australian politics? It is easier to map the shifts in opinion than to explain them. As in most Western societies, the 1950s and 1960s were a period of Cold War mentality in Australia. The manichaean split between Communism and anti-Communism permitted external adversaries and internal perils to be equated. It was an intellectual milieu in which the split within the ALP, which produced an essentially Catholic party, the DLP, was certain to place Labor on the wrong side of the political fault line.

The Vietnam years, from the mid-1960s to the mid-1970s, saw a change in the middle ground's perceptions. As in the United States, this was a slow shift, accompanied by new forms of public protest and demonstration. It was a shift that both parties were required to make. Labor's change from cautious endorsement of U.S. policies in Indochina to critical independence is sometimes overlooked. But by 1968, when the United States changed course as the coalition government in Canberra held fast, the ALP could present itself as closer to domestic opinion and allied policy alike.

Was there any middle ground in the 1975 crisis? That upheaval—and that election—stands out as the most polarized moment in postwar Australian politics. It was precisely the inability of the parties to achieve a negotiated solution to their conflict that precipitated the extraordinary intervention by the governor-general. So long as the protagonists of 1975 remained on the stage of national affairs, it was impossible to achieve a return to centrist legitimacy.

In the 1980s, the trilateral emphasis on government, business, and unions characteristic of the Hawke government's approach to industrial relations and economic management marked a new phase in the style and vocabulary of pragmatic centrism.

How has the middle ground been defined? I would argue that Australia's middle ground is chiefly defined through a "commonsense" utilitarianism. This ideology is the matrix from which the major parties emerge, which helps to account both for their similarities (the common stock of essential ideas) and for their differences (which reflect the tensions and contradictions within the inherited ideology). With its roots in the radical, chartist politics of the colonial era, it combines an individualist philosophy with a meliorist program. It maintains a commitment to representative democracy alongside a positive approach to the work of government. Its inherent legalism accommodates a juristic approach to politics in which judicial activism is more apparent than participatory democracy. It adopts an unheroic view of politics with an unabashed pursuit of individual interest. The dominance of this ideology explains the relatively restricted range of views that contest for attention in Australian politics. It may also account for the national inclination to assess the plausibility of any proposal in terms of its practicability.

But shifts in the middle ground have not been the ferment of a home brew only. Transnational influences are also evident. The Cold War rhetoric drew significantly on American statements of the same period. Equally, the slogans and styles of the Vietnam years borrowed significantly from U.S. models. In contemporary debates about the size of government and the merits of privatization, policies and authorities from the Thatcher government and the Reagan administration, and their respective critics, have frequently been cited. A country whose intellectual moorings were for a long period British and have more recently and more uncertainly been North American is bound to bear the marks of those external influences.

Yet another influence over the postwar period has been nationalism. The deliberate cultivation of nationalist symbols was a distinctive characteristic of the Whitlam government. Its legislative changes from "Commonwealth government" to "Australian government" exemplified the trend, which is surely captured in the prime minister's customary invocation, "Men and women of Australia!" In 1988 the politics of the bicentenary predictably fed on and unleashed a welter of nationalist symbols and sentiment.

To have effect, such disembodied influences as ideology, transnational ideas, and nationalist symbols require actors, interests, and structures. Given the ambitions of individual politicians, the clash of parties, the interests of particular groups and classes, and the power of modern media, mediating agents have not been wanting. Yet these agents will be mostly found jostling on the middle ground. The power of the center in Australia is most apparent when one considers the degree to which political debate is conducted within a particular vocabulary. There is a clash of views, to be sure, but not a cacophony of voices. To depart from the current orthodoxy, be it the fervent anti-Communism of the 1950s or the technocratic economics of the 1980s, is to risk leaving the narrow room in which the national debates are conducted with passion but without diversity.

CENTRAL POWER IN THE AUSTRALIAN COMMONWEALTH: EVALUATION

Where have central power and centrist politics led us? How do we evaluate the institutions and the ideology that dominate Australian life? Three sets of issues may be pursued as a partial response to these questions.

First, the capacity of the national political system has come under challenge. The growth in central power has enlarged the executive and depended on the judiciary. Although it has not been without consequence for the legislature, the representative organs have not generally kept pace with either the activism of the courts and tribunals or the administrative appetites of ministers and officials. It may be a symptom of the legislature's difficulties that the typical means for achieving a reform will be found in capturing an executive agency or resorting to a legal tribunal (such as an ombudsman or royal commission), rather than through parliamentary scrutiny. Given the importance of parliamentary accountability within the Australian system of government, how credible is this as a legitimizing principle?

The salience and the constraints of federalism have been emphasized. What cost is placed on these complications in a relatively small economy highly vulnerable to external pressures? Is the division of powers appropriate? If not, how can a conservative electorate be persuaded to amend its constitution?

Here an immediate contrast with the United States may be drawn. American politics can draw directly on American constitutional theory. Its practices and its principles may be described, challenged, and cherished in the same political vocabulary. The Australian polity lacks the means by which institutions and practices can be connected with principles and purposes. The Australian constitution is a convenient blueprint, not an embodiment of rights. Faced with more difficult choices in a less certain environment, it is not clear that the inherited ideology is strong enough either to sustain or to change the inherited institutions.

Second, how is the agenda of public debate to be evaluated? The list of issues resembles that of any other liberal democracy. But the preoccupations remain with some persistent problems long since identified as core issues in Australian politics: the social wage, protection, and immigration. And few other democracies face the same perplexities that aboriginal policies present.

Australia appears to have particular difficulty in joining expertise to politics. It is a problem in the management of the bureaucracy. It is a problem in the conduct of public debate. The debate over immigration could be used to demonstrate some of the difficulties in bringing historical and statistical evidence to bear on issues. The politics of immigration are also a cautionary study in the darker side of attempts to manipulate the middle ground and the limitations of a crudely utilitarian philosophy.

Another ongoing debate, concerning tertiary education and research funding, can be used to illustrate the force of central power within those domains it has successfully captured. Here, too, the limitations of the debate deserve remark, given the significance of research and higher education in more general fields of science and technology policy. Has the debate identified the most serious issues? Are the policies grappling with the right problems?

Finally, a generational change in Australian politics will produce new styles. It will also produce leadership without the connections in war and postwar politics that have been an often-unrecognized support to the multifarious connections between Australia, New Zealand, and the United States. If it is still important that these polities understand one another, what thought is being given to formal and informal means of maintaining the links that facilitate communication?

5

The World Turned Upside Down? Change and Continuity in New Zealand Politics in the Postwar Era

ROBERTO G. RABEL

> Like the Liberals after their victory in 1890, Labour after 1935 was able to set the terms of political debate and action for the next forty years.
>
> (Chapman 1981: 333)

> The election of New Zealand's fourth Labour Government in July 1984 brought more than simply a change in political leadership and a reshuffling of the seating arrangements in Parliament; it marked a crucial turning point in the style, character and content of the politics of the post-war era.
>
> (Boston and Holland 1987: 1)

> In the future it is likely to be the 1980s which will loom largest in historical explanation of the shape and direction of Aotearoa into the twenty-first century and beyond. Who knows? Before too long the stresses and strains in our emerging Pacific culture might even help generate an original political idea.
>
> (Vowles 1987b: 227)

Continuity was the dominant theme during the period in New Zealand political history framed by the snap elections of 1951 and 1984. There were, of course, certain evolutionary and incremental changes, often in response to external developments. New domestic issues and actors came to the fore on the political scene from time to time, leading to some fluctuations in support for the two major political parties and to occasional sharp swings in voting as in the 1972 and 1975 elections. Yet in general terms of basic world views, of political structures, of national policy agendas, and of two-party dominance, the New Zealand political landscape was not transformed dramatically in this period.

Politics essentially revolved around a set of institutions, ideologies, and general voting patterns associated with the establishment of a comprehensive welfare state by the first Labour government of 1935–49. These were only slightly modified during the terms of the succeeding National governments, which governed New Zealand for all but six of the thirty-five years from 1949 to 1984.

Voting patterns were relatively stable. National was generally assured of the support of rural and wealthier urban areas while Labour could rely on the less affluent urban electorates, leaving the two parties to compete for the socioeconomically mixed electorates whose votes usually determined shifts in party strength in Parliament. Neither major party has had a larger margin of victory than 8 percent of the popular vote in national elections since World War II. There have been occasional minor successes for other parties but no significant electoral breakthroughs (Chapman 1981: 333).

Within the framework of this closely balanced two-party system, in which National usually formed the government, there developed a complex system of interaction between powerful functional interest groups, a large bureaucracy, and elected representatives. For most practical purposes, policy was made through a process of consultative bargaining and accommodation of competing interest group objectives on issues ranging in level of significance from the national to the most local.[1] It was a system of governance that has been described by more than one observer as a form of democratic corporatism (Cleveland 1972: 2–3; Mitchell 1969: 31; Boston and Holland 1987: 4; Mulgan 1984: 90–94). Reinforced by the networks of close personal contacts characteristic of a small society, this system ensured major interest groups of influence on government decisions affecting their members and discouraged any reforms that would endanger their vested interests.

Underpinning the whole was a dominant ideology that has been variously described as "liberal-conservatism" (James 1986: 79) and "popular liberalism" (Vowles 1987a: 218), but which might equally well be labelled "pragmatic welfarism."[2] In accordance with this ideology, both National and Labour accepted—and indeed embodied—the national consensus concerning the need for an active welfare state to provide an extensive range of social services and for governmental intervention in all sectors of the economy in a regulatory fashion, though with only limited nationalization of the productive sectors of the economy. Political debate proceeded from this consensus, with the differences between the major parties and their supporters revolving around relatively fine degrees of opinion over the extent of governmental intervention. Given the character of this postwar political order, Austin Mitchell (1969: 309) had some justification for claiming that New Zealand was "the world's most stable democracy."

Such a claim could not be made today. Since the election in 1984 of the fourth Labour government, that stable postwar political and economic order has been turned upside down. Subscribing to a previously unthinkable faith in market forces, this government has initiated a process of massive economic deregulation and reorganization of the state sector. It has not only reduced previous levels of governmental intervention in the economy but has transformed political life in New Zealand by challenging some of the most basic assumptions on which both its ideological consensus and "corporate democracy" of interest group consultation once rested. Alongside—but not strictly in tandem with—the changes wrought by a rethinking of the role of the state in economic life have come significant shifts in foreign policy and defense, a new and expanded consciousness of issues relating to gender and race, and the prospect of a radical reshaping of health, education, and welfare policies.

The immediate political consequences of the post-1984 changes include a disruption of traditional voting patterns and a high level of ideological debate and confusion within—as much as between—the two major parties. As if to confirm that the postwar political pattern had indeed been overturned, Labour was reelected in 1987 to a second term for the first time since 1946. If political time was stalled in New Zealand from 1935 to 1984, it is now advancing at breakneck speed.

Despite this deluge of change, it remains unclear how, why, and to what extent the changes of the past few years mark a rewriting of the national political agenda. To understand if the "mold" of New Zealand politics has been truly broken it is necessary to look more closely at the lines of political evolution in this country in the postwar period. In fact, as Colin James (1986) has persuasively argued, the voices of challenge and change had been rising in intensity for some time and the Labour government's recent actions appear less surprising when viewed as an overdue response to those pressures. Futhermore, New Zealand's "quiet revolution," as James has dubbed it, is still in train and its destination remains far from clearcut.

CASTING THE MOLD

The roots of New Zealand's postwar political order were laid down in response to the local impact of the international depression of the 1930s. Thrown into disarray by their failure to counter problems of mass unemployment and falling export receipts, New Zealand's conservatives were soundly defeated in the 1935 election by a well-organized, energetic Labour Party which had considerably toned down its earlier more radical version of Antipodean socialism.[3]

The first Labour government extended the welfare state in far-reaching but essentially pragmatic directions. The sheer scope of the innovations was impressive: an industrial relations system based on compulsory unionism for all workers subject to national awards; guaranteed prices for sheep and dairy farmers; cooperative marketing arrangements for agricultural producers; state-funded mortgage relief schemes; an active program of state housing construction in cooperation with the private sector; expansion of the educational system; protective import licensing; full nationalization of the Reserve Bank; and, above all, a comprehensive social security system providing universal free health care, old-age pensions, and other benefits (Chapman 1981: 337–47). The general objectives of Labour's reforms were to ensure economic security for all New Zealanders and to insulate the economy as much as possible from destabilizing external influences, though without wholesale nationalization of the productive industrial or agricultural sectors of the economy.

The outcome of the 1938 election demonstrated that a majority of New Zealanders endorsed those principles. Michael Joseph Savage's government was triumphantly reelected with a large majority despite facing a united opposition in the form of the new National Party. Thereafter the pace of reform slowed.[4] The Bank of New Zealand was nationalized in 1945, but Labour took few new initiatives during and after World War II, pursuing policies of rehabilitation and stabilization, and modest extensions of the welfare system such as the universalization of the family benefit and increases in benefit rates. Electoral support for the government slipped consistently throughout the 1940s, culminating in an election victory for National in 1949.

Though ushering in a new government, the 1949 election did not mark a drastic shift in the national political agenda that Labour had defined. While nominally championing the virtues of individualism and free enterprise over Labour's alleged collectivism and state controls, the National Party, which had emerged out of the ashes of the conservative defeats of 1935 and 1938, had accommodated itself to much of the program put in place by Labour's reforms: full employment, the social welfare system, import licensing, guaranteed prices for rural producers, cooperative marketing of export commodities, protection for domestic manufacturing.

National only removed a few of the economic controls Labour had imposed and made no effort to roll back Labour's reforms in any systematic fashion. Indeed, it was unclear that National would continue to dominate (Chapman 1981: 356–58).

In that sense, 1951 was a more important year for setting the postwar mold of New Zealand politics as far as National's long-term control of the reins of government was concerned. National's leader, Sidney Holland, seized on the bitter waterside confrontation of that year to call a snap election testing public support for the government's tough response to militant unionism. With both the political and industrial wings of the labor movement divided on the issue, the government was returned with an increased majority. As Robert Chapman (1981: 358) has noted, National had succeeded in earning "recognition as the party of law and order, property, anti-communism, arbitration, and social peace." Ironically, Labour did not differ substantially from National on such issues, but the outcome of the 1951 election showed that the 1949 result had not been a temporary aberration and inaugurated a long period of National ascendancy as the new putative "natural party of government."

1951 is also noteworthy as the year in which the ANZUS agreement was signed. An alliance with the United States had been enthusiastically sought by both major parties as "the richest prize of New Zealand's diplomacy" (McKinnon 1986). The attainment of that prize marked a high point of bipartisan consensus in foreign policy, which was partly a reflection of Cold War concerns and partly a recognition of the postwar reality of New Zealand dependence on the United States rather than Britain for defense of the Pacific.

Political life in the following years was decidedly grey in tone and the period from 1951 to 1967 has been described "as amongst the most conservative in New Zealand history" (Brooking 1988). Despite the shift in dominant governing party, the basic structures created by the first Labour government and now administered conservatively by National remained in place. The ideologies of the two major parties differed only on the rhetorical level. Labour was briefly in power from 1957 to 1960, dabbled with more support for industrialization and steered the economy from recession to recovery, but introduced few reforms.

After returning to power in 1960 under a highly consensus-minded leader, Keith Holyoake, National presided over more than a decade of deliberate political stasis. Despite a steadily rising tide of change in the social, technological, cultural, and economic spheres after the mid-1960s, New Zealand's political order remained substantially unaltered.

These were the years in which New Zealand's version of democratic corporatism was perfected. Important interest groups such as the Federated Farmers, the Chambers of Commerce, the Manufacturers' Federation and even the Federation of Labour were able to exercise considerable influence over governmental regulation of those sectors of the economy that affected their interests and a burgeoning number of "quangos" (quasi-autonomous–non-governmental-organizations) appeared to link such groups to government. Given the power of these groups and the limitations of a three-year electoral term, the government proved unwilling to undertake any major reforms that would risk alienating any significant group. It was more politically judicious instead to manipulate the business cycle and stimulate the economy at appropriate times by increasing public expenditure (Boston and Holland 1987: 4–5).

National's political success in the 1950s and 1960s was underpinned by the relatively high levels of economic prosperity and full employment that prevailed. There was little incentive to undertake major changes until the British decision to join the European Economic Community raised the prospect of the collapse of guaranteed markets for much of New Zealand's primary exports.

Economic strategies remained based on the desire for security and stability and were Keynesian in thrust, with tight controls to protect New Zealand from the vicissitudes of the international economy.

Foreign policy was essentially reactive and dominated by the security link with the United States and Australia. It was the perceived need to sustain that link that led the National government to agree reluctantly to make a modest military contribution to the Vietnam war (McCraw 1981). The subsequent public controversy generated by that decision led the Labour Party to oppose New Zealand military involvement in that conflict. In so doing Labour's leaders continued to affirm their commitment to ANZUS, but a first chink in the bipartisan foreign policy consensus became evident.

Eventually in 1972, after a slow but steady erosion of electoral support in successive elections, the government was decisively defeated by a revitalized Labour Party under the leadership of Norman Kirk. Having won with the well-chosen slogan of "Time for a Change," Labour did, in fact, introduce a series of social reforms and minor extensions of the programs initiated by the first Labour government. But no major structural changes in social or economic policy were attempted, with the possible exception of an income-related compulsory superannuation (pension) scheme. It was the brainchild of Roger Douglas and foreshadowed in certain respects the direction in which he would take Labour economic policies as minister of finance a decade later.[5] Even Kirk's espousal of a "moral" diplomacy and the quest he inspired for a more distinctively New Zealand voice in foreign policy did not lead to any disavowal of the alliance linkages that had dominated New Zealand's postwar diplomatic and defense policies (Kennaway 1975: 163–67).

After Kirk's sudden death in August 1974, the government found itself increasingly beleaguered. New Zealand was hit hard by the 1973 oil shock and the new prime minister, Wallace (Bill) Rowling, had to deal with an economy weakened by rising inflation and overseas debt and rapidly moving into recession by the time of the 1975 election. Taking full advantage of public disappointment with Labour's performance, National's pugnacious new leader, Robert Muldoon, led his party to a landslide victory in 1975 that exactly reversed the margin of seats between the two parties.

Muldoon personally dominated New Zealand politics for almost a decade thereafter. His usually astute blend of populism and polarization assured National of continued control of New Zealand until 1984 in what seemed to be a rerun of the 1960s with the only significant differences being ones of style in political leadership and markedly poorer economic performance. Once again, there was a slow but steady erosion of popular support for the government (to the extent that National won two successive elections with fewer overall votes than Labour) and eventual defeat. Similarly, though differing about means and methods, both parties remained basically committed to interventionism and managing the order inherited from the 1930s. Muldoon's quintessentially conservative commitment to that order was encapsulated in his well-known comment on the eve of the 1975 election that his objective was to leave New Zealand "no worse than when I took it over" (Vowles 1987a: 225). The status quo seemed secure in the hands of such a man.

CRACKS IN THE MOLD

There is room for debate about whether Muldoon achieved his objective. What is not debatable is that he governed New Zealand pragmatically for the next nine years on the basis of assumptions formed during the post-depression years in which he had matured. Yet while the political order based on the assumptions of those years seemed intact, the social and economic realities of New Zealand's circumstances had altered markedly. Eventually, these changes would have to be acknowledged by the mainstream political system.

By the early 1970s, New Zealand was no longer simply the "quarter acre, half gallon, pavlova paradise" that Austin Mitchell (1972: 32) could satirize so mordantly as "the world's most stable and probably most conservative society." As in much of the developed world, the late 1960s were years of protest in New Zealand, inspired in part by the rejection of its parents' values by a younger generation raised in affluence. This challenging of dominant values was reinforced by such factors as the influence of television, the impact of rock music, the expansion of tertiary education as the "baby boom" grew up, and contraception and the "sexual revolution."

The issue of the Vietnam conflict and New Zealand's involvement there alongside the United States prompted some of the most heartfelt popular protests, mainly but not exclusively by younger people. It was an issue that raised important questions about New Zealand's role in the world and about the relationship with the United States that lay at the heart of its postwar foreign policy. Although New Zealand played only a minor supporting role in Vietnam, the issue's symbolic impact at home was such that the concept of a "Vietnam generation" has even been used as a general epithet to describe the generation which came of political consciousness in these years (James 1986: 30).

The Vietnam war was not the only source of protest. Environmental concerns also came to public prominence and it was noteworthy that the campaign to save the South Island lake of Manapouri from being raised for hydroelectrical development resulted in 1970 in the largest petition ever presented to the New Zealand Parliament. More unique to New Zealand perhaps were protests over such issues as sporting links with South Africa, especially with reference to the national sport, rugby. Even more significantly, there was a gradual rise of Maori consciousness and assertiveness, which began to challenge the comfortable myths of New Zealand as the world's most harmonious multiracial society. As in other Western nations, a women's movement would also arise in the wake of these protests in the 1970s to press for gender equality in various spheres.

One reason that these protests triggered such public debate and forced politicians to take notice was that they attracted so much attention from the mass media, which since 1960 had included television. Despite having been likened at times to "an amiable but stagnant branch of the civil service" (Cleveland 1972: 2), the media became more aggressive in its treatment of politicians and its analysis of political issues. Television in particular obliged politicians to deal directly with a mass public, and Robert Muldoon emerged as New Zealand's first political master of the medium. Increasingly, television would become the most influential of the media during election campaigns and in popular reporting and analysis of politics.

Media attention notwithstanding, the changes in society were not reflected in formal political structures.[6] This was probably related to the economic prosperity that prevailed until the late 1960s, and to the fact that much of the protest of these years was explicitly anti-materialistic in tone, seeking to liberate the individual from outworn cultural and moral restraints, rather than economic ones. As in the United States and Europe, this wave of protest subsided in the 1970s as boom turned to recession and as the "flower power generation" gave way to the "me generation." But some legacies of the protest era lingered.

The stirrings of the 1960s did, however, begin to bring some changes to the character of the political parties. A new party, Values, was formed in 1972, stressing the "small is beautiful" philosophy of decentralized government, no-growth economics, and environmental consciousness. Although collapsing in the later 1970s, values took almost 2 percent of the vote in 1972 and over 4 percent in 1975. Labour was considered a more realistic alternative by some young radicals and idealists, who began to join the party and helped shift it toward a more "liberal" stance on issues relating to foreign policy, race, women's rights, generational conflict, culture, and morality. It was probably due more to dissatisfaction with National's stance on such issues that Labour was elected to office in 1972, rather than to any basic challenging of the postwar political consensus in either ideological or substantive terms. Despite Labour's more "liberal" look, neither of the major political parties had changed its basic ideology and attitude toward the role of the state.

Accordingly, it is not surprising that Labour's brief stay in government did not bring major changes in the pattern of postwar political life, despite the hopes held out by some. As Colin James (1986: 37) has observed, after a flurry of bold moves in foreign policy,

> the government concentrated on incremental social improvement, principally by spending more and regulating more. It was the liberal-conservative 1960s writ a bit larger and faster; and when the money ran out in 1974 it looked increasingly like a failed and irresponsible version of the Holyoake governments.

Ironically, the quick return to National "normalcy" seemed to pose a greater challenge to the prevailing orthodoxies of New Zealand politics.

Many commentators have noted that the return of a National government under the more aggressive Muldoon brought significant changes in terms of political style. It is true that he polarized New Zealand society and in so doing laid the basis for changes that have come in the 1980s. But it was primarily a polarization of New Zealanders into pro- and anti-Muldoon camps, not a polarization that immediately created a consistent ideological division between New Zealanders on the role of the state in the economy. In many respects the nine years after 1975 brought only more of the old pragmatic methods of government, based on intervention, interest group accommodation, and political manipulation of the business cycle. The costly election bribe that was National's universal superannuation scheme was a classic example of this sort of politics. In short, Muldoon may have abandoned some of his National predecessors' consensus-minded approach in favor of a more authoritarian style of leadership, but he remained at heart an ad hoc interventionist who was committed to maintaining the essentials of the order that he had inherited (James 1986: 79–110).

Yet demands for major changes requiring a new political direction were building on two general levels, if in uncoordinated ways. The first concerned the need to reorganize an economy whose overall performance had been characterized since the late 1960s predominantly by low growth, high inflation, poor productivity, rising unemployment, outward migration of skilled workers, growing foreign debt, industrial strife, falling terms of trade, and a steady decline in living standards according to international comparisons. Apart from ad hoc interventionism, the principal response of the Muldoon government to those problems was to propose the "Think Big" program of large-scale investment in energy-based industries. There was some restructuring and deregulation as a result of pressures by a small group of "more-market" liberals in the National Party. Muldoon, however, deliberately restrained the pace of such changes, and National's term of office ended on quite the opposite note, with a final burst of strict controls regulating prices, wages, and interest rates.

The other level on which pressures for change were increasing concerned issues that had not usually figured prominently on New Zealand's domestic political agenda and involved groups who had not had great influence in Parliament or in the major organized interest groups. One of these issues was the question of greater equality for women. Another was the issue of race relations, most importantly with respect to the rights and status of the indigenous Maori people of New Zealand, but also with respect to those of newly arrived immigrants from the Pacific islands. A third was the question of opposition to nuclear weapons, manifested most particularly in growing popular opposition to visits of nuclear-armed ships to New Zealand ports. This opposition raised important questions about New Zealand's international identity and its role in the Western alliance system, most especially through its membership of ANZUS. All these issues had been initially raised but not resolved in the late 1960s—in many cases by individuals who were now moving into positions of power.

These issues and the groups that promoted them could not be easily accommodated by the old political order. The questions they raised betokened the arrival of a more complicated political society made up of shifting coalitions that did not unite on all issues. For example, the most divisive episode that arose during the Muldoon era was triggered by a rugby tour of New Zealand by the South African Springboks. The often violent clashes between protesters, police, and rugby supporters that ensued suggested that New Zealand's tradition of consensus was being shattered along "liberal" and "non-liberal" lines that did not equate strictly with either divisions based on class or on party political preferences. This pattern of polarization was intensified by Muldoon's penchant for criticizing unpopular minorities and his articulation of a sort of populism of the "ordinary bloke" (James 1986: 84–87). For a time that strategy worked in keeping the forces of change divided, enabling National to squeak back in government twice. Yet the country's dismal economic performance and Muldoon's visceral opposition to the liberal agenda on non-economic issues had triggered a sequence of subterranean shifts that would eventually shake the political landscape with devastating force. Support for the old orthodoxies was visibly eroding.

National was progressively losing the confidence both of those groups who wanted a freer economy that was more responsive to market forces and of those who wanted more liberal policies on issues of race, gender, morality, and foreign policy. Muldoonism was taking its toll.[7] Labour was still haunted by memories of its economic failures of the 1974–75 period and was perceived to have weak leadership. For a time in the early 1980s, Social Credit (now the Democratic Party) appeared to be the beneficiary of public disillusionment with the major parties, emerging as a possible vehicle for political change. Social Credit almost surpassed Labour in public opinion polls in 1980 and secured two seats in Parliament in the 1981 election and over 20 percent of the popular vote nationally. That level of support, however, declined steadily thereafter, as its policies had only limited appeal for those who wanted a freer economy and/or held more liberal views on other issues.

The emergence of two new parties underscored the dissatisfaction many felt with the existing system and highlights yet again the differing levels on which change was being sought. One was the New Zealand Party, formed in 1983 and led by millionaire businessman Bob Jones to promote a radical libertarian message of freedom from governmental controls in both economic and private life. The other was Mana Motuhake, led by Matiu Rata, a former Labour minister of Maori affairs, to champion Maori causes such as land rights in a way the mainstream parties had failed to do (James 1986: 111–32).

Ultimately, however, Labour would become the only realistic alternative for those wanting change. While retaining its greatest consistent base of support among the urban working classes, the social composition of the Labour Party's membership profile was changing to include more professionals and white-collar workers from the middle classes. This trend was even more pronounced within the parliamentary wing of the party (Vowles 1987b: 23–25). This changing social composition would make the Labour Party willing to be more flexible about its traditional commitment to interventionist economic policies, as some of its members became more interested in moving the party in more liberal rather than more socialist directions. Many of the recent converts had, in fact, joined the Labour Party because it was seen to be more progressive than National on issues of race, gender, morality, and foreign policy, rather than because of its economic policies. By 1983, Labour was in a position to capitalize on the pent-up desires for change. Its organization had been overhauled during Jim Anderton's time as president, its membership was growing, and it had a new, dynamic leader in the person of David Lange (James 1986: 144–45).

As New Zealand entered 1984, the old order no longer appeared so secure. To many New Zealanders the traditional system of government and economic management simply did not appear to be performing and radical solutions were called for. To some, New Zealand in 1984 was the incarnation of George Orwell's vision of a bureaucratic nightmare with the tentacles of government omnipresent, as Bob Jones and the New Zealand Party would argue (Jones 1987: 76). To others the central problem was a lack of national consensus because of the polarization wrought by the Muldoon years.

Muldoon realized his government's weakness and his own weakness within that government after the so-called "colonel's coup" narrowly failed to remove him from the leadership of the National Party. He decided to hold an early election at a time when the effects of his wage and price freeze seemed to be paying off and economic growth was accelerating.

Ironically, the public rationale given for calling a snap election was the unreliability of the government's majority in Parliament because of the opposition of a liberal woman member of the National caucus on a foreign policy issue—the question of a stronger antinuclear stance by New Zealand. It was an interesting commentary on the impact that non-economic issues had assumed on the symbolic level of politics (James 1986: 102–3).

The pressures for change finally burst in that election. The New Zealand Party played a pivotal role in drawing enough votes from National to allow Labour to win a decisive victory. The new government, however, was elected without a specific agenda. There was a clear mandate for change but the election result did not reveal a clear national consensus as to what precise direction that change should take.

SHATTERING THE MOLD

Labour had been elected against a general background of rising strains and divisions in New Zealand society. There were great external pressures on the economy, and the transitional period between National's defeat and Labour's constitutional assumption of power coincided with a currency crisis that forced Labour to devalue the dollar immediately. Moreover, the party had presented the electorate with only vague outlines of its intended program of government, especially as far as economic policy was concerned. The new minister of finance, Roger Douglas, would step into this policy vacuum with his own clear, comprehensive agenda for economic reform which essentially paralleled the advice Treasury officials were offering the new government on reversing the country's economic decline.[8] This agenda would quickly be accepted as the only realistic alternative by a young Labour Cabinet whose political experience to that point had coincided for the most part with a period in which interventionism had patently failed to alleviate New Zealand's economic ills.

Change followed in a deluge. Indeed, the speed and magnitude of change was such that the so-called "Reagan Revolution" in the United States and the triumphs of "Thatcherism" in Britain pale considerably in contrast. Ironically, unlike those counterparts, the new Labour government seemed at first to be embarking on a work of restoration, not revolution. Prime Minister Lange's public rhetoric suggested a determination to reinstate a consensus-oriented style of political leadership after the allegedly polarizing excesses of Muldoonism. Accordingly, a grand national economic conference was held shortly after the election, bringing together all the major interest groups. The government soon appeared to conclude, however, that to achieve a true consensus would risk perpetuating the paralysis of the past. It was in conjunction with this realization that "Rogernomics" was launched.

A list of the major changes that have resulted reads like a systematic demolition of much of the political and economic edifice constructed by the first Labour government. After terminating Muldoon's wage and price controls and devaluing the dollar, the government introduced a floating exchange regime and removed all currency exchange restrictions; financial and other domestic markets were deregulated and access to those markets for foreign companies was liberalized; agricultural subsidies and export incentives were removed; the system of protective tariffs and import licensing is being progressively dismantled; industrial relations law was amended to minimize governmental intervention; the tax system was dramatically overhauled, bringing a greater reliance on indirect taxation; the whole state sector is being reformed through "corporatization," privatization, and a major internal reorganization of the bureaucracy.

The underlying purpose of these policies has been to place more reliance on the market, to encourage competition and entrepreneurship, to stimulate growth and lower inflation, and, ultimately, to create the basis for a more prosperous and equitable society. As David Lange (1987: ix) has put it, "The politics of change . . . is about turning around the serious decline in New Zealand's economic circumstances and regaining our former position. The ultimate objective is not wealth as such, but having the economic means to attain social ends."

There has also been a significant change in foreign policy which has raised New Zealand's international profile considerably. The policy of prohibiting port visits by nuclear warships has resulted in the country's effective exclusion from the ANZUS alliance. Although such an outcome was certainly not actively sought by the government, it was committed to a strong antinuclear stand by the intensity of party opinion on this issue (Alley 1987). Accompanying this shift was a review of defense policy in which public opinion was solicited concerning New Zealand's defense options and which confirmed public support for the government's non-nuclear stand but also indicated majority support for remaining in ANZUS (Clements 1987). Such actions as the closing of the South African consulate, the imposition of some economic sanctions against South Africa, the opening of the country's first embassy in black Africa and the reopening of the Delhi post are also indications of a foreign policy that is more explicit in its opposition to apartheid and more sensitive to Third World concerns than the preceding National administrations. It may be argued that the result has been a shattering—at least temporarily—of the previous bipartisan consensus on foreign policy, with Labour appearing to hold the support of a majority of New Zealanders for its diplomatic policies.

The pace of change in social policy has generally been slower and not strictly in line with the more-market philosophy. For example, the Family Support scheme has actually extended the social welfare net. There has, however, been a major shift away from universal welfare entitlements toward the targeting of benefits to those who are deemed to require genuine assistance, while a philosophy of "user-pays" has been applied to those who do not. Thus a tax surcharge was levied on superannuitants (retirees) receiving additional income, and nominal charges have been introduced for medical prescriptions. The government made economic reform the priority during its first term and was awaiting reports of various commissions of inquiry into health, education, and social welfare. The controversies that attended the release of those reports during 1987 and 1988—and their sometimes conflicting recommendations—suggested the government remained less decided about how to tackle these areas.

In partial contrast, Labour appears to have given considerable attention to the rights of women and Maori. In general, a greater sensitivity has been evident at all levels of government and among the public on issues relating to gender and race. A Ministry of Women's Affairs was created in 1984 and the government has made a strong public commitment to pursue equal opportunities for women more vigorously. The government has also shown itself to be sympathetic to Maori rights in the areas of cultural promotion, language teaching, and land and fishing rights. Its proposal to institute a devolution of the Department of Maori Affairs to facilitate more direct tribal control of Maori affairs has not met with a generally favorable response in the Maori community. Labour leaders have, however, drawn Maori support for their endorsement in principle of the important role of the Waitangi Tribunal as an arbiter of Maori land and fishing claims dating back to the nineteenth century, especially in the wake of the landmark decision of the High Court validating the Treaty of Waitangi of 1840 as a perpetual guarantee of Maori rights. Although many recent economic changes have had disproportionately adverse effects on the Maori people, Labour has gone further than any previous administration in articulating the concept that New Zealand's future political and social evolution must be grounded in a bicultural partnership between Pakeha and Maori.

The general direction that Labour has pursued is not unique to New Zealand (Boston and Holland 1987: 2; Vowles 1987a: 15). The market liberalism typified by "Rogernomics" has not only enjoyed strong support within conservative parties in many Western nations but has also won many converts in the social-democratic and liberal parties of those countries. What remains unusual, as Jonathon Boston and Martin Holland (1987: 2) have suggested, is "the scope of the reforms and the determination and speed with which they have been instituted."

The specific reasons for Labour's rapid and thoroughgoing pursuit of reform await systematic investigation by historians, but political scientists and journalists have offered some initial explanations.[9] The personalities, ideas, and persuasive influence of Lange, Douglas, and a few other key ministers have been critical in carrying along the rest of the Labour caucus and an often reluctant Labour Party. The changing occupational and generational composition of the party leadership, membership base, and electoral support have also contributed to an ongoing shift in policy orientation.[10] The sense of urgency imparted by the 1984 currency crisis and New Zealand's high rate of international indebtedness have generated much of the momentum for Rogernomics, as have the support of Treasury and the perceived absence of alternative economic strategies. The argument that New Zealand must adjust to the realities of integration into a highly competitive world economy has been a compelling one. Finally, in a small society with a system of centralized government in which there are few constitutional checks on the executive, the government has a strong incentive to move boldly and rapidly at those times when the public mood is receptive to change—and before the vested interests have time to respond.

Though politically dangerous because of New Zealand's short electoral cycle, this strategy provided an electoral payback in 1987. That election seemed to confer an interim, if qualified, popular ratification of the government's course. The margin of victory over National in the overall popular vote was narrow, but a Labour government had been returned to office with an increased number of seats for the first time.

Yet does that election result mean the old mold of New Zealand politics has been enduringly broken? Since then the government itself seems to have been reassessing the pace of change and justifying its policies in more pragmatic terms. Geoffrey Palmer has warned his colleagues of the perils of "speed wobbles" in instituting rapid change. Dissension has been more evident within the ranks of the Labour caucus and the party at large, as arguments over social policy loom and as the costs of restructuring have begun to hit Labour's traditional constituency especially hard. Little progress has been evident on the economic front as far as higher growth, lower unemployment, and interest rates are concerned. Inflation, however, has fallen, export performance has been relatively strong, and international confidence in the New Zealand economy seems surprisingly high. Domestically, confidence in the government has nevertheless flagged and uncertainty appears to be replacing dynamism in the national political agenda.

RECASTING THE MOLD

If the world of New Zealand politics has been turned upside down by the events of the past four years, it remains unclear what the new world will look like. What does appear certain is that there can be no turning back, for Labour has indeed broken the old mold.

The fulcrum of national politics has shifted as a result of Labour's actions. Instead of pragmatic welfarism, the dominant political ideology appears to be market liberalism. The government's more-market approach has redefined the role of the state in New Zealand economic life in a way that has been substantially accepted by both major parties. Labour has also challenged the comfortable orthodoxies of New Zealand's "corporate democracy." The philosophy underlying Labour's approach in this area, as stated by Douglas, is that "the government is responsible and is answerable to the nation as a whole; not to particular interest groups, or to institutions, or to political parties" (see *The Capital Letter* 1988: 476). As a result, many of the links that bound together the government and interest groups in a sort of consultative consensus have been severed.

Given the convulsions that have shaken the political landscape, it is not surprising that the old political certainties have become confused. Labour and National are both ideologically divided (Roberts 1987: 49). Labour's leaders appear to have directly attacked their own party's heritage, and criticism of the government's direction has mounted within the party, especially by trade unionists. Although National appears to have renounced Muldoonism, that party's direction is also unclear. Some of its parliamentary team, including its leader, are ambivalent about the merits of interventionism, while others, led by the finance spokesperson, wish to go even further than Labour in deregulating the economy.

Public opinion polls reflect the confusion and internal conflicts of the parties. As support for Labour has declined, National's popularity has risen even though it offers no clearly different alternative policies. The proportion of "don't knows" is relatively high and support for the minor parties is negligible (see *Otago Daily Times*, October 8, 1988: 1). There is also evidence to suggest that membership of both parties has declined significantly in the past few years. The age of mass membership parties may be passing in New Zealand, as the policies of both major parties become increasingly dominated by a small group of "professional" politicians who rely increasingly on public relations techniques and television exposure to win elections.

The confusion and uncertainties of the present era suggest that the national political agenda is likely to be a contested one for the immediate future. The consensus that characterized New Zealand's political culture for so long has not disappeared simply because of economic decline and the combined effects of Muldoonism or Rogernomics, but also because of larger changes in New Zealand society which have complicated the lines of division and group identification in New Zealand society. Issues of race, feminism, morality, and foreign policy do not square neatly with class divisions. Though never easy in New Zealand, it is becoming even more difficult to adopt stances that are strictly left or right in a pure ideological sense.

The challenge ahead may well be to create structures to facilitate a new politics of diversity and fragmentation within and outside the major political parties, rather than to hope for a bland new consensus. In the absence of Pakeha political society's old democratic corporatism, new links will have to be forged through which people can be represented and have their voices heard in the halls of government at times other than election day. In so doing, the role of the Maori contribution to New Zealand life is a major political issue. Now that the dominant Pakeha ethos is more individualist in tone than it has been for some time, there are bound to be strains and conflicts in attempting to accommodate the more collectivist values of Maoridom in a genuinely bicultural political order. As a result of that interaction, however, it may yet be possible, as Jack Vowles (1987b: 227) has speculated, that "the stresses and strains in our Pacific culture might even help generate an original political idea."

The next stage in New Zealand's political evolution thus remains uncertain. What is more certain is that the late 1980s will rank alongside the 1890s and the 1930s as a turning point in the country's political history. The success of Labour's present economic experiment will not be the sole determinant. It is more likely that the nation's future political evolution will be determined by a dialectical interaction between economic issues and those of race, gender, foreign policy, and culture. All these issues will raise difficult questions, and turbulent political times lie ahead as New Zealanders grapple with them.

POSTSCRIPT

Since this chapter was drafted in late 1988, the world of New Zealand politics has remained volatile. While persisting with a reformist economic agenda through such moves as the privatizating of major state assets, the Labour government has been riven by factional infighting. Among other developments, Roger Douglas, the architect of "Rogernomics," was dismissed as finance minister in late 1988 by Prime Minister Lange, whom he subsequently challenged unsuccessfully for the party leadership. Shortly after, some left-wing activists, including one member of Parliament, deserted Labour to form the New Labour Party, which, ironically, sought to uphold Labour's "old" values. In an eventful month, Douglas was reelected to Cabinet in August 1989 and Lange surprised the nation by resigning as prime minister. His successor, Geoffrey Palmer, enjoyed relative success in maintaining unity within party ranks but economic recovery proved more elusive and popular support for the government plummeted to an all-time low, auguring almost certain defeat in the elections scheduled for late 1990. Though National differs with the government somewhat on labor market reform and race issues, the general thrust of its policies as outlined to date does not differ substantially from Labour's and it has even embraced the government's antinuclear policies. It remains to be seen if the 1990s will produce a new structure of political alignments to accommodate the convulsions wrought during the past decade by the dynamic interaction of the issues of economic reform, gender, race relations, and national identity.

NOTES

1. In this context, Les Cleveland (1972: 3) has noted that "government by committee is not just an expedient to make an old fashioned political machine of piecemeal design work more smoothly; it is a mode of existence, an expression of the political culture."

2. The "pragmatic" character of New Zealand political thought has been stressed ever since Albert Metin (1910) used the phrase "socialisme sans doctrine" to describe the reforms of the Liberal government of the 1890s. Jack Vowles (1987b: 216) does, however, succeed in demonstrating that the mixture of derivative ideas that constitutes "the liberal democratic tradition in Pakeha New Zealand, in certain principles and in their emphasis, is significantly different from its counterparts elsewhere." For other analyses of New Zealand political thought, see Mulgan (1984); Vowles (1987a: 16–22); Mitchell (1969: 190–94).

3. For a fuller analysis of the changing ideology of the Labour Party in the first half of the twentieth century, see Vowles (1987a: 16–20).

4. The reasons for this gradual slowdown in reformist zeal include the death of Savage, intra-party conflict, the limitations of a small, trade-dependent economy, the

outbreak of war, and the limits of electoral support for more radical change (Chapman 1981: 347–55).

5. This scheme was much criticized as collectivist in philosophy because of the large state-administered investment fund that would be created. In contrast, National in 1975 offered a financially costly but electorally popular scheme that was universal and non-contributory.

6. As Robert Chapman (1981: 365) has observed, "The underlying changes in society in the golden 1960s were social rather than political, technological rather than legislative, individual rather than public. If they took a mass form they did so as protest movements, confronting or, at the most, working alongside the party structures."

7. The term "Muldoonism" has generally been used in a critical sense to refer to the style of government associated with Robert Muldoon's time as prime minister. It tended to be closely equated with "polarization," as suggested in this contemporary definition of Muldoonism: "an emphasis on divisiveness; the subordination of principles to tactics; the inability to unite his countrymen behind compelling national goals" (Garnier and Levine 1981: xi).

8. Douglas was actually demoted from Labour's shadow front bench while Rowling was leader because he issued an alternative economic policy statement without prior party approval.

9. The fullest and clearest explanations to date of the reasons that Labour has so vigorously pursued a market-driven economic strategy have been provided by two journalists, Colin James (1986) and Simon Collins (1987). For a leftist critique of Labour's policies, see Jesson (1987).

10. For evidence of the changing profile of Labour Party support, see the opinion poll results published in the *New Zealand Listener*, May 16, 1988, pp. 12–15, and August 8, 1988, pp. 28–29. See also Vowles (1987a).

6

U.S. Political Change and the ANZUS Relationship

DONALD E. STOKES

Is the stance of the United States toward its ANZUS partners an important element of recent American politics? Although the answer to a comparable question asked of Australia or New Zealand would almost certainly be yes, in view of how large America looms in the Antipodes, it is impossible to give an affirmative answer for the United States.

The question is nonetheless interesting, since the reasons for a negative answer throw light on America's political development. I will use this query as an opportunity for tracing the international context of U.S. politics in past eras and a profound shift in the popular role of the American presidency from the nineteenth to the twentieth centuries, before examining how the course of U.S. political change since World War II helps explain why the ANZUS relationship has no more than a marginal place in American politics today.

THE INTERNATIONAL CONTEXT OF AMERICAN POLITICAL CHANGE

Americans have never been disposed to think of their politics as closely linked to international factors, for reasons that lie deep in our history. The remoteness of North America from Europe and Asia, the energy required by the economic and political development of the American land mass, the Washingtonian tradition of freedom from foreign entanglements, reinforced by the Monroe Doctrine, the inward-turning challenge of the frontier all created a view of America's politics as self-contained. But this view misses an interplay of international and domestic politics older than the Republic. If we take "external context" to mean both the projection of international affairs onto our domestic politics and the projection of domestic politics onto international affairs, this context has been important since the late eighteenth century. It was overwhelmingly so in the Revolution and its aftermath, as the new nation dissolved the bonds with Britain and prevented them from re-forming in the War of 1812.

This external context was no less important as the conflict between North and South deepened in the first half of the nineteenth century. It is indeed essential for explaining why the North did not ultimately let the South go. Beyond the hold of the ideal of Union and the horror of slavery, the North saw that it would be in conflict with an independent Confederacy over the dream of a slave-holding empire in the Caribbean and Central America—as well as over the control of the western territories.

Once the Civil War began, the conflict of North and South was projected onto a far wider international arena. The Confederacy sought to enlist Britain's support to breach the Union blockade. But as northern ships and marines sealed off the southern ports, the Union government kept the British navy at bay by playing on Britain's abhorrence of slavery and reluctance to undercut its own future use of the blockade as an instrument of war. Indeed, the timing of the Emancipation Proclamation owed as much to this international context as it did to political or military considerations at home.

The conflict of North and South in the antebellum and Civil War era ultimately restructured the party system. Northern and southern Democrats were deeply divided by the idea of new slave-holding domains to the south and west. The Republicans used the issue to break the existing party system and emerge from the Civil War as the dominant political force in the restored Union.

The goal of developing the western territories as a hinterland of the industrial North and Midwest was a prime objective of Republican administrations in the unparalleled economic expansion after the Civil War. Moreover, the Republicans used the tariff to keep in place a barrier to southern imports of foreign manufactures after the Union blockade was lifted. By the 1890s this economic conflict was sharp enough to produce a sectional realignment between the Republicans as the party of the modernizing, industrial, high-tariff North and Midwest and the Democrats as the party of the rural, agrarian, low-tariff South and West, a realignment that remained in place until the Depression of the 1930s.

The most important international dimension of the party alignment in the first half of our own century was the struggle over isolationism after

World War I and before World War II. The defeat of the League of Nations sharply split the parties along internationalist-isolationist lines. This was only a secondary ground of the party battle as the nation turned inward during the economic expansion of the 1920s and the economic misery of the 1930s. But it reemerged as a paramount issue with the approach of a new war in Europe. The isolationist Republican challenge hampered Roosevelt's efforts to prepare America for war, and only the attack on Pearl Harbor produced, albeit overnight, the consensus that made World War II more of a "great patriotic war" than any other in our history, including the Revolutionary War. The consensus between the parties at the war's end readily extended into the Cold War, with the Soviets now cast as the principal enemy.

No aspect of external affairs has been woven into the alignment of the parties since the internationalist-isolationist cleavage disintegrated with Pearl Harbor. The popular backlash created by the Korean and Vietnam wars sharply altered the party balance for a time. But each of these conflicts left the more lasting popular alignment between the parties remarkably intact, for reasons I will explore. There has in fact been a fundamental change in the international context of domestic politics, one with sources in the nature both of presidential leadership and of the public's response. I will set out some observations on each of these things before connecting the argument to our relationship with part of the Pacific rim.

THE EVOLUTION OF PRESIDENTIAL LEADERSHIP

The idea of a strong president is so firmly rooted in the late twentieth century that most Americans would be astonished by the recency of its origin. It is in fact a conception of our own century that had little place in American government to the time of McKinley. The way this change has transformed our politics bears on our central question.

The framers had no intention of recreating the executive power they had fought in their long struggle with the English king. On the contrary, the Federal Convention of 1787 and the Washington and Adams presidencies created the expectation that the leadership of the president would be exercised within sharp limits.

This was first of all to be true of the president's dealings with Congress. He was required to submit an annual message on the state of the union, but by Jefferson's time the president no longer gave them in person. The president was to respect the legislative initiative of Congress, although he was given the countervailing power of veto. Even less was it imagined that the president would work his will with Congress by directly appealing to the people.

This constitutional etiquette bound the president throughout the nineteenth century. Until McKinley's time most presidents were sparing in their messages to Congress and circumspect in their appeals to the people. Even in their election campaigns, most stayed on their front porches while the electorate was mobilized by party lieutenants and the partisan press. The exception that proved the rule was Lincoln's embattled successor, Andrew Johnson, who carried directly to the people his struggle with the Radical Republicans and paid a grievous price; the scandal of this appeal helped his adversaries carry the vote of impeachment in the House of Representatives.

Of course, the nineteenth century had presidents whose greatness lay partly in their ability to evoke a deep popular response to their vision of the nation's future. This was true of Jackson and Lincoln as well as Jefferson. How can we reconcile this with their limited direct appeals to the people, or even to Congress, as president?

The key to this puzzle is that the popular response was structured in terms of broad issue dimensions these leaders helped define on the road to the presidency. By the time Lincoln became president he long since had defined the goals of union and freedom for the western territories that evoked the support he needed to deal with secession. In the White House he saved the Union and freed the slaves by strong executive action—but not by repeated, modern appeals to Congress or the people. His unprogrammatic addresses at Gettysburg and the second inaugural are testaments to the gulf that separates nineteenth- from twentieth-century practice.

The watershed was a period of brilliant improvisation by two presidents who expressed the aspirations of the Progressive movement early in this century. Theodore Roosevelt converted the presidency into a "bully pulpit" from which he raised the consciousness of his countrymen on all manner of emergent issues, such as the conservation of natural resources. Woodrow Wilson was still more programmatic as he mobilized support for the New Freedom proposals he carried to Congress in the great legislative session of 1913–14. Wilson revived the moribund practice of personally delivering the state of the union message, testified before congressional committees, and even lobbied members of the House and Senate in the congressional cloakrooms. His failure at the end of his presidency to rally the country for Senate ratification of the League Covenant was a caution to his Republican successors in the 1920s. But Wilson's demonstration of the power of the "rhetorical" presidency (in

Tulis's phrase) was not lost on Franklin Roosevelt, who completed the modern presidency by adding the institutional resources of the Executive Office.

So complete is this transformation that the president is expected to give strong leadership on all major issues confronting the nation today, whether or not these played a role in the campaign that brought him to office. Although he is constrained by Congress and the media, his mandate is a general one, and it is by now a commonplace that our system works well only with this sort of leadership. What this means for the public's response to foreign issues will be clear in a moment, when we trace certain changes in the parties' support in the electorate.

THE TRANSFORMATION OF CONGRESSIONAL AUTHORITY

A further mark of the strong presidency is today's presumption that the Constitution entrusts foreign affairs to the president. The Constitution does give the president a large foreign-policy role. He dispatches and receives ambassadors, negotiates treaties, and is commander-in-chief of the armed forces, a power that made a lion out of such an obscure nineteenth-century president as Polk. But the framers were careful to check each such grant of authority to the president with a balancing grant to Congress, in line with the doctrine they absorbed from Montesquieu. The president's ambassadors are sent only with the advice and consent of the Senate. His treaties need the approval of two-thirds of the Senate. Only Congress can declare war. And Congress always can withhold appropriations for foreign ventures, the power that was at the heart of Mr. Reagan's frustrations over Central America. The tension between the two branches is not some aberration from constitutional intent brought on by the misadventures of recent presidents; it was as real in the time of Adams and Madison as in the time of Nixon and Reagan. But by the late twentieth century it is the president who has the initiative, and it is his stewardship of foreign affairs that can shift the balance of party support in the electorate.

The reasons for the primacy of the president lie partly in the complexity, pace, and degree of threat in our international relations. There was never the slightest doubt that it should be the president's finger on the trigger when the country entered the nuclear age. But the president has also the priceless advantage of being a single voice in the cacophony of modern American government, an asset that is reinforced by the mass media, for whom it is a gift sent by the gods. Roosevelt and Kennedy held the White

House reporters, and beyond them, the country, spellbound. The spell was not much less with Eisenhower's fractured syntax or Truman's Missouri twang. More recent presidents and their staffs have skillfully exploited the media's need of photo opportunities and sound bites.

But the president's one-versus-many advantage lies also in the fact that our system is utterly without an opposition leader or president-in-waiting, apart from the few short months in which the rival party has nominated a candidate for president. In modern times only Lyndon Johnson had the stature of a true opposition spokesman, when as majority leader of the Senate, flanked by fifty staff aides and buttressed by his friend and Texas patron Sam Rayburn's control of the House, he confronted Eisenhower in his second term.

The president's position is reinforced by the fragmentation of power in Congress. The awesome authority of nineteenth-century speakers of the House, which gave them a major role in defining the party battle, was demolished by the revolt against Speaker Cannon at the beginning of this century. The seniority system remade Congress into a baronial world of powerful committee chairmen and ranking minority members loosely responsible to the party leadership in the two houses. This system flourished in the postwar decades and created congressional leaders who were substantial foreign-affairs figures in the eyes of presidents and the public, although Congress had nothing like the parity or preponderant authority it enjoyed in the nineteenth century.

Congress's chance of seeming to the public a coherent, independent actor on foreign policy was further reduced by the rapid decentralization of congressional power in the 1970s, especially in the House of Representatives. Reforms initiated by the House Democrats sharply curtailed the seniority system, making committee chairmen responsible to the party caucus, dismissing several long-term chairmen, and limiting the authority of those who survived. Individual congressmen used the fragmentation of power to prefer local interests over party positions and strengthen their electoral base on trade and other issues. But they thereby abandoned still further the possibility of structuring the foreign-policy debate for the country at large. It is the president's handling of foreign affairs that at times moves the electorate, for reasons we should now explore.

THE EVOLUTION OF PARTY ALIGNMENTS

When the findings of survey research on electoral behavior began to appear a generation ago, they made clear that the civics-course image of an electorate listening to both sides and reaching a decision in the course of a campaign bore little relation to the realities of electoral choice. Millions of voters had instead what V.O. Key once called a "standing decision" to support one party or the other, a decision they reexpressed in each election unless deflected by strong issues or events.

It was also clear that millions of voters first developed these "party identifications" in the childhood home, although their loyalties were reinforced in later decades. This reinforcement was due partly to the psychological value derived from these loyalties in successive elections. Since a sense of citizen duty required the electorate to act toward a remote and confusing realm of affairs, one with issues complex enough to defy the experts, many voters cut through this dilemma by falling back on their standing decisions, and each time they were served in this way their standing decisions become more deeply rooted. But social processes also reinforced these party identifications in later decades as millions of voters found their early partisanship shared in their neighborhoods, their schools, their workplaces, and their partisan newspapers.

These processes, acting across the electorate as a whole, were the reason for the rise and aging of political alignments. Some issues and events acted on the electorate strongly enough and over a long enough time to produce a lasting alignment of party strength. This happened in the Civil War era when the conflict of North and South remade the party system. But as the decades go by the alignments produced by the primary influence of great issues and events will be kept in place by secondary processes, especially the cloning of partisanship in the early home.

An alignment weakens in time as the generation that experienced the forces that produced it gives way to generations that did not. An aging and weakened alignment may be displaced by a new alignment produced by new forces. This happened in the 1890s when the loyalties created by the Civil War were displaced by a new alignment reflecting the regional economic interests of the time. It happened again in the 1930s when the powerful forces unleashed by the Great Depression allowed Franklin Roosevelt to build a new coalition of have-nots within the Democratic Party.

The Roosevelt alignment is still in place, but it is very weak. What has happened in the decades since the earliest survey findings on voting became available should be understood less as a realignment of party strength than as a progressive dealignment of the electorate. There are a number of signs of the loosening of the old alignment. One is the falling proportion of the electorate that identifies with the parties strongly or at all when asked about their loyalties in opinion surveys. A second is the greater amplitude of the electoral swings between the parties. A third is the soaring fraction of the electorate that splits its vote rather than voting a "straight ticket" for the multiple offices on the long American ballot. A final mark of the aging alignment is the falling fraction of the electorate that casts a vote at all, since the older party loyalties helped get voters to the polling place.

The reasons for this dealignment are easily identified in general terms. One is rising education, since a more educated electorate has less need of standing loyalties to make sense of politics. Another is increased mobility, since an electorate moving from the farms to the cities, from the central cities to the suburbs, and from the rustbelt to the sunbelt is less likely to have its early loyalties reinforced in stable, politically consistent surroundings. Another is the change in mass communications. The partisan press of an earlier day, angling its political coverage to hold partisan readers, has been displaced by politically bland papers all alone in their metropolitan newspaper markets and reluctant to reveal a political bias that could drive still more readers to television. The electronic media have been relatively bland from the beginning, by law and tradition. The political Right may see a bias in the CBS evening news, but any hue that the networks give their stories is a pale reflection of the old-time bias of the partisan press.

A further reason for the progressive dealignment of the electorate, a reason closely linked to the changing character of the media, is of the highest relevance to our argument. I distinguish here between two basically different kinds of issues that move the electorate, separating two types that are rarely distinguished in popular commentaries on politics. The most familiar kind of electoral issue is one on which the rival parties or candidates appeal to the voters by taking different positions on questions that divide the electorate itself. Each of the issues that have been the basis of lasting party alignments have been position issues of this kind. The western territories—slave or free?—was a position issue. So was the issue of the League of Nations—in or out? So are a number of other issues, such as whether the United States should have free trade with Canada, but these are of far less impact.

But the electorate is also moved by issues of a fundamentally different kind. An example is the issue of economic prosperity or hard times. In this case the parties and candidates do not take diverging positions on an issue that also divides the electorate. Both parties and all voters are of one mind—that we want prosperity rather than hard times. The issue acquires its electoral potency because one of the parties, typically the one in power, is linked in the public's mind with the condition everyone wants or the condition no one wants. Thus, the Democrats were driven from power in the election of 1840 because the country held President Van Buren responsible for the severe economic hardship following the panic of 1837, although no one supposed Van Buren was less in favor of prosperity than his victorious opponent, William Henry Harrison. This was not a position issue but rather a consensus or *valence* issue, since everything turned on the bonds or valences formed in the electorate's mind between the rival leaders and conditions that are universally approved or disapproved.

There is little doubt that valence issues have been increasingly important in recent decades and have contributed to the dealignment of the electorate—for reasons that tie into the changing character of the mass media. It was very difficult to make an old-time political speech without talking about position issues. But it is easy to avoid such issues in a 30-second television spot. As a result, our heavily televised election campaigns are increasingly exercises in which the candidates and their media advisers seek to bond themselves in the electorate's mind to such universal positives as competence, experience, integrity, or success and to bond their opponents to such universal negatives as corruption, weakness, crime, or failure.

The appeal of valence-issue campaigning to the parties is that a successful issue of this kind need not cost any votes, whereas a position issue always has this down side. A candidate who successfully appeals for support by stressing integrity in government will not lose the votes of those who prefer dishonesty in government because there aren't any. However, a candidate who takes a "pro-choice" position on abortion can expect to lose support among voters who believe in the "pro-life" position, just as Lincoln, in advocating freedom for the territories, inevitably lost support among those who believed the territories should be slave.

But it would be a mistake to see valence issues simply as a pathology of modern politics. There are fundamental reasons for the rise of such issues and of retrospective voting on the record of incumbents, including, par excellence, incumbent presidents. The range of issues and the pace of events facing modern government are difficult to reconcile with the broad position alignments of an earlier era. Here the argument links up with the profound difference in presidential leadership between Victorian times and our own. The late twentieth century is a different world, one in which it is hard to structure politics along the lines of the enduring position issues of the age of Jackson or Lincoln. We might want large-scale electorates to follow the debates of national policy in position terms. But they will want to convert their role into the plebiscitary one of judging the success of leaders and governing parties in valence terms.

This tendency is very marked in foreign affairs. Each foreign conflict that has powerfully moved the electorate since World War II has been seen by the public more in valence than position terms. This was true of the Korean War, which helped turn the Democrats out of office in 1952. With mounting American casualties after China's entry into the war, the Republicans called Korea "Truman's War" and nominated a military hero for president. But it was not the military hero, Douglas MacArthur, who had been relieved of his command by Harry Truman for wanting to bomb Manchuria. Although we might suppose that the ensuing election campaign would have been structured by the position issue of how forward a strategy America should pursue, from bombing China to pulling back to Japan, the electorate instead treated the war as a valence issue, linking the Democrats with failure and Eisenhower with the prospect of success. The public neither demanded to know nor was told what position Eisenhower would take on the war—and readily acquiesced when an armistice was negotiated along the Panmunjom line.

Still more surprising is the extent to which the Vietnam War, which lasted far longer and was structured both for political leaders and the press by a hawk–dove position dimension, was instead seen by the public largely in valence terms. An incumbent president was again linked with failure in the electorate's mind. The survey evidence shows that the public wanted the problem solved and did not much care whether by hawkish or dovish means. In particular, when Senator Eugene McCarthy administered the coup de grace to President Johnson in the New Hampshire primary of 1968, the survey evidence showed that voters supporting McCarthy were surprisingly unclear as to whether he was a hawk or dove; indeed, almost as many who gave a view thought he wanted to bomb North Vietnam into submission as thought he wanted to withdraw from the war. He was simply the instrument by which the public signaled its desire for a new beginning. Similarly, in the general election of that year Nixon held an edge in terms of Vietnam neither as hawk nor dove but as an experienced leader who was more likely to heal an open national wound. In office he and his remarkable foreign affairs lieutenant Henry Kissinger used hawkish means, including the Cambodian incursion and Christmas bombing of Hanoi, to pursue the dovish end of terminating direct U.S. military involvement in the war, as they simultaneously pursued rapprochement with the Chinese and detente with the Russians.

Clearly, the lesson of Vietnam limited America's involvement in civil and regional conflicts—in Angola, in the Horn of Africa, in Central America—over the next decade, just as the lesson of Munich stiffened America's resolve to play a role in such conflicts, including Korea and Vietnam, after World War II. The view might indeed be pressed that a new involvement–disengagement dimension, created by Vietnam, structured Reagan's conflict with the Democrats in Congress over U.S. involvement in Central America. Undoubtedly it did, at a leadership level—just as a hawk–dove dimension structured attitudes toward the Vietnam War at a leadership level. But in neither case was this sort of structure very prominent at the level of the mass public. Although many Americans who opposed aid to the contras thought the jungles of Central America looked uncomfortably like the jungles of Vietnam, there was in neither case evidence that a more general involvement–disengagement dimension structured popular thinking, as an isolationist–internationalist dimension structured popular attitudes before World War II.

POLITICAL CHANGE SINCE WORLD WAR II

Several insights from this analysis can help us understand the evolution of party strength in recent decades. A clear mark of the Roosevelt alignment, now far removed from the forces that created it, is the preponderant Democratic strength in Congress and the state houses—indeed, in all offices other than the presidency. In the fifty-eight years since Franklin Roosevelt became president, the Republicans have controlled the U.S. House of Representatives for only four, from 1946 to 1948 and from 1952 to 1954. They have fared little better in the Senate, adding only the six years from 1980 to 1986.

But the high politics of the presidency are something else again, since the choice between rival candidates for the nation's most visible office is least likely to be left to the voters' standing decisions. We may pick up the account of the influence of foreign and domestic issues on contests for the presidency with the Kennedy administration's skillful use of Keynesian measures to unleash a long demand-led, low-inflation economic expansion in the 1960s. The resulting economic surplus was partly dedicated to extending the welfare state. Lyndon Johnson's landslide victory of 1964 was the high-water mark of postwar support for government intervention in behalf of social-welfare goals, and the Democratic majorities swept into Congress by Johnson's triumph used the fruits of economic expansion to promote the Great Society. If the welfare state was born of the hardships of the 1930s, it came of age in the prosperous 1960s.

The Congress elected by the Johnson landslide also wrote the first significant civil rights legislation since the Civil War era, and the drive for minority rights widened the reform agenda of the 1960s; the prosperity and rising education of the postwar decades helped foster the belief that the American dream might be within the reach of minorities too. The drive began in the South, with the boycott of segregated buses in Montgomery, Alabama, and the sit-ins of segregated lunch counters in Greensboro, North Carolina. Participants from across the country joined in the march in Selma, Alabama, and this and the moving events that followed reinforced the demand for basic extensions of civil rights, especially for guarantees of equal access to the ballot, and intensified the mood for change. As the decade progressed, the protest took more violent forms, particularly after the Watts riot of 1965, and the goal was more often thought to be a radical restructuring of society.

This transformation was paralleled by the increasingly violent protest over Vietnam. After his 1964 victory, Johnson escalated U.S. involvement, and the protests that focused initially on civil rights soon spread to the war. The civil rights movement showed the efficacy of action mounted outside the electoral or legislative arena, and both strains of protest rested on an increasingly radical critique of American society. The riots that swept through the black ghettoes were matched by the disruptions on a number of college campuses. The violence unleashed by the assassinations of Martin Luther King and of Robert Kennedy and renewed on the streets of Chicago during the 1968 Democratic convention was a substantial challenge to civil order.

The backlash helped elect Nixon president in 1968. He benefited both from a deeply unpopular war and the increasingly hostile reaction to the protests against it. Nixon was helped to office by the country's yearning for order—just as, by a supreme irony, he was later driven from office by the belief that his response to Watergate was undermining the constitutional order.

But it is important to note that the preoccupation with Vietnam did not call a halt to the Great Society. One of Johnson's most deliberate decisions was to sustain his social-welfare initiatives in the midst of the war. Neither did Nixon call a halt. Despite his conservative rhetoric, his budgets continued to fund the new social programs and signaled an emerging bipartisan consensus on the extensions of the welfare state.

The brakes were applied only when the external context of our domestic politics weakened the economic base of the social policy initiatives.

Johnson's desire for guns and butter unleashed severe inflationary pressures, which Nixon's direct wage and price controls did little to contain. Indeed, the pressures were soon amplified by the oil shocks of the 1970s. The decade's stagflation, adding rising unemployment to soaring inflation, led Americans to take a very different view of the welfare state. If economic adversity provoked the leftward move toward government intervention in the 1930s, it inspired a rightward move toward market economics in the 1970s. A tax revolt spread eastward from California, and the stage was set for Ronald Reagan.

That the new president was as much the instrument as the source of the new mood is shown by the parallel experiments with market economics in other countries experiencing stagflation—and the fact that Reagan's program was anticipated by the policies of Jimmy Carter, the president he displaced. It was Carter who launched the effort to control expenditures on the social programs, as his budgets also launched the effort to rebuild the nation's defenses. But Carter's base in his own party was undercut by these steps, and he was in the end a victim of the strongly valenced issue of the hostages in Teheran.

There is no doubt that Reagan came to power with a program defined partly in position terms: He wanted to shrink the role of government and widen the role of the market economy. Toward this end he was committed to tax cuts and sharp reductions in social expenditures, as he was also committed to increased outlays for defense. But we should not miss how skillfully he relied on the valence issue of the stalled economy.

He exploited this issue with consummate skill in the single television debate of the 1980 campaign. In the summing up at the end of this debate, his Democratic opponent came first. Believing Reagan vulnerable because of his extremist positions on a series of issues, Jimmy Carter told the television audience that he was the mainstream candidate of the mainstream party, whereas his opponent was an extreme right-wing candidate of the right-wing party. Therefore, Carter said, his TV viewers should vote for him if they belonged to the American mainstream. But when Reagan summed up he said the choice facing the electorate was nothing like that. He told his viewers that they should ask themselves whether they were better off than four years before, whether America was better led and more respected in the world. If their answer was yes, they should vote for his Democratic opponent. But if their answer was no, they should vote for him —a master valence-issue politician plying his trade.

It would also be wrong to miss the degree of improvisation in the Reagan presidency, even when it dealt with issues closest to the president's core program. There was an almost accidental quality to the fiscal measures of Reagan's first term. In particular, the president and his senior lieutenants failed to foresee the stupendous size of the budget deficits that lay in store. But as this became clear, Reagan correctly saw these deficits as an effective weapon for restraining social policy initiatives by his opponents in Congress. The Reagan legacy may be less that he persuaded the country to a different view of the role of government than that he left his successors in a very tight spot, fiscally speaking.

Indeed, the polling evidence shows that the public has by no means lost its appetite for the benefits government may confer, even if the public is reluctant to pay for them. Surveys have recorded substantial majorities in favor of government protection of the environment, government funding of economic development, government interdiction of the flow of drugs, government funding of better schools and health care, even government provision of a safety net for the poor and homeless. Hence, the pendulum is likely to swing back toward greater government intervention if Congress and the new president can extricate the country from the fiscal fix in which it was left by the Reagan administration.

The improvisation of the Reagan years brought changes in America's trading position that may take a long while to reverse. As the deficits piled up and domestic savings and investment held steady, the United States had to borrow funds abroad, and huge deficits in current account took their place alongside the massive budget deficits. America was transformed in eight years from the leading creditor to the leading debtor nation, and our net overseas investment was reduced as dramatically as Britain's over the period of World War II—except that we had not fought a war. I will note a further result of these developments as we explore the implications of U.S. political change for our relations with our southern partners.

THE ANZUS RELATIONSHIP

We may now ask what all this has to say about America's ties with Australia and New Zealand. First, despite the importance of the external context of our politics from the beginning of the republic, Australia and New Zealand have been only a marginal part of this context since the ANZUS alliance crystallized almost four decades ago. The situation might have been transformed during the Vietnam era if the parties had been aligned along a more general involvement–withdrawal position dimension that also divided the electorate. A party battle structured in these terms might have given a far greater visibility in our domestic politics to actions by our ANZUS partners that aligned themselves with the goals of the rival parties. In this situation the offer of Australian troops by the Holt government and the withdrawal of these forces by the Whitlam government would have been a significant part of the context of domestic politics and might have left a marked residue in popular attitudes.

If the decision to end America's role in Vietnam had been more tightly constrained by a continuing alignment of our parties and their supporters along an involvement–withdrawal dimension, Australia and New Zealand might have loomed far larger in our political consciousness as events unfolded. The constraint on our leaving the war would have sustained an identity of interest between the Soviets and Chinese and precluded our playing the "China card" that transformed our relationship with East and Southeast Asia and that relieved not only ourselves but our ANZUS allies of the fear of a "domino effect" from the loss of Vietnam. Under these circumstances, the impact of our regional allies on the goals that divided our parties could have made Australia and New Zealand a lively part of the international context of U.S. politics.

But this conjecture is about a world that might have been. The Vietnam controversy was actually structured in the very different valence-issue terms I have described and involved a much simpler response to the president's stewardship of foreign affairs. Johnson's failure was the issue, and the Democrats, driven from the White House, were replaced by an administration that "solved" the problem by a mixture of hawkish means and dovish objectives.

How little our relationship with our ANZUS partners has subsequently penetrated to the core of U.S. politics can be seen by tracing America's handling of defense and trade issues that have caused a considerable stir in New Zealand and Australia in recent years. The first of these arose from the decision of the Lange government to bar from New Zealand's ports U.S. ships that might be nuclear powered or armed. The American government saw this decision as touching defense interests extending far beyond the South Pacific and worked to keep the ban from spreading to more sensitive parts of the world. The American response therefore made clear that no ally could follow New Zealand's example and expect its defensive arrangements with the U.S. to remain intact.

This confrontation held center stage in New Zealand for a number of weeks and was highly visible in Australia as well. But the U.S. policy response was worked out within a fairly small leadership circle, involving the president and National Security Council staff, the State and Defense Departments, the Central Intelligence Agency, and the relevant committees of Congress. No broader debate was needed to authorize our policy actions or to convey our message to other governments.

The U.S. government would not have welcomed a broader public debate, and the administration was nonplussed when a House subcommittee proposed to hold hearings on this turn in our relations. Although New Zealand has an exceedingly low profile for Americans and is scarcely mentioned outside of a common breath with Australia, such visibility as it has is distinctly favorable. It would not have been easy to cast this small country in the villain's role and to take a broader public through the administration's two-step reasoning that it was wiser to suspend our defensive commitments to New Zealand than to run the risk of our allies in more sensitive places following New Zealand's example. In the event, this case needed to be made only in Foggy Bottom, Arlington, Langley, and the White House and Executive Office Building. For the broader public it was simply one of the myriad details of foreign affairs that are left to the stewardship of the president.

The stand of Australia helped to contain the issue. The Hawke government in Canberra had already faced down the idea of denying entry to nuclear armed or powered ships, first broached by the left-wing Labor government in the state of Victoria, when the New Zealand government announced its ban. The crisis in the alliance would have been far more serious if our ANZUS partners had presented a common front.

It is by no means unimaginable for the issue to have become more visible to the American public and to have raised a serious question as to the president's stewardship of foreign affairs. For example, a massive radioactive leak from a U.S. ship in southern waters would have created a sensation, one that would have set a good many Americans to thinking about visits to U.S. ports by ships with nuclear power or arms. In the absence of such a triggering event, the issues surrounding the nuclear-ship ban were less salient to the public because they could not readily be assimilated to broader position dimensions that structured American thinking about international affairs.

The absence of this sort of structure also fragments public response to the issues of trade policy that have vexed America's relations with its southern partners in recent years. In the early postwar world the huge and relatively open U.S. market seemed a bright substitute for the increasingly problematic markets in which New Zealand sold its lamb and butter and Australia such products as wine under the old system of imperial preferences. As Britain set its course toward Europe, with its Common Agricultural Policy and high external tariffs, Britain's willingness to negotiate concessions for its imperial offspring only muffled the sound of the closing door.

By contrast, U.S. farmers believed they could compete with the world and stood in the vanguard of free trade. Even in the postwar world there were exceptions in the never-never land of U.S. agricultural supports and production controls; a plan for stabilizing sugar prices born in the Great Depression had been converted to a system for transfering monopolistic profits from the American consumer to domestic producers of cane and beet sugar—and to foreign governments that were assigned quotas to sell on the rigged U.S. market. But the general postwar stance toward agriculture by the United States was strongly free trade.

In subsequent decades American farmers too have heard the sound of the closing door in a world of trading blocs and mercantilist governments. Even grain farmers, once the most confidently free-trade part of American agriculture, came to think in these terms after Richard Nixon's wheat sale to the Soviets and Jimmy Carter's wheat embargo, a fact not lost on later candidates for president. Our ANZUS partners have paid a price as the U.S. government has increasingly taken up the cause of its agricultural producers.

This was very clear to Australia's farmers when the U.S. government offered wheat to the Soviets and sugar to China at subsidized prices. The international markets for these commodities are well enough integrated for this dumping to depress the world price of wheat and sugar—and the income of Australia's farmers. The sharpness of the reaction throughout Australia was noted with dismay in the councils of American government but not on the American farm. This international context failed to deflect the play of the issue in domestic U.S. politics.

The low visibility of Australia's distress for the American public is not due to a simple view that Russia and China count for something in the world whereas Australia does not. The deals with Russia and China were equally invisible, except to those whose economic interests were directly involved. Moreover, Australia is a country of standing in the American psyche. It is far more salient than New Zealand and just as favorably seen. Americans with even a primitive sense of geography think that a country occupying an island continent between the Pacific and Indian Oceans is a substantial entity. And cultural factors, however elusive, count for a good deal too. Large numbers of U.S. servicemen visited Australia during World War II and the Vietnam War. Australians are superb at tennis, a game Americans play, while New Zealanders are superb at rugby, a game Americans don't. Australia enhanced its reputation as a rogue competitor by making off with the America's Cup. Most Americans can whistle "Waltzing Matilda," although most Australians wish they would not. And Americans widely if mistakenly believe that Australia is the last refuge of the extreme individualism of the American frontier. *Crocodile Dundee* didn't create this view; indeed, the reverse is more nearly true, with the misplaced belief creating a market for the Hogan films.

In view of all this, extraordinary events might in this case too have made Australia's anger over U.S. dumping more visible to the American public and have raised questions as to the president's stewardship of foreign affairs. But the trigger would have been the pleas of Australian rock stars or a "Sydney tea party" dumping American products overboard or other events outside the compass of any broader position dimensions that structure American thinking about international affairs. Lacking such pre-cut channels into the main stream of political discourse in America, this worsening of Australia's trading position, although it was of deep concern to Australia itself and of interest to the leaders in Congress and the executive branch whose stakes were involved, was consigned to the many things on which the government's handling of foreign affairs will be judged by the electorate, if at all, largely *ex post* and in valence terms.

Yet if the external context of U.S. politics has been transformed over half a century by the need to deal with a more complex and rapidly changing world, this context is still very much with us. Indeed, no policy sector makes this point more clearly than trade. Although it is difficult to say how many hostages the U.S. has given its trading partners—especially Japan—by inviting the rest of the world to finance the budget deficits of the Reagan years, we have as a result less freedom to pursue a strongly protectionist course. A president who seeks to close our trading gap by reducing the level of American living may yet pay a price at the polls, as the workings of our predominantly valence politics would lead us to predict.

Comment

CHARLES E. MORRISON

The three country chapters reveal at least one undeniable element of commonality between the political experiences of Australia, New Zealand, and the United States in the postwar period: All three societies have undergone major political change during this time.

Clearly there are numerous important differences between the three polities and their postwar histories. Their political systems vary in important ways, from New Zealand's unitary parliamentary system through Australia's parliamentary/federal amalgam to the American presidential/federal formula. The starting points for their postwar evolution also differed. New Zealand had—and for some time continued to elaborate—a highly corporatist system of policymaking not found in equal measure in either of the other two, thus giving it further to go when the tide turned toward a more competition-based system. Australia shared with New Zealand a strong social democratic ideological tradition and a history of government interventionism quite foreign to American experience except perhaps at the height of the New Deal era.

Both the timing and the pace of change have differed also in the three cases. As described in Roberto Rabel's account, the changes in New Zealand, long postponed, were all the more dramatic and extensive when they came—and as a consequence may also be most vulnerable to subsequent adjustments or reversals. The major trends in Australia described by Hugh Collins have been more gradual and steady, although the policy innovations of the Hawke government have also been quite striking when compared with traditional Labor policy and even the practice of previous conservative governments. Donald Stokes's analysis of political change in America sees an even more measured pace but also more of a pendulum motion of swings between periods of interventionism and social reform, and periods of contraction and caution.

Finally, an obvious if somewhat ironic contrast between the most recent experiences of the three countries is that the key agents of change toward more traditionally "conservative" approaches in Australia and New Zealand have been Labor governments, while the U.S. version of the neo-conservative formula was implemented largely by a Republican administration.

But beneath these different specific situations and experiences, several even more fundamental common trends stand out. These trends appear to reflect still more basic shifts in the nature and dynamics of advanced representative democracies in the late twentieth century.

First, in each of the societies there has been a progressive weakening of the historical political alignments within the electorate. Party loyalties have become less important in determining individual voting behavior, and the numbers of independent, ticket-splitting or "swing" voters have been growing. New political interest groups, particularly single-issue groups (e.g., antinuclear, environmentalist, women's and minority rights) have also assumed increasing influence. The appearance of various new splinter and minor parties as well as independent candidates in all three countries has been one visible symptom of these trends. These processes have not (yet) come to threaten the dominant positions of the traditional major parties, but the major parties have increasingly been forced to cater to the new groups in their campaign strategies and political programs. Electoral outcomes and even legislative action increasingly reflect shifting coalitions of voters and interest groups. Fragmentation seems to be the order of the day, and the outlook for the future.

In part, the decline in traditional party loyalties reflects social changes: rising education levels, higher incomes, increasing proportions of the work force in white-collar jobs, greater mobility and the general spread of a common "middle-class" identity among the bulk of the voting population. With the previous lines of conflicting political interests becoming less clear, the traditional structures of political organization have also lost much of their salience and appeal.

Another common theme is the importance of what Donald Stokes terms "valence" politics, that is, the linking of parties or candidates to general conditions or values rather than specific policy positions. In all three societies, elections for national leadership (the presidency in the United

States and the national parliaments in the other two) essentially function as referenda on the performance of the government in power and/or the basic circumstances of the country. When the problems being faced appear to exceed the capabilities of the government, the government is replaced. The "electoral centralism" (competition for the middle ground) described by Hugh Collins in Australian politics is another way of describing competition by parties for the endorsement of the electorate in valance terms. In New Zealand, the ultimate rejection of Muldoonism and the end of the long period of National dominance in 1984 can be similarly seen as a judgment on overall performance rather than a vote for any specific new set of policies, as witnessed by the fact that the dramatic Douglas economic program was only adopted and announced after Labour was in government. The public mandate had been to "do something" about the country's increasingly serious economic circumstances, but neither Labour's platform nor the electoral outcome were very specific in terms of precisely what the government would or should do.

A corollary of valence politics has been a centralization of the political process—for example, the growth of central power in Australia as described by Collins, and the increased focus on the Presidency in the United States identified by Stokes (New Zealand's unitary system was already as centralized as is probably feasible in a parliamentary democracy). There is an expectation that the national leadership is ultimately responsible for the country's welfare and must take the initiative in identifying solutions to national problems. This expectation holds even if the solutions themselves are not necessarily government-centered, as seen in the recent common moves toward reducing the regulatory and managerial roles of government.

A third common trend, another outgrowth of the changing nature of the electorates and of political competition, is the high degree of pragmatism that characterizes practical policymaking by the governments in all three countries. Collins speaks of the dominance of "common sense utilitarianism" in the determination of Australian political programs. Stokes describes the improvisational aspects of decision-making even under the ostensibly program-oriented Reagan administration. And Rabel recounts the early effort of the Lange government to return to the traditional consensus processes of government decision-making and its abandonment of that effort when it became clear that a consensus approach would make it impossible to take bold action to deal with the nation's urgent problems. The Lange Labour government's adoption of extreme Thatcherist economic policies and the Reagan administration's adoption of tax policies that produced massive deficit spending must stand as classic demonstrations of the ultimate triumph of practical politics over ideological preconceptions. And Paul Keating's embrace, in effect, of Milton Friedman ranks only slightly behind.

A fourth common factor affecting political change in all three countries is the involvement of transnational influences. The influence of British and American models and policies, from anti-Communism to Thatcherism and Reaganomics, is noted in both the Australian and New Zealand studies. And while Stokes emphasizes that events in Australia and New Zealand have little impact on American political processes, he cites the major impact of international issues (the Cold War, Vietnam) on American domestic politics and paints some conceivable circumstances in which Antipodean developments could play these roles. It has become a commonplace to speak of the increasing international interdependence of the modern world. The three experiences recorded here provide specific illustrations of the impact of this phenomenon on the substance and process of domestic political change.

A final commonality in these three stories, which again reflects a broader international phenomenon, is the role of economic imperatives in stimulating the political changes described. In all three countries the movement toward a greater reliance on market competition, individual incentive, and the private sector has been directly triggered by consciousness of lagging international economic competitiveness and the looming prospect of declines in national living standards. That the changes were implemented by Labor governments in Australia and New Zealand, and that the start of the redirection process in the United States can be traced to the Democratic Carter administration again point to the influence of economic (and associated political) reality rather than party principle in motivating these decisions.

The three polities face some common questions for the future as well. In all three, the traditional political structures do not seem to be well equipped to accommodate the fragmentation and lack of consensus that now pertain in their electorates. The combination of weakened political bases and heightened expectations of performance by leaders is a prescription for failure and frustration. It is clearly desirable that new mechanisms be developed to facilitate the formation and maintenance of stable new political coalitions and to provide a more reliable basis on which governments can develop and implement broad programs. Otherwise, electoral fragmentation may lead simply to government impermanence and inability to deal with fundamental problems.

Opinions differ as to the likelihood that such new mechanisms can be developed. Rabel is relatively pessimistic for New Zealand in this regard, although given the particularly traumatic upheaval through which New Zealand has recently traveled, some of the elements of the current situation that most arouse his concern may only be transitional. Collins is concerned over the relative weakness of the representative mechanisms in Australian politics, and also questions whether the processes of competition for the middle ground are actually identifying the correct political agenda for the country. But he points to the experience of economic policy change under the present Australian government as illustrating the positive aspects of these dynamics. And Stokes believes the pendulum in the United States is bound to swing again in the direction of somewhat greater interventionism.

A second question facing all three societies concerns the philosophical basis of government policy in an era in which government programs are increasingly determined by essentially pragmatic processes. In each of the countries at present, the serious concerns over the nation's international economic competitiveness have led to the focusing of government attention and effort on the prosperity and welfare of the mainstream. This emphasis in turn inevitably detracts to some degree from attention to social welfare issues and the condition of the poorer and non-mainstream groups. The traditional political philosophies of the major parties in all three countries have, in one way or another, dealt with both sets of concerns and attempted to accommodate the conflicts between them. These conflicts are in many ways starker and more difficult to resolve in the present, economically straitened circumstances.

Thus in New Zealand a Labour government has had to deal with—and justify—historically unacceptable levels of unemployment that were at least in part a direct result of its own policies. In Australia the Labor Party's Left regularly and vocally challenges the dominant Right faction with neglecting the party's electoral roots and its traditional dedication to social reform. The Democratic Party in the United States suffers from an agonizing and debilitating split between advocates of its "liberal" reform tradition and social and fiscal conservatives. And the conservative movements in all three countries are torn between the pulls of their traditional philosophies, which would counsel even further movement in the direction of laissez faire and a reduced government role, and the electoral pragmatists who argue that the best way to compete with the political Left is to demonstrate both compassion and a superior ability to manage social problems.

It can only be expected that this struggle will continue, both between and within the major parties in each country. Whether the eventual result will be a new philosophical synthesis, deeper polarization, or simply continued eclecticism and incoherence is difficult to predict, although as suggested by Stokes, a return to more prosperous conditions would clearly make it easier at least to paper over some of the differences in priorities. One reasonable guess, however, would be that whatever the overall direction of the outcomes, reflecting the parallels in the forces at work there is likely to continue to be a broad degree of similarity among the three cases.

SECTION III

Images and Attitudes

In this section we examine the national self-images of the peoples of Australia, New Zealand, and the United States, and their related perceptions of their roles in the world and of each other. We are interested in changes in the way the peoples in each country define their identities, international roles and relationships, what national filters they apply to information about the outside world, and particularly how their perceptions of the nature and degree of external threats have been changing in each case. We also consider the special factors that have influenced each country's evolving perceptions, and to what degree the present outlooks in each country can be described as characterized by consensus or internal differences.

The measurement and description of self-images and attitudes remains a very imprecise science, and inevitably individual interpretations and emphases vary. This is the case in the chapters that follow. Partly for this reason, the section begins with a review by William Watts of some of the major survey research data bearing on attitudes in each of the countries toward the others. Although the data base is still partial and limited, it does paint a picture of basically positive relationships punctuated by distinctive national perspectives and some negative factors and trends.

Against this background, the country chapters explore significant aspects of each nation's individual experiences and attitudes. Trevor Matthews and John Ravenhill describe the evolution of Australian attitudes from those of an insecure British outpost facing European imperial predators and "Asian hordes" and taking a highly defense- and alliance-based approach toward relations with the outside world, to an increasing though still qualified emphasis on independent policies, self-reliance, and a regional orientation in the post-Vietnam period.

Jock Phillips focuses on New Zealand's 1984 decision to deny entry to nuclear ships as illustrative of what he sees as the quite recent emergence of a distinctive New Zealand national self-consciousness and a new vision of itself as Aotearoa, a Maori and South Pacific country and a moral exemplar to the world, with America having had the misfortune of being on the "receiving end" of this process.

Matthews and Ravenhill and Phillips also comment on the contrasts between the Australian and New Zealand world views, with Australian attention concentrating on the United States and Asia, while New Zealanders give a corresponding importance to their relationship with Australia which most Australians do not reciprocate.

James Rosenau's essay on changing American international orientations emphasizes the post-Vietnam breakdown of the American Cold War consensus world view and the likelihood of even greater disarray in American belief systems if present trends toward a more benign international environment continue. He concludes, however, that none of the recent or foreseeable trends is likely to make peripheral relationships such as those with the ANZUS partners more central to American perceptions or policymaking.

In the concluding commentary, the editor notes that a number of similar forces have influenced the changing attitudes in the three countries, including conflicting pulls between the desire for autonomy and the imperatives of interdependence as well as a growing need to reconcile national policies with the constraints imposed by location and resource limitations. These common dynamics, however, have tended to produce quite distinctive outcomes in each case.

7

Australia, New Zealand, and the United States: Mutual Perceptions

WILLIAM WATTS

The following pages attempt to summarize some of the prevailing perceptions and attitudes held in each of the three ANZUS countries toward the others, drawing on opinion surveys conducted in all three countries as the main source of information.

WHOSE RADAR SCREEN?

Americans view the world around them, and others view the United States, through the prism of very different radar screens.

For the United States—in the eyes of both leaders and those who take more than a passing interest in international affairs—the radar screen is jammed with blips throughout its entire 360-degree sweep. It is jammed, furthermore, by blips representing countries and problems with which the United States is deeply involved. To name but a few: trade differences to the north; debt problems and hostile insurgencies to the south; superpower rivalry; strained relations with combatants in the Middle East; suspicions about policies in Africa, including both involvement and disengagement in the volatile southern end of the continent; trade frictions across the Pacific with America's second largest trading partner, accompanied by strains with other dynamic exporting powers in the region; and a frayed alliance with old friends in the South Pacific, the focus of this chapter.

These are all problems of substance. The list, furthermore, is easily expanded. Each item demands the time and energies of key figures in both

Table 7.1. American Views of Other Countries: Like/Dislike

Country	Most Positive 1980 %	Most Positive 1985 %	Most Positive % Shift	Most Negative 1980 %	Most Negative 1985 %	Most Negative % Shift	% Net Shift
1. Canada	75	78	+3	1	—	−1	+4
2. **Australia**	49	49	—	1	—	−1	+1
3. Japan	30	35	+5	3	3	—	+5
4. West Germany	33	34	−1	4	3	−1	—
5. Israel	28	29	+1	5	4	−1	+2
6. **New Zealand**	28	27	−1	2	2	—	−1
7. China	17	16	−1	8	6	−2	−1
8. Brazil	21	14	−7	2	2	—	−7
8. Philippines	21	14	−7	2	4	+2	−9
10. Saudi Arabia	15	11	−4	17	8	−9	+5
11. Taiwan	13	10	−3	6	5	−1	−2
12. India	9	9	—	6	5	−1	+1
13. South Korea	9	8	−1	8	8	—	−1
14. Singapore	9	7	−2	4	3	−1	−1
15. Thailand	9	5	−4	7	7	—	−4
16. Malaysia	5	4	−1	4	4	—	−1
16. Indonesia	5	4	−1	5	4	−1	—
16. Nigeria	7	4	−3	7	8	+1	−4
16. Soviet Union	6	4	−2	47	47	—	−2
20. Cambodia	n/a	2	n/a	n/a	20	n/a	n/a
20. North Korea	2	2	—	28	30	+2	−2
20. Vietnam	5	2	−3	33	34	+1	−4

n/a = not available.

Source: Potomac Associates.

the public and private sectors. In the process, numerous other plaints of a lesser nature—lesser in American eyes, that is—get lost.

The world is viewed somewhat differently from Wellington and Canberra, for example. On their radar scopes there are fewer major blips in the course of each swing. The United States is almost always one of them, frequently the largest. There are, furthermore, aspects of American thinking and actions of its leadership that many thoughtful people find disconcerting. It is on the basis of those concerns that leaders and peoples in these and other countries will act.

THE UNITED STATES

Let us start with a look at some perceptions (and misperceptions) held by Americans. To provide a comparative setting, we will first present

Table 7.2. American Views of Importance of Other Countries
(Ranked in order of those who said "very important" in 1985)

Country	Very Important 1979 %	Very Important 1985 %	Very Important, Fairly Important/ Not So Important, Not Important at All 1985 %
1. Canada	76	77	96/3
2. Soviet Union	67	68	88/11
3. Japan	58	62	94/5
4. West Germany	54	58	91/7
5. China	57	55	92/7
6. Saudi Arabia	63	49	87/11
7. Israel	57	44	85/14
8. **Australia**	41	42	87/12
9. Brazil	34	29	80/18
10. Philippines	n/a	28	74/23
11. South Korea	35	28	73/25
12. Taiwan	44	24	72/25
13. India	33	22	69/29
13. Vietnam	n/a	22	52/45
15. **New Zealand**	n/a	21	65/31
16. North Korea	29	20	52/44
17. Singapore	n/a	19	59/35
18. Thailand	n/a	17	58/37
19. Indonesia	n/a	14	52/41
19. Nigeria	n/a	14	49/44
21. Malaysia	n/a	13	47/43

n/a = not available.

Question: "When it comes to pursuing our interests all around the world, how important do you think it is for the United States to try to get along well with each of the following countries—very important, fairly important, not so important, or not important at all?"

Source: Potomac Associates.

findings of surveys that measure attitudes toward both countries, and then look separately at views toward each.

Some General American Images of Australia and New Zealand

Comparative Levels of Like and Dislike. How do Americans rate Australia and New Zealand in terms of relative levels of like or dislike? In an effort to measure such feelings, Potomac Associates asked Americans

Table 7.3. American Views of Trustworthiness of Other Countries (percent mentions)

Country	1979	1980	1981	1982	1983	1984	1985	1986	1987	1988	1989
Canada	69	77	72	73	74	75	76	70	73	76	73
UK	43	56	48	54	55	54	55	54	58	52	52
Australia	47	46	41	42	43	49	46	45	44	50	48
Switzerland	35	31	32	37	33	41	38	38	36	44	41
Sweden	30	24	29	31	31	33	28	31	30	35	37
France	29	27	21	22	29	32	27	23	25	29	33
FRG	24	28	24	21	23	26	28	24	24	25	23
Norway	22	16	15	20	19	20	22	23	23	22	23
New Zealand	13	11	9	14	14	12	14	12	13	16	19
Italy	13	9	8	12	13	17	15	12	13	13	17
Holland	16	12	13	19	14	17	13	14	15	17	15
Japan	17	22	26	18	23	23	24	23	20	15	15
Mexico	18	17	25	16	16	17	20	14	15	14	13
Israel	14	18	15	12	17	17	17	17	17	13	11
Philippines	n/a	n/a	10	9	11	10	9	9	7	5	6
Brazil	6	6	5	5	5	7	5	5	5	4	5
China	5	8	7	7	7	6	8	7	6	4	4

n/a = not available.

Question: "Listed below are the names of several countries. Which five do you regard as especially trustworthy?" (Multiple answers, so totals exceed 100 percent. Only those countries mentioned by at least one respondent in twenty are included.)

Source: The *Yomiuri Shimbun*.

in 1980 and again in 1985 to express their feelings about various countries worldwide on a scale that ranges from plus 5 ("highly favorable") to minus 5 ("highly unfavorable").

For purposes of simplicity, Table 7.1 shows only most positive and most negative responses, that is, totals of those who give a country plus 4 and plus 5, or minus 4 and minus 5. Shifts in attitudes from 1980 to 1985 are also included. Australia ranked second only to Canada (invariably first in American eyes, since most of them think of Canada as an extension of their own country, making highly favorable ratings virtually inevitable); New Zealand ranked sixth. And if all favorable responses are added together, Australia and New Zealand rank second and third, evidence of considerable warm feelings.

Importance to U.S. Interests. Another, more demanding assessment of how Americans feel about specific nations stems from the perceived importance such nations are given in terms of U.S. interests, as shown in Table 7.2. The upper end of this list represents a realistic, sophisticated ordering. The first six countries—Canada, the Soviet Union, Japan, West

Germany, China, and Saudi Arabia—comprise a logical selection. But Australia ranks close behind, marginally below Israel and substantially ahead of New Zealand. Australia's continental dimensions, in sharp contrast with New Zealand's island status, undoubtedly play a role in these assessments.

Trustworthiness. Largely favorable ratings apply to the theme of trustworthiness as well, more so in the case of Australia than New Zealand.

For several years the *Yomiuri Shimbun*, Japan's largest circulation daily newspaper, has commissioned an annual survey of Japanese and Americans, asking their views about the relative "trustworthiness" of a number of countries around the world. Table 7.3 shows the question and selected American responses. Only Canada and Britain outrank Australia. As in the case of perceived importance to U.S. interests, New Zealand ranks farther down the list. But the official storm over port calls of U.S. naval vessels appears to have had little effect on the public at large; the most recent rating was the highest in this particular series.

Perceptions of Australia

Stereotypes. It is clear that Americans in general have a very high regard for Australia and Australians. Unlike the stereotypes Americans hold for for Asia as a whole—"overcrowded," "underdeveloped," "political unrest," and "poor sanitation" were most often mentioned in our 1980 and 1985 surveys—those chosen for Australia were among the most positive: "modern" (selected by 54 percent in 1985, the highest for any country in the region, and up 9 points from 1980), "peace-loving," "industrialized," and "well-educated."

Australian government is thought of by a clear majority of Americans (66 percent) as democratic—the most positive views we recorded about

Table 7.4. American Characterizations of Australians

Characteristic	% Mentions		Characteristic	% Mentions	
Peaceful	94	(+5)	Warlike	2	(−1)
Hardworking	89	(+2)	Lazy	5	(−1)
Straightforward	89	(+3)	Deceitful	4	(—)
Individualistic	70	(—)	Group oriented	23	(+4)
Competitive	70	(+1)	Noncompetitive	22	(+2)
Creative	66	(−1)	Imitative	27	(+4)

Note: Change in points, 1980–1985, in parentheses.
Source: Potomac Associates.

systems of governance in the region. (For Japan these numbers were barely more than one in three.)

Americans also characterize Australians as individuals with attractive, positive personal attributes, as shown in Table 7.4. This generally flattering listing conforms to what most Americans would like to attribute to themselves. Most other peoples in the region do not fare as well. And while most Americans think of Australians as "hardworking" (a point of amusement to some Australians) and "competitive," that does not translate into concern about Australian imports threatening jobs of U.S. workers. Only about one American in twenty thinks of Australia in such terms—a far cry from the eight in ten who see a threat in Japanese imports.

Table 7.5. American Willingness to Defend Other Countries (percentage)

Country	1972	1974	1976	1978	1980	1984	1985
Major European Allies (if attacked by Soviet Union)							
Agree	52	48	56	62	74	69	76
Disagree	32	34	27	26	19	18	16
Japan (USSR or China)							
Agree	43	37	45	50	68	59	70
Disagree	40	42	37	35	28	26	21
Australia (enemy of the U.S.)							
Agree	*	*	*	*	70	64	70
Disagree	*	*	*	*	21	24	20
Philippines (enemy of the U.S.)							
Agree	*	*	*	*	65	58	63
Disagree	*	*	*	*	25	28	25
China (Soviet Union)							
Agree	*	*	*	*	45	41	42
Disagree	*	*	*	*	42	43	44
South Korea (North Korea)							
Agree	*	*	*	32	38	36	41
Disagree	*	*	*	52	51	48	48
Taiwan (China)							
Agree	*	*	*	32	43	34	37
Disagree	*	*	*	48	42	47	46
Thailand (Vietnam)							
Agree	*	*	*	*	30	*	32
Disagree	*	*	*	*	55	*	55

* = not asked.

Note: "Don't knows" were omitted.

Question: "Please tell me whether you agree or disagree with the following statements: The United States should come to the defense of (country "x") with military force if it is attacked by (country "y")."

Source: Potomac Associates.

Australia is also given high marks in terms of "the degree to which the rights and liberties of individual citizens are protected." Almost nine Americans in ten rated the situation in Australia as either "very favorable" (54 percent) or "somewhat favorable" (35 percent). Among other countries in the Pacific region included in this particular question, only Japan comes close as far as Americans are concerned (31 percent "very favorable," and 45 percent "somewhat favorable").

Security Commitment. Australia is regularly ranked near the top of the list of countries for which Americans would be willing to commit U.S. military might, including combat personnel, should it be attacked from without. Since the early 1970s, Potomac Associates has been tracking American willingness to defend certain friends (see Table 7.5). For both European allies and Japan, support for their defense—including the use of U.S. military force—has climbed almost without interruption since the low point of 1974. By 1985, such willingness had reached a new peak. Australia and the Philippines are the only other countries in the region for whom support is in the majority column. One can argue that the wording of the question, specifying the attacker in both cases as "an enemy of the United States," may have biased respondents toward the "agree" column. But even allowing for such potential influence, the levels of support are high.

Why So Popular? We noted earlier that Americans ascribe considerable importance to Australia as a country with which it is important "for the United States to try to get along well." What explains the remarkably favorable feelings that Americans in general hold about Australia and its people? Australia is, after all, far removed from the continental United States, and the number of Americans who have visited Australia or have had much direct contact with the country and its people is not large. Several factors come to mind:

- common cultural, historical, and social values
- alliance relationships, especially during World War II, and the ANZUS link
- Australia's frontier image, with the conquering of the outback raising memories of America's drive westward across a new continent
- the expanding Australian cultural presence in the United States (Diva Joan Sutherland; rock artists Olivia Newton-John and the Bee Gees; film hits from the *Mad Max* series, *My Brilliant Career*, and *Breaker Morant*, to Paul Hogan's 1987 smash *Crocodile*

Dundee; Colleen McCollough's hugely popular novel *The Thorn Birds* and the more surprising 1987 historical bestseller *The Fatal Shore* by Robert Hughes)

- the strong sports/outdoors image (international tennis stars such as Hoad, Rosewall, Laver, and Yvonne Goolagong; golf's Greg Norman, the "Great White Shark"; America's Cup yachting prowess; and the general allure of the outback, beaches, the Great Barrier Reef, and the remarkable variety of wildlife)

Some Negatives. It would be mistaken, however, to assume that the array of bilateral interests, buttressed by a common language and common historical antecedents, ensure smooth sailing for relationships between Australia and the United States.

Thus, while Americans profess considerable warmth and admiration for Australia, there is also much ignorance about the country. Even its location is often mistaken by many Americans. If most Americans know that Australia has a democratic political system, 17 percent identify it as having a "civilian-authoritarian" government. Large numbers of Americans fault Australia for one area in particular. Its immigration policies, measured in a perceived lack of willingness to open doors to non-Anglo-Saxons and non-Europeans, are viewed with considerable skepticism. Australia is seen as exclusionist, particularly toward non-whites, a view that fails to take into account sharp revisions in recent years of immigration policies as well as Australia's positive efforts in helping to resettle refugees from Indochina.

We noted above that Australia has come into American consciousness through a variety of channels, with films and novels playing an important role in recent years. The images being transmitted by such books as *The Thorn Birds* or the *Mad Max* films may be outdated, marked with an undeserved overlay of violence, or just plain inaccurate.

Australia does not command much attention on a day-to-day basis in the United States. We discussed at the outset the problem of the "overloaded radar scope." With big countries dominating the radar screen, others tend to get crowded out. This certainly applies to Australia, as it does to so many other countries in East Asia and the Pacific.

Perceptions of New Zealand

New Zealand, because of its smaller size (population of 3.2 million in 1984, similar to that of Chicago, and land area roughly the size of

Colorado) and lesser impact on the U.S. economy, has tended to command less attention than neighboring Australia both in the U.S. media and in various governmental and other policy councils. As already noted, New Zealand trails Australia by considerable margins in terms of both perceived importance to U.S. interests and "trustworthiness."

The Port-Call Crisis. Until quite recently, there were no overriding problems on the bilateral U.S.-New Zealand agenda. Comfortable and friendly relations are clearly reflected in the high "like" rankings given New Zealand in the first opinion studies cited in these pages. This generally positive mood evoked widespread public tolerance toward New Zealand when policy differences surfaced. Prime Minister David Lange stated at the time the crisis erupted in 1985 that the "nuclear ship ban [was] anti-nuclear, not anti-American or anti-ANZUS." The upshot nevertheless was the suspension of the U.S. security commitment to New Zealand under ANZUS.

American Images. The impact of this substantial policy move on the American public at large appears to be minimal. In our 1985 assessment of opinion, attitudes toward New Zealand remained overwhelmingly positive, almost unchanged since the comparable testing carried out five years earlier. (The latest questioning, it should be added, was conducted after the initial U.S. port-call request under the new policy had been turned down by New Zealand.)

Particular note might be made of the ranking given New Zealand in terms of its perceived "trustworthiness." Its rating actually moved up two points from 1984 to 1985, putting it at the highest in a series going back to 1978—again, after the port-call issue had been fully vented. Marginal shifts have occurred in subsequent years, with the most recent rating the highest in the series. New Zealand was also seen, next to Australia, as the country in the region with the most democratic form of government. A majority of 56 percent chose this label, although over one American in five (21 percent) viewed the government in Wellington as "civilian-authoritarian."

Many Americans tend to lump New Zealand and Australia together, meaning that they ascribe to both countries the "ANZAC" image, outpost of British Empire, pioneering spirit, and some of the other plusses noted in the previous section. New Zealand itself is widely pictured in terms of extraordinary landscape, an unusual ratio of sheep to humans, esteemed cultural influences such as the powerful "Te Maori" exhibit and the operatic skills of Kiri Te Kanawa, and, most recently, the America's Cup yachting challenge. Such overall positive factors tend to soften the negative impact of any policy disagreement—especially when the disagreement is, for the public at large, not all that immediate or clear. For the vast majority of Americans, problems associated with the right to make port calls fall into just such a category.

AUSTRALIA AND NEW ZEALAND: DIFFERING PERCEPTIONS OF THE UNITED STATES

The United States occupies a very different position in the thinking of Australians and New Zealanders, as documented in a 1984 study conducted for the Australia New Zealand Foundation by McNair Surveys (*A Report* 1985). Among Australians, for example, 62 percent of those interviewed said that the United States was the country with which they have the most in common. Britain followed with 57 percent mentions, while New Zealand lagged behind with 37 percent. Among New Zealanders, on the other hand, Australia ranked first (79 percent), followed by Britain (37 percent), and the the United States (only 14 percent).

In ranking peoples with whom they have the most in common, Australians put the British into the first position (37 percent), followed by Americans and New Zealanders (29 and 25 percent, respectively). For New Zealanders, Australians again ranked first with 59 percent, 32 percent named British, while a scant 3 percent mentioned Americans.

Australians ranked the U.S. first in terms of current importance (countries considered to be "generally of importance to Australia"), as the one country most important to Australia, and as the country likely to be of most importance to Australia in the future (see Table 7.6). For New Zealanders, as shown in Table 7.7, the "importance" picture is quite different. New Zealanders look first to Australia on all three counts, and only then to the United States and Japan, with Japan overtaking the United States in terms of future significance.

Table 7.6. Australian Views of Importance of Other Countries (percentages)

Country	Present Importance	Single Most Important	Future Importance
United States	74	59	48
Japan	46	17	37
United Kingdom	29	7	14
Asia/Pacific	21	3	26
New Zealand	17	1	10
European countries	9	1	5

Source: McNair Surveys.

Table 7.7. New Zealand Views of Importance of Other Countries (percentages)

Country	Present Importance	Single Most Important	Future Importance
Australia	62	34	48
United States	58	25	39
Japan	44	13	41
United Kingdom	35	14	15
Asia/Pacific	17	2	20
European countries	14	2	6

Source: McNair Surveys.

Table 7.8. Australian Views of U.S. Society (percentages)

Characteristic	Very Favorable	Somewhat Favorable	Unfavorable
Science and technology	69	22	4
Potential for future progress	42	42	8
Higher education	38	43	8
Art and literature	25	46	9
Economic opportunity	26	44	12
General quality of life	13	55	22
System of government	13	49	25
Social welfare, such as care of sick and aged	6	26	36

Source: United States Information Service.

Table 7.9. Australian Views of U.S. Problems (percentages)

Problem	Very Serious	Fairly Serious	Not Serious
Crime and violence	84	14	1
Drug abuse	83	14	1
Environmental pollution	49	33	7
Racial prejudice	44	38	12
Poverty	41	42	11
Unemployment	39	39	9

Source: United States Information Service.

AUSTRALIA

Overall Perceptions of the United States. A national survey in Australia in October 1983 found a strongly favorable balance of positive versus negative views of the United States: 69 percent favorable and 24 percent unfavorable. An extensive 1986 study commissioned by the United States Information Agency (USIA) found that 73 percent of Australians had a very favorable (23 percent) or somewhat favorable (50 percent) opinion, as opposed to 25 percent who had a somewhat unfavorable (19 percent) or very unfavorable (6 percent) opinion. A follow-up survey in October 1988 recorded a 75 percent favorable rating (25 percent very favorable and 50 percent somewhat favorable) against 24 percent unfavorable (19 percent somewhat and 5 percent very unfavorable).

America's Impact and Life Style. Australians also see the United States as having a major impact on Australian life. Another 1986 USIA-commissioned undertaking found that a total of 85 percent thought that "American ways and things" have had either a "great deal" (43 percent) or a "fair amount" (42 percent) of influence "on our life here in Australia." That influence is not seen in entirely favorable terms, however. Less than a majority (48 percent) saw it as either "much more beneficial" (9 percent) or "somewhat more beneficial" (39 percent), while more than one in three (36 percent) saw it as "somewhat more harmful" (27 percent) or "much more harmful" (9 percent).

Such ambivalence about the American impact notwithstanding, Australians appear to have generally positive views about most aspects of U.S. society and the American way of doing things. Low marks on social welfare stand out in the negative column, as Table 7.8 illustrates. Australians were clearly of the opinion that social and economic problems in the United States are "more serious" than in Australia (60 percent to 7 percent), with another 28 percent seeing the situation as roughly equal in

Table 7.10. Australian Views of U.S. Alliance (percentages)

View	Oct. 1982	Sep. 1984	Jun. 1985	Dec. 1985	Oct. 1986	Oct. 1988
Continue U.S. alliance	83	77	78	79	76	78
Get out of ANZUS	7	13	12	11	16	14
Don't know	10	10	10	10	8	8

Question: "All things considered, do you think it is better for Australia to continue to be allied with the United States under ANZUS, or do you think it would be better for us to get out of ANZUS?"

Source: United States Information Service.

Table 7.11. Australian Views of Beneficiaries of ANZUS (percentages)

Beneficiary	Oct. 1982	Oct. 1983	May 1984	Sep. 1984	Jun. 1985	Dec. 1985	Oct. 1986	Oct. 1988
United States	25	29	35	34	31	35	45	41
Both about equally	32	36	34	33	38	35	31	32
Australia	31	24	20	24	24	23	18	21
Don't know	12	11	11	9	7	7	6	6

Question: "On balance, who do you think benefits more from our alliance with the U.S. under ANZUS—the United States or Australia—or do you think both benefit about equally?"

Source: United States Information Service.

both countries. High on the list of perceived problems in the United States were crime and drugs (Table 7.9).

It would be a mistake to read into these findings, when taken in their totality, an overly uncritical view of the United States. America's role and influence is a subject of large, often heated interest in Australia. There is a considerable U.S. economic presence in Australia, with direct investment reaching $8.8 billion in 1985. For some, this investment and the general visibility of the American economic reach have sparked concern about American domination. There is an uneasy sense among a number of Australians that Australia is selling its birthright to foreign capital (a concern currently rising in the United States in the wake of massive flows of Japanese investment into the American marketplace), allowing its culture to be overwhelmed by such American symbols and/or traditions as Coca-Cola, Levis, and the latest in the "rock" scene, and ceding national interest to the whims of U.S. foreign policy.

When sensitive bilateral policy issues arise, the failure of American leadership to give Australia greater salience in policy terms can be a galling experience (more on this shortly).

Attitudes about the Alliance. Recent surveys suggest that these and other concerns may have caused some erosion in public support for the alliance relationship. While the shifts have not been major, they are noticeable (see Table 7.10). In just four years, from 1982 to 1986, a 76 percentage point margin in favor of continued alliance with the United States dropped to a 60 point spread.[1]

There also appears to be a growing tendency among Australians to think the United States is the principal beneficiary of the alliance links (Table 7.11). The shifts here could cause considerable concern to policymakers and strategic planners. Early in this decade, the alliance link was seen as mutually beneficial, with even a slight plurality thinking that Australia was

Table 7.12. Australian Views of U.S.-New Zealand Dispute (percentages)

View	Mar. 1985	Dec. 1985	Oct. 1986
Support the U.S. position and try to get New Zealand to change its policy	35	27	20
Support the New Zealand position and try to get the U.S. to change its policy	22	20	22
Remain neutral in the dispute	37	49	56

Question: "Please use this card to tell me what you think we should do in the current dispute between the United States and New Zealand:"

Source: United States Information Service.

Table 7.13. Australian Views of U.S. Nuclear-Powered Ship Visits (percentages)

View	Oct. 1982	Oct. 1983	May 1984	Sep. 1984	Jun. 1985	Dec. 1985	Oct. 1986	Sep. 1987	Oct. 1988
Strongly favor	21	16	18	17	20	24	24	19	20
Somewhat favor	34	36	31	36	35	32	37	36	39
Subtotal	65	52	49	53	55	56	61	55	59
Somewhat oppose	14	17	17	17	16	16	15	17	17
Strongly oppose	16	18	21	18	16	17	17	16	15
Subtotal	30	35	38	35	32	33	32	33	32

Question: "Next, about visits by American nuclear-powered warships to Australia's ports. Do you favor or oppose visits by American nuclear-powered warships? Strongly or only somewhat?"

Source: United States Information Service.

Table 7.14. Australian Views of U.S. Nuclear-Armed Ship Visits (percentages)

View	Dec. 1985	Oct. 1986	Sep. 1987	Oct. 1988
Strongly favor	20	21	16	17
Somewhat favor	29	34	32	36
Subtotal	49	55	48	53
Somewhat oppose	16	15	20	17
Strongly oppose	26	24	22	22
Subtotal	42	39	42	39

Question: "And do you favor or oppose visits to Australia's ports by American warships that might be carrying nuclear weapons? Strongly or only somewhat?"

Source: United States Information Service.

getting the better of the bargain. But in the most recent years there has been a surge in the numbers of those who think the United States is the prime beneficiary, even approaching majority opinion in 1986. And that has been accompanied by a substantial drop-off among Australians who see their own country as the one that benefits more. Should the perceived imbalance in alliance benefits continue to grow, a considerable weakening in long-term alliance support may result.

On an issue of more immediate moment, there appears to be waning enthusiasm for the U.S. position in the dispute between the United States and New Zealand over port calls of U.S. vessels in New Zealand waters. Shifting Australian attitudes are noteworthy, as seen in Table 7.12. Declining support for the U.S. position does not translate into increased backing for New Zealand's stance. Rather, a hands-off attitude has come to command majority favor. At the same time, and in what can be viewed as an implicit rejection of the New Zealand policy, visits to Australian ports by American warships that are nuclear-powered or that may carry nuclear weapons appear acceptable to a majority of the population (Tables 7.13 and 7.14).

Declining Trust in the United States? One striking trend in the ongoing series cited in these pages has been the long-term drop in confidence among Australians in the U.S. security commitment (Table 7.15). The slippage, while not drastic, is considerable. What was a 60 percentage point margin on the "trust" side in 1975 had eased to a 41 point spread thirteen years later.

The low point reached in 1986 may have been influenced by President Reagan's decision that summer—reportedly over the strong opposition of

Table 7.15. Australian Confidence in U.S. Security Commitment (percentages)

Amount	Sep. 1975	Mar. 1978	Oct. 1982	Oct. 1983	May 1984	Sep. 1984	Jun. 1985	Dec. 1985	Oct. 1986	Sep. 1987	Oct. 1988
Great deal	37	34	36	31	28	27	29	30	24	25	24
Fair amount	40	45	43	43	44	43	41	40	44	45	44
Subtotal	77	79	79	74	72	70	70	70	68	70	68
Not very much	14	13	12	17	18	19	18	21	22	21	23
None at all	3	3	3	4	4	4	5	3	6	5	4
Subtotal	17	16	15	21	22	23	23	24	28	26	27

Question: "If Australia's security is threatened by some other country, how much trust do you feel Australia can have in the United States to come to Australia's defense–a great deal, a fair amount, not very much, or none at all?"

Source: United States Information Service.

Table 7.16. Australian Views of Impact of U.S. Alliance (percentages)

View	Oct. 1982	Oct. 1983	Sep. 1984	Oct. 1986	Sep. 1987	Oct. 1988
Reduce the risk	36	28	28	31	30	35
Increase the risk	22	29	29	26	29	23
Make no difference	33	36	35	37	35	36
Don't know	9	7	8	6	6	6

Question: "Do you think that our defense alliance with the United States under ANZUS is likely to reduce the risk of an attack on Australia, increase the risk of attack on Australia, or make no difference to the risk of an attack on Australia?"

Source: United States Information Service.

both Secretary of State George Shultz and Secretary of Defense Caspar Weinberger—for the subsidized sale of wheat to the Soviet Union. As far as many Australians are concerned, this only says that talk about American good will is hollow, that good will fails to impress American policymakers, even at a time when trade imbalances unfavorable to the United States are playing so large a role in other bilateral relationships. What about the imbalance favorable to the United States with Australia? What is the benefit of all the American good will, observers ask, if it doesn't affect policy? As one Australian wheat farmer put it, "It was always assumed in this country that if there was a fuss, the Americans would come to our aid. Good alliances are built on trust, and this sort of thing undermines that trust, and among those who have been strongest in that trust. The feeling is, if they've done this to us, what will they do to us on some other issue?"[2] Some Australians showed the depth of their anger by calling for the end of U.S. base rights.

Beyond this, and at least as worrisome for the future, is some Australians' belief that close security and military links with the United States may actually do more to endanger Australia's security than to enhance it. The alliance structure, some say, commits Australia to the whims and vagaries of America's foreign policymakers, with whom critics frequently disagree. The joint defense facilities are looked on as magnets for Soviet missiles. Why, then, should Australian leaders knowingly and willingly submit Australia to this assured cataclysm? While not a majority view, there are impressive proportions who worry that the alliance relationship carries high risks for Australia (Table 7.16). Unlike some of the other alliance-related findings already noted, these do not indicate any particular opinion shift. But there is a consistent one-in-four core who sees an increased risk of attack on Australia as a result of the alliance ties.

These symptoms of generally flagging trust in the United States are paralleled by declining Australian confidence in the United States as an international actor (Table 7.17). In 1978, the margin on the favorable side was better than four to one, with a 60 percentage point spread. Ten years later, that margin had shrunk to a simple majority, with only a 12 point differential—and that represented an improvement over the previous year, when the margin had almost disappeared. It should also be noted, however, that these confidence ratings are probably influenced by developments in the arms control field, with confidence increasing when arms control agreements are reached. The recent developments in U.S.-USSR relations, including the accord on Intermediate Nuclear Forces (INF), are likely responsible for the rebound between 1987 and 1988.

There is another twist to the concern felt by some Australians about the security relationship with the United States. One hears regularly that the United States is so exercised about the Soviet threat as a global worry that American policymakers fail to take into account local realities. Australia is no exception where this gripe is concerned. "What about Indonesia?" is a question asked at most foreign policy discussions. "Will you defend us against attack from the real threat to the north?" Ongoing research illustrates this concern (Table 7.18). In the 1980s, a hostile Indonesia next door seemed at least as ominous as the Soviet superpower thousands of miles away.

A Generation Gap? Australian opinion on the range of security issues just discussed shows important variations on the basis of age and education. A 1987 study sponsored by USIA, for example, found differences almost across the board when respondents with some college education or higher were divided into groups under forty years of age, or forty and above. The younger group was less inclined than the older to: favor visits of U.S. nuclear-powered or nuclear-armed ships; rate the importance of

Table 7.17. Australian Confidence in U.S. International Role (percentages)

Amount	March–April 1984	Sept. 1985	March 1987	Sept. 1988	Oct. 1978
Great deal	26	15	18	11	13
Fair amount	52	49	39	39	42
Subtotal	78	64	57	50	55
Not very much	15	27	30	37	35
None at all	3	5	11	10	8
Subtotal	18	32	41	47	43

Question: "How much confidence do have in the ability of the United States to deal responsibly (wisely: 1978 wording) with world problems—a great deal, a fair amount, not very much, or none at all?"

Source: United States Information Service.

ANZUS for Australia's security as "very" or "fairly" important; and believe that the benefits of the joint defense facilities were worth the added risk they may entail. At the same time, the younger cohort was more likely to think that the United States was the main beneficiary of ANZUS, and that the joint defense facilities increased the risk of attack.

This generational split carried over to views of the United States and specific U.S. policies. The under-forty better-educated were more prone than their elders to think that the impact of U.S. actions and policies on the Australian economy is "harmful" and that U.S. agricultural policies, rather than those of the European Community, cause most problems for Australia. The younger segment was also less favorable in its overall opinion of the United States and displayed less confidence in the U.S. ability to deal responsibly with world problems.

It is quite possible that views of the younger generation will change over time. In the case of Japan, for example, many of those who led demonstrations outside the American embassy in Tokyo in 1960—protesting the U.S.-Japan mutual security treaty and forcing the cancellation of a visit by President Dwight Eisenhower—are now among the leadership group in working with the United States and promoting closer ties between the two countries. But the Australian findings are important, and should be followed over time.

Table 7.18. Australian Views of External Military Threat (percentages)

View	Sep. 1975	Mar. 1978	Sep. 1984	Oct. 1986	Sep. 1987	Oct. 1988
See a military threat	41	35	43	46	30	24
Soviet Union	11	16	21	16	8	6
Indonesia	—	8	21	21	7	12
China	25	17	7	2	2	2
Japan	3	6	3	2	2	2
Vietnam	—	4	3	1	1	1
United States	—	—	1	6	4	2
Other	8	4	4	10	3	2
See no threat[a]	59	65	25	44	60	63
Don't know	—	—	32	10	10	13

Question: "Do you think any countries will pose a military threat to the security of Australia over the next 5 years?" [If 'Yes']: From which country or countries do you think this threat will come?"[b]

a. "Don't know" combined with "see no threat" in 1975 and 1978.

b. Question was asked in terms of a military threat "five years from now" prior to 1986; it was asked in terms of a military threat "over the next ten years" in 1986.

Source: United States Information Service.

Table 7.19. New Zealand Choice Between ANZUS and Nuclear Ship Ban (percentages)

Choice	1985 Mar.	1985 Oct.	1986 Apr./May	1989 June
Break defense ties with the U.S.	45	44	44	52
Allow ships that could be nuclear armed into New Zealand ports	45	48	52	40
Don't know	10	8	4	8

Question: "If you had to choose between breaking defense ties with the U.S., or allowing ships that could be nuclear armed into New Zealand ports, which would you prefer?"

Sources: 1985/1989: Heylen Research Center; 1986: National Research Bureau.

NEW ZEALAND

Differing Perspectives. At least since the end of World War II, New Zealand has tended to see itself more closely aligned to Britain and the Commonwealth, while Australia has moved into a more complex set of ties with the United States. This has stemmed from a number of economic, political, and sociological factors.[3]

New Zealanders tend to see their country as small, isolated, rural, and economically limited. Happy with the Commonwealth connection, New Zealanders have not been all that anxious to get involved in great-power politics and alliance arrangements. New Zealand has not seen itself as particularly threatened militarily from without, and did not turn to the United States with the same level of interest as did Australia when Britain's regional influence and power declined. In short, New Zealand has kept a greater psychological distance from the United States than has its giant neighbor to the west.

The Port-Call Crisis: Some New Zealand Reactions. The port-call issue assumed considerable national importance, generating intense political debate and discussion. As noted earlier, Lange has insisted that his position should not be seen as "anti-American or anti-ANZUS." Rather, he has stated, it is "anti-nuclear." The views of his fellow citizens have been ambivalent.

Let us look at comparative testings carried out in New Zealand in March and October 1985. Earlier opinion samplings, taken without direct reference to the nuclear question, recorded large majorities (at the 70 percent level or better) favoring continued participation in ANZUS. With the crucial nuclear issue factored in, the 1985 readings indicated a virtual standoff—but with a slight shift over the seven-month interval in favor of ANZUS, nuclear or not (Table 7.19). The timing of the 1985 surveys is important. The second survey came after Prime Minister Lange had implied publicly that the ANZUS treaty might have to be sacrificed if it required acceptance of U.S. nuclear-armed vessels, and after statements by U.S. Defense Secretary Caspar Weinberger, over New Zealand TV news, that the United States might have to consider alternative security arrangements in the Pacific if New Zealand went ahead with proposed antinuclear legislation. Some of the potential impact of the new policy position, in other words, had been clearly foreshadowed. Although New Zealanders as a whole were split almost down the middle, there were important variations within some subgroups. Those most in favor of allowing ship visits included conservative National Party supporters (84 percent) and those over forty years of age (58 percent). Those most in favor of breaking defense ties with the United States included democratic socialist Labour Party supporters (65 percent) and those fifteen to twenty-four years of age (52 percent). The age differential parallels similar questioning about the United States on the part of younger Australians.

The debate was intensified by release of the findings of a special Defence Committee of Enquiry, appointed by Lange and headed by former Secretary of Foreign Affairs Frank Corner, in August 1986 (Defence Committee of Enquiry 1986). The committee report was accompanied by results of an extensive survey of New Zealand opinion. Here are some of the key findings of the study, conducted in late April and early May 1986 by the National Research Bureau:

- New Zealanders ranked Americans third, after Australians and the British, as people they "would get on with."
- Most New Zealanders identified Australia as the country toward which "a great deal of effort" should be expended to be on good terms with, followed by a grouping of Britain, the South Pacific countries, and the United States.
- There was widespread support (82 percent) for forming alliances, with seven out of ten New Zealanders (71 percent) in favor of ANZUS—92 percent among the National Party, and 58 percent among Labour.
- In specifying countries with which New Zealand should form alliances, Australia came first, followed by the United States and Britain (68, 52, and 35 percent, respectively).

- There was overwhelming opposition (more than nine in ten) to stationing in New Zealand of any weapons of mass destruction, whether nuclear, chemical, or biological.
- When asked about banning nuclear-powered or nuclear-armed ships, 38 percent opted for banning both kinds of vessels, 28 percent favored banning nuclear-armed ships only, 3 percent opposed just nuclear-powered ships, and 28 percent preferred to ban neither. Along party lines, 55 percent of Labour Party supporters favored banning both types of ships, while 51 percent of National Party backers favored banning neither.
- When asked what kind of defense arrangements they preferred, 72 percent of the respondents believed that New Zealand should remain in alliances (of which 66 percent wanted alliances with the United States and Australia).
- At the same time, illustrating the dilemma that New Zealanders face, 73 percent said they want defense arrangements to be nuclear free.
- Concerning membership in ANZUS and nuclear ship visits, 37 percent said "yes" to ANZUS and "yes" to visits by nuclear ships, 44 percent said "yes" to ANZUS but "no" to nuclear ship visits, while 16 percent said "no" to both.
- Confronted with the bottom-line choice (what should New Zealand do if a nuclear-free presence in ANZUS is impossible—allow nuclear ships or get out of ANZUS?) then a 52 percent majority said New Zealand should stay in ANZUS and allow nuclear ships, while 44 percent opted for getting out of ANZUS with no visits by nuclear ships.

The results of the 1986 study are not fully comparable to those recorded in 1985, noted above. It is worth noting, however, that there was a

Table 7.20. New Zealand Views of Nuclear Ship Ban (percentages)

View	Aug. 1984	Mar. 1985	Jun. 1989
Approve	45	52	63
Disapprove	46	41	32
Don't know	9	7	5

Question: "Do you approve or disapprove of the Labour Government's policy to ban nuclear-powered ships from New Zealand ports?"

Source: Heylen Research Center.

Table 7.21. Australian and New Zealand Views of Other's Importance (percentages)

Importance	Overall importance of other country to: Australia	New Zealand
Of major importance	28	62
Of some importance	52	33
Of little or no importance	17	4

Source: McNair Surveys.

four-point increase during the roughly six-month interval in the ranks of those who wanted to stick with ANZUS—nuclear or not. The U.S.-New Zealand negotiations on the issue broke down in mid-1986, and it is also noteworthy that over the following two years New Zealand public opinion swung around to support the actual state of affairs by an even stronger margin. Those views were matched by a steady increase over time in support for the ship ban policy (Table 7.20).

AUSTRALIA AND NEW ZEALAND: PERCEPTIONS OF EACH OTHER

Like Australian and New Zealand attitudes toward the United States, the basic atmosphere of trans-Tasman relations can only be considered positive and close by any international standard. Again, however, interesting differences of intensity and emphasis emerge. We noted earlier that New Zealanders tend to give a high ranking to Australia (well above the United States) in terms of both affinity and importance, while Australians rank New Zealand much lower and behind the United States on most of these measures.

Table 7.22. Australian and New Zealand Views of Other Countries with which Closer Relations Should Be Developed (percentages)

Country	Australia	New Zealand
United States	23	19
Japan	21	18
China	21	13
New Zealand/Australia	18	48
United Kingdom	13	10
Asia/Pacific	13	8
Soviet Union	11	5
European countries	9	5
Indonesia	7	1

Source: McNair Surveys.

Table 7.23. Australian and New Zealand Views of Each Other: Likes/Dislikes (percentages)

Likes/Dislikes	Australian	New Zealand
Aspects Liked About the Other		
Friendliness	73	50
Casual/easy going	14	13
Honest/decent/genuine	9	—
Hardworking/good workers	8	3
Similar people/no difference	7	9
Hospitable/sociable	5	21
Willing to help/generosity	5	8
Open/straightforward/frank	5	12
Aspects Disliked About the Other		
Nothing disliked	64	29
Brash/loudmouthed	2	24
Arrogant/superior/over confident	3	20
Boastful/brag a lot	—	18
Rude/pushy/cocky/crude	2	8
Bad sports/need to win at all costs	—	7
Dislike the way they speak/accent	2	6
Lazy/don't want to work	2	2

Source: McNair Surveys.

These differing ratings find further reflection in the data from the 1984 Australia New Zealand Foundation study, in which Australians and New Zealanders were asked to rank the overall importance to their own country of the other. Australians were considerably less inclined to find their neighbor "of major importance" than were New Zealanders (Table 7.21). Another indicator of significant divergence in views was revealed in ratings given by Australians and New Zealanders of countries seen "as best to develop closer relations with" (Table 7.22). Australians were at least marginally more inclined than New Zealanders to think that better relations with other countries were more important—with one glaring exception. On the relative merit of better relations across the Tasman Sea, New Zealanders were markedly more anxious than their neighbors, placing by far the highest level of importance on these ties.

It has been noted that Americans tend to have extremely favorable attitudes toward Australians, as measured in 1980 and 1985 studies. That warmth, extended to New Zealand, also helped to explain the minimal public response in the United States to the port-call controversy. What about views that Australians and New Zealanders have about each other?

Some selected findings from the ANZF report are shown in Table 7.23. On the positive side, assessments of one another are relatively similar, stressing elements of friendliness and overall likability (though little respect for each other's work ethic). On the negative side, however, striking differences emerge, with New Zealanders considerably more prone to finding flaws in the Australian character than the reverse. While almost two-thirds of Australians interviewed (64 percent) could think of "nothing" they disliked in New Zealanders, less than three New Zealanders in ten (29 percent) were correspondingly charitable toward their Australian neighbors, with roughly one New Zealander in five thinking of Australians as "brash," "arrogant," and "boastful." As in the attitudes of the Antipodean states toward America and Americans, across the Tasman the bigger brothers seem to be less interested and less well informed but inclined to be well disposed, while the small partner is both the more knowledgeable and more skeptical of the two.

NOTES

1. One 1985 survey showed clear majority backing for U.S.-Australia defense links, even without New Zealand participation. When asked: "ANZUS is a defence alliance of Australia, New Zealand and the United States. If New Zealand is no longer in ANZUS, do you favor or oppose the same kind of mutual defence alliance between Australia and the United States?" 75 percent were in favor as against only 17 percent opposed (Campbell 1986).

2. "Australian Wheat Farmers Reap Bitter Feelings," *The New York Times*, February 2, 1987, p. D8.

3. See, for example, Campbell (1985 and 1987).

8

Adrift in an Alien Sea? Australian Perspectives on the World

TREVOR V. MATTHEWS AND JOHN RAVENHILL

Australians have long had difficulty in coming to terms with their location in the Asia-Pacific region and in effecting an accommodation between the geographical proximity of Asia and their sense of Asia's cultural remoteness. Instead, Australians were highly conscious of themselves as an isolated, threatened, and vulnerable country—as "a small nation in an alien sea." This sense of being a vulnerable European outpost on the edge of Asia shaped the Australian national identity, the Australians' outlook on the world, and the role they chose to play in the world.

The overriding goal in foreign policy was to secure the protection of the two great English-speaking powers. In return for this protection, Australia was willing to play the part of loyal and dependent ally of Britain and the United States. As a consequence of this insecurity, Australia's foreign policy took on a peculiarly defense-centered character. In the postwar period the ANZUS treaty has been its linchpin. In the aftermath of Vietnam, however, amid increasing doubts about the capacity and willingness of great and powerful friends to come to its protection, Australia has moved toward a more independent and self-reliant posture. In this chapter we examine the factors that have shaped Australia's defense and foreign policies and its definition of its role in the world.

PERCEPTIONS OF EXTERNAL THREATS

A former head of the Foreign Affairs Department has described Australia as "the frightened country" (Renouf 1979). This fear was originally rooted in the Australian colonists' sense of being remote from Britain (on whose navy they depended for their security); of being a sparse settlement in a large, richly endowed, and fundamentally indefensible continent; and of being a culturally and racially isolated European outpost. For most of the nineteenth century, Australians looked on Britain's European enemies as the most likely source of danger. The fear was that France—later Russia and then Germany—might challenge Britain's dominance in the Southwest Pacific.

By the end of the nineteenth century, stirred by China's awakening, by Japan's rapid rise as an industrial and military power and by Social Darwinist notions of Anglo-Saxon racial superiority, Australians saw Asia and its "teeming millions" as the major threat to their living standards, national security, and racial superiority. The "yellow peril" now loomed on "White Australia's" horizon. The full impact of this threat came in May 1905 with the news of Japan's signal victory over the Russian fleet at the Battle of Tsushima. Australia, with a population of four million people and with no navy of its own, felt defenseless and vulnerable to invasion. The lesson of the Japanese victory, Prime Minister Deakin warned, was that Australia could no longer "depend on its isolation for its security" (Meaney 1976: 122). For the next sixty years the threat of Asia sustained Australia's defense and foreign policy. The fear of a Japanese invasion—intensified by the Japanese bombing attacks on Darwin and submarine raids on Sydney Harbor in 1942—lasted well into the 1950s. With the Communist victory in China in 1949, China and "Asian Communism" became the object of Australia's fears. The red star replaced the rising sun.

Sir Robert Menzies spoke for many in the 1960s when he argued that Vietnam was but the first step in China's southward expansion. For other Australians Indonesia was the wild card. In a speech in 1959, Arthur Calwell—who was soon to become the parliamentary leader of the Labor Party—expressed the range of strategic and racist anxieties that Australians felt toward Asia in general, and Indonesia in particular:

Table 8.1. Percentage of Australian Public Perceiving Countries as Threats to Australia's Security, by Year

	1967	1968	1969	1970	1976	1978	1980	1982	1983	1984
Threat perceived	52	52	51	54	43	46	63	51	57	53
No threat perceived	32	34	36	36	46	42	34	37	31	37
Not sure/DK	16	14	13	10	10	12	3	12	12	10

Question: "In your opinion are there any countries which are a threat to Australia's security?"
Source: Morgan Gallup Polls.

Table 8.2. Percentage of Australian Public Perceiving Threats to Australia in the Next Fifteen Years, by Year

	1971	1974	1976	1977	1979	1980	1985
Will be threatened	42	36	51	49	51	65	46
Will not be threatened	45	51	38	41	39	28	45
Not sure	13	13	11	10	10	8	9

Question: "Do you think Australia will be threatened from outside its borders in the next 15 years?"

Source: ANOP Polls.

> If Indonesia took over West New Guinea, there would be nothing to prevent the Indonesians from allowing the Japanese or some other people—Chinese Communists or some other potential enemy of this country—to flood in and become a menace to the future security of the people in Australia. (quoted in Camilleri 1979: 13)

According to polls over the last two decades, approximately one-half of adult Australians on average have believed there was a threat to Australia. The results, however, have been influenced not only by the timing but also by the wording of the question. One series of Morgan Gallup Polls between 1967 and 1984 asked voters the question: "In your opinion are there any countries which are a threat to Australia's security?" In the late 1960s a little over half the electorate agreed that some country or countries threatened Australia's security; another 10 percent indicated that they were not sure (Table 8.1). During the years of detente between the superpowers in the 1970s this proportion fell. In April 1980, doubtless as a result of the Soviet invasion of Afghanistan, the proportion rose to more than six in every ten (with only 3 percent undecided).

Another series of polls has used a somewhat different question. On various occasions since 1971 Australian Nationwide Opinion Polls (ANOP) has asked: "Do you think Australia will or will not be threatened from outside its borders in the next 15 years?" A more relaxed attitude to threats is evident in the responses to this more specific question (Table 8.2). They also show a sudden escalation in threat perception in 1980. Otherwise, the pattern has been that around one-half the electorate since the mid-1970s has been of the opinion that Australia will be threatened externally over the next fifteen years. In other polls, the more specific the definition of threat, the fewer the respondents who stated that it was a likely occurrence. References to a "military" threat, an "attack" on Australia, or a shorter time period have markedly reduced the level of threat perception

Table 8.3. Percentage of Australian Public Specifying Threats to Australia's Security, by Country Name and Year

Year	China	Russia	Vietnam	Indonesia	Japan	America
1968	32	11	14	6	5	3
1969	30	16	9	8	7	3
1967-9	31	14	11	7	6	2
1975	21	12	13	7	6	-
1976	17	20	2	10	7	4
1978	14	16	8	14	9	3
1980	14	40	7	11	6	7
1982	7	26	2	17	5	6
1983	13	37	7	15	6	5

Source: David Campbell, *Australian Public Opinion and National Security Issues,* (Working Paper No. 1, Peace Research Centre, Australian National University, 1986), p. 27.

among those polled. Polls in 1986 and 1987 for the Murdoch press group showed that 40 percent and 37 percent of respondents thought Australia would face a military threat in the next ten years (Campbell 1988).

What countries did Australians see as the major threat? In the 1960s voters were most concerned about China, followed by the Soviet Union and Vietnam (Table 8.3). In the 1980s the Soviet Union was seen as the greatest source of threat, followed at some distance by Indonesia and China.

There has been a clear divergence since 1972 between the concern felt by half the electorate about threats that face Australia and official thinking on this question. The Whitlam government rested its defense policy on the official assessment that there would be no foreseeable major threat to Australia for a period of ten to fifteen years. Similarly benign strategic assessments (albeit in the context of a shorter time span) have been endorsed by the Fraser and Hawke governments. According to the paper on the Strategic Basis for Australia's Defense Policy that was current at the time the Hawke Labor government came to office in early 1983, there was "substantial prospect" that the central strategic balance between the nuclear superpowers would be maintained; no present or prospective military threat to Australia from the Soviet Union (even though U.S. defense-related facilities might be targeted by Soviet nuclear weapons); "no likelihood" of a major power, such as China or Japan, deploying forces in areas of direct defense concern to Australia; and no evidence that any government in Southeast Asia would have the military capability for posing a significant threat to Australia. More recently, the 1986 Dibb report on Australia's defense capabilities and the 1987 Defense White Paper endorsed the judgment that, except for the remote possibility of global war, Australia faces no presently identifiable major military threat.

Surveys of elite opinion have shown Australian leaders to be less concerned about external threats than the electorate. In a 1975 survey of national leaders, Higley, Deacon, and Smart (1979) found that 54 percent of their 370 respondents agreed that Australia was under no foreseeable military threat over the next ten to fifteen years. A 1983 survey of the Australian foreign policy elite (Meaney, Matthews, and Encel 1988) found the 200 leaders who were interviewed to be markedly closer to the reassuringly optimistic official views than the concern about external threats displayed in the opinion polls. On being asked whether they agreed with the statement that there were no likely threats to Australian security in the foreseeable future, 69 percent agreed, 30 percent disagreed, while only 1 percent were unsure. In both elite surveys, public servants and those whose party sympathies lay with the Australian Labor Party contributed disproportionately to those who did not perceive a threat. However, business and rural leaders and sympathizers of the Liberal and National parties were notably less inclined to agree that there were no likely threats to Australian security.

Many of those who refuted the notion of a likely threat used the same terminology as that employed in the official reports. Almost six in every ten who perceived no threat to Australia explained their position by stating that they could discern no country with both the will and the capacity to threaten Australia. Interpreting threat as invasion, they saw only the Soviet Union and the United States as having the capacity to so threaten Australia, but neither superpower was believed to have any reason to do so. Certain countries in the region—for example, Indonesia—might develop the will but they would lack the capacity to mount and sustain a major military action against Australia. Only two respondents specifically referred to the deterrent character of the ANZUS treaty as the reason they agreed with the statement that there was no likely threat to Australia's security in the foreseeable future.

One reason for disagreeing with that statement was the argument that no country can be certain of its security in an anarchical international system. These responses were couched in traditional conservative language: Prudence dictates that a country must always be prepared for the unpredictable. One group referred to regional instability as the ground for its belief that a threat to Australia's security was likely. This group was particularly troubled by developments that might take place in Australia's relations with Indonesia; for example, leadership changes in Jakarta or hostilities between Indonesia and Papua New Guinea. Others feared nuclear proliferation and an outbreak of global conflict involving the superpowers. As one senior diplomat put it: "Superpower rivalry is a threat to us all." But despite the official admission by government ministers that the U.S. communications bases were likely nuclear targets, only two leaders mentioned them as constituting a threat to Australia's security.

DEPENDENCE ON GREAT AND POWERFUL PROTECTORS

The correlate of Australia's preoccupation with external threats and the belief that the defense of Australia was beyond Australia's own capacity was a tradition of devoted dependence on powerful protectors. For the first century and a half following the establishment of the British penal colony at Sydney in 1788, Australians looked to Britain for their security. With the imminent fall of Singapore at the end of 1941 they turned to the United States. In 1951 that dependence on America was enshrined in the ANZUS treaty, which to this day has been the foundation of Australia's defense and foreign policy. The chosen stance of being a dependent and dependable ally gave Australia's foreign policy its other two characteristic features: the exceptional degree to which it has been dominated by questions of national security; and the reluctance of Australian governments to articulate policies that reflected Australia's own interests if there was any possibility that these would endanger the relationship with the powerful protector.

Even with the federation of the six Australian colonies in 1901 to form the Commonwealth of Australia, Australian governments had no desire to loosen Australia's dependency on Britain in matters of defense and foreign policy. They were proud of Australia's place within Britain's great empire and believed that both Australia and Britain could only stand to benefit from the imperial relationship. When asked about the possibility of a clash between Australian and imperial interests, Prime Minister Deakin replied: "The interest of the Empire as a whole and the interest of Australia are one" (Murdoch 1923: 225). Along with the other dominions of white British settlers, Australia saw its role in the empire in familial terms: Having recently gained its adulthood, it expected the mother country to inform and consult it about imperial policy and to allow Australia to participate in the empire's councils. But the underlying Australian stance was that of loyalty, manifest in the enthusiasm to rush to Britain's assistance whenever Britain was involved in imperial wars. The expectation was that Britain, in return for these demonstrations of Australia's loyalty, would guarantee to defend Australia when Australia's hour of need arose.

This imperial loyalty was not inconsistent with Australian nationalism, for many Australians defined their national identity in the words Deakin used—as "independent Australian Britons," with the stress on the word "Britons." Australians prided themselves on being "98 percent British" and the "crimson thread of kinship" tied Australia closely to Britain.[1] This pride of race, which according to historian W.K. Hancock (1930: 66) "counted for more than love of country," was reassuring in a threatening world: It expressed a provincial identification with a great power and a claim to cultural and racial superiority. Even the nationhood that the ANZAC legend claims was forged in 1915 on the shores of Gallipoli was attained in fighting a war "for King and Country."

Australia's reliance on Britain in matters of defense and foreign policy, at least in the years up to World War I, reflected a belief that Australia as an integral part of the wider British empire was legally not a fully sovereign nation. Deakin, who was prepared vigorously to question Britain's strategic priorities, assumed that not even in theory did Australia have the power to conduct direct negotiations with foreign powers. Although Australia had signed the Treaty of Versailles in 1919 and joined the League of Nations, it continued to be reluctant to play an independent role in world affairs. Australia did not set up its first fully independent diplomatic missions until 1940, when it opened legations in Washington and Tokyo. During the 1930s, the predilection of Australian non-Labor governments to cleave to Australia's dominion status hindered Australia's playing an independent role in foreign affairs. So too did the strong sense of isolationism in the Labor Party (which was in opposition between 1932 and 1941).

Yet as the 1930s unfolded, Australian governments and their advisers became increasingly concerned lest Australia find itself without a protector in the event of Britain's facing a war on a European as well as a Pacific front. There was also the realization that Australia and Britain might not necessarily share the same strategic interests in the Pacific region. R.G. Menzies captured this nicely in 1939 in his first speech as prime minister: "What Great Britain calls the Far East is to us the near north" (Meaney 1985: 450). Nevertheless, he also stressed that in defense matters Australia must always act "as an integral part of the British Empire." So when Britain declared war on Germany in September 1939, Menzies announced that "as a result, Australia is also at war."

Although Japan's entry into the war was not unexpected, the speed of Japan's advance in December 1941 sent enormous waves of alarm through the Australian government and people. Australia clearly could no longer rely on the British navy: The nightmare scenario of a Japanese invasion became a distinct possibility. In a New Year message to the Australian people, newly installed Labor Prime Minister John Curtin announced that Australia would perforce be looking to the United States for its protection against Japan in the Pacific War. He stressed that he was doing so "without any inhibitions" concerning Australia's "traditional links or kinship with the United Kingdom" (Meaney 1985: 473–74).

This did not represent, however, a turning away from Britain, or a distinct watershed in Australian foreign policy (Edwards 1975). Australia had on previous occasions looked to the United States when Britain was unable to play the role of protector. And ties with Britain remained strong. Curtin's statement was not a signal that once the immediate dangers of the war were past Australia would spurn its old allegiance.

By 1944 Curtin's government was resentful of Washington's failure to involve Australia in Allied consultation and planning, and suspicious that the United States would pursue imperial ambitions in the South Pacific after the war. The government's hope was that British power and influence in the Far East would be reasserted. Public opinion heavily favored this approach: 64 percent of respondents in a 1945 poll asserted that Australia should "join with Britain and other Dominions in a common foreign policy" whereas only 30 percent believed that Australia should "decide for herself how she will deal with foreign countries" (Campbell 1988: Appendix A, Table 3).[2] In the years immediately after the war, Australia engaged in the standardization of military equipment, organization, and doctrine with Britain; joined in military planning with other Commonwealth countries over Malaya; took responsibility for Commonwealth intelligence-gathering in the Pacific; and offered facilities to Britain for testing rockets and nuclear weapons in South Australia (Pemberton 1987: 3).

By April 1946, however, the Chifley government had realized that Britain would be unable to resume the role of protector of Australia in the Pacific. Despite Australian reservations about U.S. intentions in the Pacific, and concerns at Washington's efforts to promote multilateral trade liberalization, Foreign Minister Evatt in 1946 made his first proposal to the United States for a Pacific pact (Bell 1977: 164). Washington, preoccupied with Soviet expansion in Eastern Europe, was not interested. But the Communist victory in China and China's entry into the Korean War turned America's attention to Asia. These developments offered Australia an opportunity to obtain a defense pact with the United States in return for dropping its insistence on a harsh peace settlement with Japan. The signature of the ANZUS treaty in 1951 was the outcome.

Under Sir Robert Menzies, prime minister from 1949 to 1966, Australian governments looked to both the United States and Britain for protection against the perceived threats from the north. "If a war comes," wrote Menzies, "the business of foreign policy is to see that we enter it with great and powerful friends" (Menzies 1970: 94). During most of that period, dependence on the United States through ANZUS for the ultimate guarantee of Australian security rested comfortably with a continued identity with the old British Commonwealth, and with the integration of Australian forces with those of Britain in the defense of Malaya. Only on occasion was Australia forced to choose between Washington and London—the most notable example being at the time of the Suez crisis, when Menzies was outspoken in his support of Britain. The Suez debacle, however, served only to reinforce perceptions of the United Kingdom's decline as an international power of the first rank. The British decision in 1967 to phase out its military forces from East of Suez terminated any lingering hopes that Australia might look to Britain for protection. America became the sole protector.

The alliance with the United States shaped, as had the prewar imperial relationship with Britain, Australia's perception of the world and the role that Australia should play in world politics. The role was that of a loyal ally. Projecting the world in bipolar Cold War terms, Australia's leaders spoke of Australia as a "partner" and "supporter" of the United States in upholding the values of the "free world," in withstanding "aggressive Communist expansion," and in keeping Asia "free for democracy." They also assumed that Australia and the United States had identical strategic interests.

The traditional fear of Asia—now portrayed as Asian Communism—also gave to Australian foreign policy its distinctively defense-oriented stamp. Australia's relations with countries in Southeast Asia were largely defined by Australia's defense relations with the British in Malaysia-Singapore and with the Americans in SEATO. Assuming that Australia's enemies would also be America's enemies, Australian governments made the idea of "forward defense" a key element in its strategic thinking. The objective was to have the United States (and the British) operationally engaged in Southeast Asia so as to act as a distant buffer between Communist expansionism and Australia. It was believed that the more the United States was involved in Asia, the more certain would be the United States militarily to protect Australia. Australia's role was to support its great-power protectors by sending expeditionary forces to fight overseas in Korea, in Malaya (and Malaysia), and in Vietnam.

The policy of "forward defense" thus brought with it the obligation for Australia to participate militarily in overseas theaters, an obligation that affected the role and structure of the Australian defense force. Having the function of acting in concert with and in support of major allies overseas, the Australian Defence Force was not equipped to enable it to act alone or to provide the most effective defense of mainland Australia and its maritime approaches. Australia's actual expenditure also remained low by Western standards; the resources committed in support of the United States in Korea and Vietnam were privately criticized by Washington as inadequate, and perceived as at best a token gesture.

The Liberal and Country Party coalition government exploited the alliance for electoral purposes. The issue was not the alliance itself but the price Australia should pay for the alliance. To demonstrate Australia's dependability, the government agreed to host U.S. defense installations at Pine Gap, Nurrungar, and North West Cape and to go "all the way" with the United States in Vietnam. The government argued that opposition to Vietnam was disloyalty to the alliance. This posed an embarrassingly difficult dilemma to the Labor Party: "How to oppose American intervention without opposing America; how to denounce the war without denouncing the United States" (Whitlam 1985: 36).

As Goot and Tiffen (1983) demonstrate, the Vietnam debacle divided Australians in a way that few other issues have done. A majority of Labor voters opposed Australia's sending combat troops, opposed the dispatch of conscripts to Vietnam, and opposed American bombing of North Vietnam. The Vietnam episode, however, appeared to do little to change the importance that Australians gave to the defense relationship with the United States. Australians overwhelmingly continued, at least until the mid-1980s, to perceive the defense alliance to be of "real value" and "very/fairly important."

AUSTRALIAN PUBLIC OPINION ON DEFENSE, THE ANZUS TREATY AND THE ANZUS PARTNERS

In Australia, professional polling organizations have been regularly surveying the electorate's opinion on domestic and international issues since the 1940s. We know that the political parties now carefully watch the polls and adjust their electoral strategies accordingly. But what impact does public opinion, as reported in the polls, have on foreign and defense policy?

Australian experience suggests that public opinion on foreign policy issues acts more as a constraint or brake on policymakers than as a positive determinant of policy. Public opinion is sometimes ignored: Governments have acted in the face of clear public opposition, as the Menzies government did in 1957 when it signed the trade agreement with Japan. The Whitlam government's decision to recognize Soviet sovereignty over the Baltic States and the Fraser government's decision to accept large numbers of Vietnamese refugees are more recent examples. Whether a government decides to ignore or heed majority opinion depends on a variety of considerations. One of these may be a conviction that an issue is so important that the government has an obligation to lead public opinion. But a government will also be influenced by pragmatic judgments concerning the strength and intensity of the public's opinion; the opportunities that interest groups and the opposition have in using the issue to mobilize opinion against the government; the risk that voters will desert the government on the issue; and the chance that the issue will inflame factional discord within the party.

Because it is rare for foreign policy issues to dominate federal elections and because, since the mid-1970s, the political parties have been in quite wide agreement on foreign and defense policy, it might be argued that governments have considerable leeway to act independently of public opinion. However, the observed decline in party loyalty among electors, the consequent rise of electoral volatility, the frequency of federal elections (on average once every two and one-half years), the relatively high number of marginal seats, and the heightened domestic sensitivity of some international issues, which would otherwise be far from Australia's concerns, as a result of the ethnic character of the electorate all serve to increase the government's concern with adverse shifts in public opinion, especially if the critics are geographically concentrated or associated with disaffected interest groups.

What has been the shape of Australian public opinion toward defense issues, the ANZUS alliance, and the ANZUS partners?

Campbell (1986: 11–12) has surveyed the Australian poll data on these issues. He has shown that, in line with the public's awareness of threats, Australians have consistently given majority support for increased defense spending and compulsory military training. In no poll has there been more than 17 percent in favor of reducing defense expenditure.

Strong majorities have also favored the need for military alliances (Campbell 1986: 13–15). In 1950, nearly nine in ten Australians favored an agreement with the United States that would automatically require each

Table 8.4. Australian Public's Perception of the Adequacy of Australian Defense Forces

Date	Yes	No	Other
1986	20%	68%	12%
1987	25%	58%	17%

Question: "Do you think Australia has adequate defense forces to defend its national interests?"
Source: Campbell (1988), "The Social Basis of Australian and New Zealand Defence Policy," Appendix A, Table 2.

party to join the other in the event of a Pacific War. The data cited by William Watts in the previous chapter indicate that substantial majorities continue to believe Australia should remain in the American alliance. However, these and other recent polls (March 1988) also show that the level of support for ANZUS and the relationship with the United States has eroded, as has Australians' confidence in the U.S. defense commitment. As also noted by Watts, various polls consistently have shown that younger Australians have a less favorable overall opinion of the alliance regardless of their education or party preferences.

Continued conflict with the United States over economic issues is likely to further sour the public's perception of the value of the relationship. But Australians' confidence in their ability to defend themselves, although gradually increasing, appears to be far from a stage where they would feel comfortable in jettisoning the alliance with their most recent and powerful protector (Tables 8.4 and 8.5).

One additional trend in public opinion in the 1980s that reflects a generational cleavage is the appearance of a small proportion of Australians who point to the United States as a threat to Australia. In the late 1960s and 1970s only about 3 percent of those who believed that some countries were a threat to Australia's security (around half of the sample) specified America. By 1980 the proportion was 7 percent and in 1982 and 1983, around 5–6 percent, placing the United States among the five or six most frequently mentioned threats (Table 8.3). The young and college-educated are disproportionately represented in this group. According to Goot and King (1988: 126–27), "Anything from one-sixth to a quarter of those who are young, or tertiary educated, or professional, or Democrat" think that the United States is a threat. It is not at all clear, though, what the respondents have in mind when they specify the United States. It is most unlikely that they actually feared direct U.S. aggression against Australia. It is more likely that they saw the policies of the Reagan administration as ones that could provoke a nuclear conflict that would necessarily involve Australia (because of the strategic importance of the U.S. communication bases).

Australian hostility to the United States has usually been located within the left wing of the Labor Party. In the 1960s this extended not only to U.S. involvement in Vietnam but also to the growing direct investment by U.S. corporations in the Australian economy. Under the Hawke government, the views of the ALP Left on most foreign policy issues have been ignored. With both major parties committed to strengthening the security relationship with the United States, dissidents have expressed their opposition through minor parties. In the 1984 election, when concern with the foreign and defense policies of the Reagan administration was at its peak, two antinuclear parties, the Democrats and the Nuclear Disarmament Party, together polled 14.8 percent of the Senate vote. In the 1987 Senate election, they polled 10 percent. (The fall in the NDP vote from 7.2 percent to 1.5 percent suggests that the antinuclear vote lacks solid, organized support.)

The poll data demonstrate the inclination of most Australians to see the United States in a favorable light; to view the United States as the country of most importance to Australia and with which Australia has most in common; and to believe that the basic interests of Australia and the United States are in agreement. Their image of America is strongly shaped by television. Over one-third of Australians in a 1984 survey listed television entertainment programs and American films on television as among their main sources of information about the United States (USIA 1986). The most important source, however, was television news programs (mentioned by 74 percent) and Australian newspapers and magazines (58 percent).

How do Australians see Australia's relations with New Zealand? And how knowledgeable are Australians about New Zealand? As indicated in the previous chapter, polls conducted in Australia and New Zealand by the Australia New Zealand Foundation (ANZF) in 1984 show a stark asym-

Table 8.5. Australian Public's Perception of the Effectiveness of Australia's Defense

Date	Very Effectively	Fairly Effectively	Not Effectively	Unsure
1980	4%	20%	72%	3%
1987	5%	37%	53%	5%

Question: "How effectively could Australia defend itself?"

Source: Campbell (1988), "The Social Basis of Australian and New Zealand Defence Policy," Appendix A, Table 2.

Table 8.6. Priority of Australia's Bilateral Relations, According to Australian Leaders (ranked by mean)[a]

Political/Strategic Priority	Mean	Economic Priority	Mean
USA	1.12	Japan	1.01
Japan	1.16	USA	1.15
ASEAN	1.32	ASEAN	1.46
Indonesia	1.35	New Zealand	1.66
Papua New Guinea	1.38	EEC	1.85
China	1.62	China	1.95
New Zealand	1.69	OPEC	2.05
USSR	2.09	South Korea	2.21
United Kingdom	2.30	United Kingdom	2.23
South Korea	2.39	Indonesia	2.36
OPEC	2.55	Papua New Guinea	2.38
United Nations	2.57	USSR	2.89
India	2.81	Canada	2.90
Commonwealth	2.81	Arab League	3.01
NATO	2.83	India	3.23
Canada	2.86	Brazil	3.25
Israel	3.13	Commonwealth	3.41
Arab League	3.25	United Nations	3.51
North Korea	3.28	Eastern Europe	3.64
South Korea	3.38	South Africa	3.64
Eastern Europe	3.64	Latin America	3.69
Brazil	3.81	Israel	3.87
Zimbabwe	3.83	North Korea	4.14

a. Mean derived from 5-point scale with 1 representing "very important" and 5 "not important at all."

Source: Meaney, N., T. Matthews, and S. Encel, *The Japanese Connection: A Survey of Australian Leaders' Attitudes Towards Japan and the Australia-Japan Relationship,* Melbourne: Longman Cheshire, 1988. Reprinted by permission.

metry in the external outlooks of Australians and New Zealanders. Australia's perceived importance for New Zealanders far exceeded the significance Australians accorded New Zealand. Many Australians seemed to be barely aware of their Tasman neighbors. It should be stressed, however, that this assessment was not shared by Australia's foreign policy elite, more than half of whom (in 1983) judged New Zealand to be "very important" to Australia both economically and politically (Table 8.6).

The Australian public, in the ANZF poll, displayed a marked ignorance of New Zealand. More than half the New Zealand sample claimed to have a good or fair amount of knowledge about Australia, whereas only 27 percent of Australians made the same claim. That the Australians were not being overly modest in their claims was shown by the small percentage of

Australians who were able to name the capital of New Zealand: 37 percent correctly named Wellington as compared with 76 percent of New Zealanders who correctly identified Canberra as Australia's national capital.

Travel may be a factor at work here. Of those interviewed, there was a much larger percentage of New Zealanders who had visited Australia than Australians who had been to New Zealand. Another reason for Australians' ignorance of their neighbor is the lack of attention given to New Zealand in particular, and the South Pacific in general, in the Australian media. Australians are quick to take offense at the lack of attention that their country receives in the American press, but fail to see the similar shortcomings of the Australian media in its coverage of countries within the South Pacific region. Some changes have occurred in the geographical sources of overseas news in the Australian media, but the United States, Asia, and Western Europe continue to predominate. A study of overseas news stories in a national newspaper and on TV stations from June 4 to July 1, 1979, found only seven stories devoted to New Zealand out of a total of 799 broadcast or printed in this period. No coverage whatsoever was given to the Pacific Islands (Overton and McKenzie 1982).

TOWARD A MORE INDEPENDENT AND SELF-RELIANT STANCE

Significant reorientations of Australian foreign policy have usually been associated with perceptions that a "great and powerful friend" could no longer be relied on to provide for Australia's protection. President Richard Nixon's proclamation of the Guam Doctrine in 1969 is the most recent instance. Nixon stated that the United States would henceforth be expecting its Asian allies to handle their own defense against local and internal enemies. While indicating that the United States would honor its treaty commitments and would come to the assistance of a nation threatened with nuclear weapons by a major power, the doctrine made it clear that the United States was no longer willing simply to fight its allies' wars for them. The initial reaction of the incumbent Liberal-Country Party coalition to the new American strategy was to express shock and to seek clarification from Washington of America's security guarantee to Australia under ANZUS. Subsequent governments acknowledged that Australians could not rely on the United States for an open-ended commitment to their protection, that the traditional policy of "forward defense" was no longer viable, and that Australians would have to make greater provision for their own protection. The changing perception of overseas threats facilitated this reorientation as did the detente between the two superpowers and the normalization of relations between China and the United States.

The Whitlam Labor government, its three years of office coinciding with the period of detente, used the changed international atmosphere to announce a more independent foreign policy stance for Australia. It asserted Australia's right to criticize American policy, strengthened Australia's relations with the Third World, voted at the United Nations in support of anti-Rhodesia resolutions, denounced French nuclear tests in the Pacific, attempted to develop a resources diplomacy, recognized the People's Republic of China, and opened diplomatic relations with a number of other Communist countries, including North Vietnam and North Korea. But when it came to the alliance itself—in the form of the ANZUS treaty and the defense installations—the Whitlam government, for all its rhetoric about foreign policy independence, never seriously questioned it. As far as the prime minister was concerned, his government had a "mandate and a duty" to maintain the alliance. ANZUS, he asserted, was the "legal embodiment of the common interests of the people of Australia, New Zealand and the United States. Those interests remain constant beyond changes of administration in Washington, Wellington and Canberra" (Whitlam 1973: 2–3).

Australia's strategic doctrine evolved in the post-Guam decade from forward defense to something that came closer to what was often referred to, although misleadingly, as continental defense. Credit for the change belongs not to the Whitlam government alone. Prime Minister John Gorton spoke favorably of a "fortress Australia" approach, and analysts within the Department of Defence had for some years been rethinking the assumptions of Australia's defense policy.[3] While it was the Whitlam government that emphasized one aspect of this new thinking—that Australia faced no major threat in the next ten to fifteen years—it was the Fraser government's 1976 Defense White Paper that provided the first comprehensive statement of the new Australian position. Acknowledging that the alliance with the United States "gives substantial grounds for confidence that in the event of a fundamental threat to Australia's security U.S. military support would be forthcoming," the paper also emphasized that Australia could face a range of threat situations that "we should expect to handle more independently" and that "we owe it to ourselves to be able to mount a national defense effort that would maximize the risks and costs of any aggression" (quoted in Babbage 1980: 8). Subsequent assessments by the Parliamentary Joint Committee on Foreign Affairs and Defence (Katter Report 1981;

Shipton Report 1982) have endorsed the position that while Australia can count on assistance from the United States in the event of conflict, the form of assistance will vary according to circumstances. No longer was it assumed that ANZUS gave any iron-clad guarantees to Australia.

Neither the Whitlam nor the Fraser governments, however, developed a strategic doctrine that integrated a strategy of national defense self-reliance with a commitment to the alliance relationship. That integration has been one of the achievements of the Hawke government. This involved two steps. The first was a review in 1983 of Australia's membership of the ANZUS alliance. The review reaffirmed the alliance as fundamental to Australia's national security and to its foreign and defense policies. It argued that ANZUS continued to provide a level of assurance in the event of a major threat to Australia's security and bolstered Australia's deterrent capability by greatly complicating the planning of any country that might be contemplating hostilities against Australia. But it also acknowledged that the treaty did not absolve Australia from the responsibility of providing its own security.

The second step was a thorough review of Australia's defense capabilities (Dibb 1986). That review and the response to it (both public and official) became the basis for the government's Defence White Paper issued in 1987 (Department of Defence 1987).[4] The emphasis of these two reports was on defense self-reliance, which was to be achieved through a substantial modernization and upgrading of defense capabilities. When the Dibb Report was first published, it occasioned some concern in U.S. defense circles that it marked the first step in a retreat into "fortress Australia." A more self-reliant Australia preoccupied with low-level local threats, it was feared, would lose both an interest in the Western alliance and the capability of contributing to it. These fears were assuaged with the publication of the Defence White Paper. In fact, the White Paper emphasized that a strategy of defense self-reliance was not to be equated with a narrow, inward-looking policy. Self-reliance, it argued, was made possible because of Australia's alliance with America and its defense agreements with countries in the Asia-Pacific region. The alliance enhanced self-reliance by giving Australia privileged access to defense technology and to vital political and military intelligence; by providing joint training opportunities for Australia's armed services; and by obliging a potential enemy to contemplate the prospect of an allied response should it choose to attack Australia. The strategy of defense self-reliance was described as "defense in depth," with priority given to meeting any credible level of threat in Australia's area of direct military interest. The strategy would, the paper also claimed, strengthen Australia's ability to meet the mutual obligations Australia shared with its chief allies, the United States and New Zealand.

As Australian governments moved toward a greater self-reliant posture in defense, so too they moved away from a subservient follower role in foreign policy. The Whitlam government asserted this most loudly (and on occasion abrasively) in its efforts to deemphasize the dominating role of the ANZUS alliance in Australian foreign policy and to project "a more independent Australian stance." Prime Minister Malcolm Fraser warned that the interests of the United States and the interests of Australia were not necessarily identical. "In our relations with the United States," he proclaimed, "our first responsibility is to assess our own interests" (cited in Bell 1983: 34). The Hawke government has also claimed the right to exercise independent judgment—but "within the framework of a firm commitment to ANZUS" (Beazley 1985: 608–9)—and when necessary to criticize the U.S. policies.

This emphasis on the need for Australia independently to assess its own interests within the context of its alignment with the West has been one element in the articulation by the Fraser and Hawke governments of a middle power role for Australia. The other two elements have been a recognition of Australia's limited power and influence in global politics and an assertion of the Asia, Pacific, and Indian Ocean areas as Australia's primary focus of attention.

The most sophisticated statement of this role was by A. A. Street, foreign minister in the Fraser government in 1981–83. He argued that Australia's difference lay in its having a colonial history, in its economic dependence on the export of primary commodities, and in its location in the Asia-Pacific region, where its regional relationships were largely with Third World countries. No other Western country except New Zealand was in a comparable position. Street cautioned that it was necessary for a middle power like Australia to strike a careful and sensitive balance between ambition and resources, opportunity and constraint: "A middle power has more opportunities and therefore more temptation to over-reach itself than a small power; and it faces more constraints, and therefore greater danger that it will be unduly cautious and timid, than a great power" (Street 1982: 308). Nevertheless, he suggested that in certain circumstances a middle power could be more effective than a great power, precisely because it does not bring too much power or authority to bear on a situation and does not automatically engage the interest of the other great powers (Street 1982: 311).

The idea of a middle-power role has also been developed by ministers in the Hawke government. Hawke and Hayden have argued that Australia must be careful not to seek an exaggerated international role for itself. There must be a realistic appreciation of the limits of Australia's capabilities and influence. At the same time, Australia should realize that it is "uniquely well qualified" to play a constructive bridging or facilitating role in certain international conflicts—especially in its own region.

Australia's ability to play this role depends heavily on the willingness of other parties to accept its intervention. Foreign Minister Hayden was singularly unsuccessful in attempting to play a "bridge-building" role between the contending parties over Cambodia. And even in the South Pacific, where the Fraser and Hawke governments have felt that Australia's size, resources, and military capability enable it to play the role of a regional leader, the country's capacity to influence events is limited. Nowhere has this been more evident than in Fiji, where Australia was powerless to prevent an unwelcome coup. Similarly, Australia has had negligible impact on French policy toward decolonization of New Caledonia and nuclear testing in the Pacific.

AUSTRALIA AND THE ASIA-PACIFIC REGION

Along with the attempt to fashion a middle-power role for Australia has gone a keen willingness by policymakers in the post-Guam period to commit Australia to the Asia-Pacific region. "Partnership" and "interdependence" became the favored words. This development was the product of a series of economic and political changes in Asia: Japan's attaining the status of an economic superpower; the stand-off between the great powers in East and Southeast Asia in the 1970s; the rapid emergence of the newly industrializing countries of East Asia; China's benign relations with the West and ASEAN; and the development of ASEAN as a strong, cohesive force for stability in Southeast Asia. Once viewed as a threat, Asia was now spoken of as a region with which Australia's future was "inevitably interdependent" (Hayden 1983: 580–81).

Statistics tell part of the story. In the past thirty years, Australia's trade has been redirected from Europe to Asia. In 1954–55, 57 percent of Australia's trade was with Britain and Europe while barely 12 percent was with Japan, the ASEAN states, or the countries of Northeast Asia. In 1984–85, 41 percent of Australia's trade was with the latter countries and only 16 percent was with Britain and Europe. In the mid-1960s, when "White Australia" was still the unofficial immigration policy, Asian

Table 8.7. Helpfulness in Solving International Problems and Problems in the Asia-Pacific Region in Next Ten Years, According to Australian Leaders (percent)

International Problems	%	Regional Problems	%
ASEAN	86.0	Australia	93.0
United States	78.5	ASEAN	91.5
United Nations	76.5	Japan	89.5
Japan	74.5	South Pacific Forum	83.0
Canada	73.5	United States	80.0
Australia	73.0	Canada	74.5
NATO	71.0	Pacific Basin Economic Community	73.0
United Kingdom	69.0	China	71.0
China	67.0	US–Japan Security Treaty	75.5
Pacific Basin Economic Community	65.5	ANZUS Alliance	67.0
US–Japan Security Treaty	65.0	United Nations	65.5
Sweden	60.0	Indonesia	57.0
ANZUS Alliance	58.5	Multinational enterprises	48.5
EEC	50.0	United Kingdom	42.5
Multinational Enterprises } Non-Aligned Movement	43.5	OPEC	19.0
		Brazil	17.5
USSR	35.0	USSR	12.5
OPEC	33.0		
Arab League } Indonesia	31.0		
Organization of African Unity	28.5		
Brazil	27.0		
Israel	18.5		
PLO	8.5		
South Africa	6.0		

Questions: "How helpful or unhelpful do you think each of the following countries, groupings of countries, and organizations is likely to be in solving international problems in the next ten years?"

"How helpful or unhelpful do you think each of the following countries, groupings, and organizations is likely to be in solving the problems of the Asian and Pacific region in the next ten years?"

Source: Meaney, N., T. Matthews, and S. Encel, *The Japanese Connection: A Survey of Australian Leaders' Attitudes Towards Japan and the Australia-Japan Relationship,* Melbourne: Longman Cheshire, 1988. Reprinted by permission.

migrants accounted for just 3 percent of the total intake. In 1984–85 that share had risen to one-third.

The survey of the opinions of the foreign policy elite in 1983 indicates that Australia's leaders were convinced that Australia's future lay with the Asia-Pacific region (Meaney, Matthews, and Encel 1988: 50–60). The leaders interviewed for that survey saw the countries (and groupings of countries) of the region as having high economic and strategic priority for Australia and, with the partial exception of Indonesia, as helpful rather than unhelpful in solving regional problems and as having friendly relations with Australia. Moreover, fully 85 percent of the 200 respondents thought that Australia needed "to attempt to reconcile its European heritage with its Asia-Pacific location."

When asked to assess the importance that Australia should ascribe to various countries, the leaders gave priority to countries in the Asia-Pacific region. They rated Japan, ASEAN, and China along with the United States and New Zealand as most important to Australia from both a political-strategic and an economic perspective (Table 8.6). Their responses displayed a high level of bipartisan agreement (Matthews and Ravenhill 1988). The fact that Britain's political and economic ranking was almost identical to South Korea's is a telling index of the priority Australia's leaders now accord relations with countries in the Asia-Pacific region.

The Australian elite were also of the opinion that countries in the region, with the notable exceptions of the Soviet Union and Indonesia, would play a positive role in world and regional affairs (Table 8.7). ASEAN was looked on more favorably than any other country (or group of countries) in its helpfulness in solving international problems generally (86 percent rated ASEAN as helpful) and second only to Australia in solving regional problems (91 percent). The exceptionally favorable assessment of ASEAN—in contrast to the uncertain and reserved response to Indonesia—no doubt indicates an appreciation of ASEAN's effective role in containing political divisions and maintaining regional stability. More than eight in ten leaders also rated Japan, the South Pacific Forum, and the United States as helpful in solving regional problems.

When asked to estimate the degree of friendship between Australia and six other countries, the leaders placed Australia's relations with Japan as just a fraction below what they perceived as Australia's exceptionally friendly relations with the United States and Britain (Table 8.8). A majority thought Australia's relations with China to be more friendly than unfriendly. The assessment of Australia-Indonesia relations was ambiguous (only one-third judged them to be "friendly") while Australia-USSR relations

Table 8.8. International Friendship/Hostility Among Countries in Asia-Pacific Region (expressed by mean)[a]

Countries	Mean
Australia-USA	**1.29**
Australia-UK	**1.37**
Australia-Japan	**1.88**
Japan-USA	2.01
Japan-Canada	2.18
Australia-China	**2.32**
Australia-Indonesia	**2.68**
Japan-China	2.71
USA-China	2.92
Japan-Indonesia	3.10
Japan-USSR	3.81
Australia-USSR	**3.89**
China-USSR	4.24
USA-USSR	4.52

a. Mean derived from 5-point scale where 1 represents "friendship" and 5 "hostility." The Australian relationships are in boldface type.

Source: Meaney, N., T. Matthews, and S. Encel, *The Japanese Connection: A Survey of Australian Leaders' Attitudes Towards Japan and the Australia-Japan Relationship,* Melbourne: Longman Cheshire, 1988. Reprinted by permission.

were almost universally judged to be hostile (a reflection no doubt of the Fraser government's anti-Soviet stance).

LOCATION AND IDENTITY

A large majority of the leaders in the 1983 survey were keenly aware of what Grant (1983) had called "the Australian dilemma." More than eight in ten of them agreed that Australia needed to reconcile its European heritage with its Asia-Pacific location, but they were divided on how this should be done. The most approved course of action was to improve trade and aid links. Around half rather grudgingly accepted the desirability of promoting the study of Asian languages and cultures and of "identifying more closely with countries in the region that possess democratic forms of government." The leaders solidly rejected the notion that Australia should join ASEAN. They believed that such an approach would be unwelcome and counterproductive; the ASEAN countries did not want Australia as a member. They also solidly opposed the proposal that Australia should encourage more Asian migration. This was not because of any desire to return to the "White Australia" policy; most seemed content to accept the existing level of the Asian migration intake. But many were worried that the Australian public would not accept a policy that promoted more migration from Asia either in absolute or relative terms. Others rejected the proposal on the grounds that any decision to take more Asian migrants was inconsistent with having a racially non-discriminatory policy. Whatever the reasons, the unwillingness of all but 17 percent of the respondents to approve the step showed the political sensitivity of the immigration question, as did the divisive debates in 1984 and 1988 on Asian migration.

These debates indicated that many Australians had misgivings about the rising level of Asian migration. A Morgan Gallup Poll in 1988 found that 57 percent of people interviewed said that there were too many Asians being granted permanent residential status, the same result as in a 1984 survey. It also found that this response was not simply an artifact of a wider set of misgivings at a time of high unemployment about immigration in general; the level of opposition to Asian immigration remained static between 1984 and 1988, while the level of opposition to all immigration fell.

The debates on immigration and the voices raised against Japanese investment in tourist resorts and Asian investment in residential real estate also showed that segments of the Australian public were not yet prepared to accept some of the implications of Australia's interdependence with the Asia-Pacific region. So, too, did the campaign in 1988 against the official policy of multiculturalism. While this critique took a variety of forms, one strand portrayed multiculturalism as an attempt to "Asianize" Australia. To the critics, the adoption of the multicultural slogan "Living Together" as the official theme for the 1988 Bicentenary rather than "The Australian Achievement" (which the Fraser government had favored) was but another instance of what they saw as an insidious belittling of the Anglo-Celtic Australia they once knew. Australia, they claimed, was on the verge of losing its identity. Sensing mileage in the issue, the leader of the Liberal Party announced an end to the bipartisan backing of multiculturalism by hoisting the banner of "One Australia."

But what was that "One Australia?" In the early months of 1988 Australian radio and television were alive with the Bicentennial theme song "Celebration of a Nation." Many Australians, remembering their country's brutal treatment of the aborigines, were unsure what white Australians should be celebrating.[5] Others were simply confused about what constituted the identity of the nation they were celebrating. "Talk to 36 people about the notion of national identity and what it means to be

Australian," wrote *Time* magazine in its first Australian edition, "and you get 36 opinions" ("Our Elusive Soul" 1986: 49). The challenges facing Australia are old ones: to attain an accommodation with the Asia-Pacific region in which Australia is physically located, and to accept that Australia's identity and role should be as a nation of the region.

ACKNOWLEDGMENTS

We wish to thank Lyn Fisher and Liz Kirby for research assistance and Valerie Jones for typing the chapter.

NOTES

1. Hancock (1930: 53) pointed out that Australians had misrepresented the official figures, which referred not to the proportion of the population who were of British blood but to the proportion who were British subjects. He suggested that 10 percent of the population were of non-British ethnic origin, a figure that accords with the recent estimates by Price (1987).
2. Indicative of the sentiment of the times, an alliance with the United States was not offered as one of the alternatives by the pollsters.
3. As far back as 1959 the forward defense orthodoxy was challenged by an official assessment of the strategic basis of Australia's defense policy prepared for the Menzies government. It declared that the prime task of the Australian Defence Force was to "ensure the security of Australian territory and its sea and air approaches." The Menzies government rejected the assessment (Beazley 1985: 607–8).
4. The implications of the new defense posture for the ANZUS alliance are discussed by Mack (1989).
5. The celebrations in 1988 commemorated the two-hundreth anniversary of the first European settlement in Australia. The six colonies did not come together as the Commonwealth of Australia until 1901.

9

New Zealand and the ANZUS Alliance: Changing National Self-Perceptions, 1945–88

JOCK PHILLIPS

Writing contemporary history is always a treacherous undertaking. Memory must take the place of secondary literature; personal feelings about events overpower the historian's mythical objectivity ("mythical" because I believe it is always impossible). It is therefore important for me to state four matters of opinion and perspective that, for some readers, may well invalidate much I have to say henceforth in this chapter. First, I must admit that I am an unabashed enthusiast for New Zealand's nuclear-free policy and I do not write this chapter in the tacit hope that in understanding New Zealand we might be able to restore the country's participation in the ANZUS alliance. Rather, in explaining the changed national self-perceptions that impelled the antinuclear stand, I may be inclined to exaggerate the extent and historic nature of those changes so that they will be accepted as irreversible. Perhaps another scholar, hoping to show that the 1984 crisis was an aberration, might emphasize continuity and tradition. I believe that attitudinal change in New Zealand over the past generation has been considerable and I seek to provide evidence of this.

Second, I do not pretend to have any great expertise in the history of foreign relations. That history always seems to me to be about trade and capital flows and the detailed negotiations of very clever diplomats. It is high-level stuff, whereas my preferred area of history is social and cultural change. I have spent my academic career both as a student and a teacher strenuously avoiding the study of foreign policy. Yet when it comes to explaining the so-called ANZUS crisis, scholars of foreign relations seem to agree that they must turn for explanations to the wider context. For this is the second time in two years that I have been asked as a cultural historian to throw some light on the situation. I am flattered to do so, but warn readers that my perspective is not that of the foreign policy expert.

Third, although I have been asked to examine the whole pattern of changing attitudes and self-images since 1951, I propose to focus directly on the 1984 decision by New Zealand to refuse entry to nuclear ships and ask what changes in self-perceptions have had a fundamental influence on that decision. The New Zealand mentality has been transformed in a multitude of ways in the last forty years; many of those changes, especially ideas about the family, about social welfare, about economic relationships, will barely be touched in this chapter.

Finally, I confess to a certain unease at attempting to discuss attitudes and images in isolation from social dynamics. This is partly because I believe that ideas usually have their source in social developments and partly because I don't believe you can easily talk about national self-images in a blanket manner. Not everybody in a country shares the same sense of that nation's identity. Different groups put forward different visions, and the vision that is claimed to speak for the nation as a whole usually reflects the dominance of the group articulating that particular vision. As we shall see, the emergence of new policies by the government of New Zealand is partly the consequence of a new social group obtaining political and media control.

THE GROWTH OF A NEW ZEALAND NATIONAL CULTURE

What changes in attitude, then, can explain the fact that in 1951 New Zealand signed the ANZUS pact with Australia and the United States, while in 1984 New Zealand refused entry to American nuclear ships?[1] One possible hypothesis, that New Zealand has become a socialist society ideologically opposed to the "capitalist" or "free" world, can be immediately dismissed. Although elected under a Labour Party label, the Lange government of 1984 has shown itself in domestic and economic policies to be the most enthusiastic believers in free-market capitalism for over fifty years. Although their policies have been described as "market socialism," they are far more market than socialism, and are barely indistinguishable from the goals of Margaret Thatcher. The Labour government has not even followed a policy of economic nationalism or autarchy, but has thrown open doors to foreign investment. Economic and foreign policy seem to be heading in opposite directions.

Another possible explanation for the nuclear ships ban is that it reflects a growing sentiment of anti-Americanism in New Zealand. This is not an easy issue to prove one way or the other, but hints at an answer emerged out of the work I prepared for my previous foray into this field. For the 22nd Foreign Policy School in Dunedin in May 1987, I was asked to examine the impact of American culture on New Zealand since World War II. In exploring that issue, I attempted to quantify the levels of American culture in New Zealand. This may help us in our present question. If, for example, the exposure of American culture in New Zealand declined drastically since the war, this may indicate a general hostility to things American and it would certainly imply that the New Zealand public were less exposed to the propaganda effect of Hollywood culture.

I don't want to rehearse the details of a highly statistical and rather technical paper here, but the evidence did not support this hypothesis. The remarkable finding was how constant had been the exposure of New Zealanders to American popular culture. Although there has evidently been a slight decline in American influences in records and on the radio, the proportion of programs from the United States on prime-time evening television has increased from about 30 percent in 1967 to 40 percent in 1987, and the commercial showing of American films has not declined since the 1940s and 1950s. In May 1987 over 80 percent of the films showing in Wellington were of American origin, as has been the case every decade back to 1957 (Phillips 1987a: 31–34).

One had the paradox that the New Zealand people were in fact watching as many American films and enjoying more American television programs at the very time they were saying "no" to American nuclear ships. However, the increase in American influences was not sufficiently dramatic to support the alternative theory—that in rejecting its ships New Zealanders were reacting against a surfeit of American culture. It is true that one does hear occasionally complaints about the "Americanization" of New Zealand life, but that has been a fairly constant refrain since World War II. It reflects more an unease about the pace of social change than any particular hostility to the United States. Further, there was no evidence that New Zealanders were unwilling partakers of American culture. In 1985 American programs were actually better represented in the top twenty most popular shows than their total representation on television.[2] To suggest that New Zealanders refused entry to American ships because they felt queasy about America, whose culture they were lapping up, is to stretch credibility too far. We are not that masochistic.

My figures suggested that there was no obvious relationship between the nuclear ships policy and the general public's attitude to American culture, and even, perhaps, to America itself.

Perhaps, however, we have in this case gone against one of my first principles by treating the New Zealand public as a monolithic whole. Could it be that while most New Zealanders continue to accept American popular culture, there may have been a growing resistance to American influences by the literate educated elite who, one could argue, are the real determiners of foreign policy? Here again the thesis falls on fallow ground. Looking at the elite literary journal *Landfall*, I discovered that interest in things American became somewhat greater after the 1960s than previously, while among university staff in arts subjects only two people out of ninety-nine (about 2 percent) had American degrees in 1947, but this rose to 10.4 percent in 1967 and over 17 percent today. Statistical evidence of the import of printed material (books and papers) showed that although the proportion of material of American origin fell briefly from 17.04 percent in 1947 to 9.01 percent in 1957, the figure then rose to 28.29 percent in 1967 and has hovered around 20 percent ever since. In 1985–86, 34 percent of imported school texts were American (Phillips 1987a: 38–42). Arguably, American influences among the literate high culture have become stronger, not weaker, since World War II. Again we have another paradox that the cabinet that kicked out American ships contained two men, Michael Bassett and Geoffrey Palmer, who had graduate degrees from the United States.

Both the statistical and impressionistic evidence suggested that it was during the 1960s that some New Zealand intellectuals turned for inspiration to the United States, but significantly, the American groups and individuals attracting interest were the alienated and the critical. While New Zealand poets were reading the Beats, social critics were reading Betty Friedan on the pain of being female, or Malcolm X on the pain of being black, or Noam Chomsky on the atrocities in Southeast Asia. Opposition within the United States to racism at home and imperialism abroad attracted adherents within this country; if there is any connection between American culture and New Zealand's response to American foreign policy, this is perhaps where a connection may be found. But at best the connection is a weak one. It would be going too far to blame the American counterculture of the 1960s for New Zealand's present foreign policy. There are many leading antinuclear activists who owe nothing to American influences, and the real question is why American self-criticism began to appeal to New Zealanders. I believe that it began to appeal because New Zealand intellectual life in the 1960s was struggling to get out from under British gentility, and that New Zealanders turned to American influences as a refreshing inspiration.

This is not a diversion but central to my argument. As I compiled my profile of American culture in New Zealand, two things became obvious that were far more striking than any dramatic change in the level of American culture. The first was the extraordinary decline in the impact of British culture in New Zealand since World War II. The second was the dramatic rise of a self-derived New Zealand culture over that period. Now it may not seem at all obvious why these two changes should have anything to do with New Zealand's relations with the United States, but I believe they do so. I therefore wish to rehearse briefly the evidence on these two points.

The British decline was evident on the radio, where BBC programs seem now to survive, almost by stealth, on the all-night session; on television, where the proportion of British productions has dropped from about 35 percent twenty years ago to under 25 percent today; at the cinema, as evidenced by the reduction in films shown in Wellington and reviewed in the *New Zealand Listener* from about 25 percent in 1947 to about 10 percent in 1987; and finally in books. In 1957 about half the books reviewed in the *New Zealand Listener* were from Britain. Today the figure is under 10 percent. Meanwhile, the New Zealand figure for books reviewed has risen from about 7 percent in 1957 to over 65 percent in 1987 (Phillips 1987a: 34, 35, 43). Where once this country's publishing center was London and New Zealand authors wrote consciously for a British audience, there are now a score of publishers producing New Zealand books for a local audience. Bookshops in the 1950s usually had one small table carrying New Zealand books, and often these consisted of glossy picture books designed as souvenirs for tourists or as Christmas gifts for sending to the relatives back "home." The Book Publishers' Association claims today that about 50 percent of the books sold in New Zealand bookshops are domestically published. Each year there are over twenty novels and about half a dozen major works of historical interpretation. In other fields too the local voice has begun to be heard. Let me cite only the emergence of a New Zealand film industry and playwriting for professional theater; the creative vitality displayed in our art galleries and slowly, too, our museums; the introduction of New Zealand history and literature into our universities; and the growth of a large corpus of New Zealand social science and economic research (Oliver 1981: 430–61).

Neither is it only high-level culture that reflects this change. As New Zealanders start to dream their own dreams and wrestle with their own problems, so their magazines and newspapers come home to focus on domestic matters. The *New Zealand Listener*, which has been since World War II the nearest thing to a national journal, provides evidence of this. When I examined the editorial content and cover illustration for the first six months of every year ending in "7" from 1947 to 1987, I discovered that the American content rose significantly to a climax in the 1960s and then fell away again, but that there was a steady decline in the choice of British subjects until in 1987 only 6.2 percent of the editorials concerned that country. Conversely, domestic editorial topics rose from a low of 15.4 percent in 1957 to over 93 percent in 1987 (Phillips 1987a: 44). Lest this pattern be thought to reflect the particular biases of individual editors, I examined the editorials in the Wellington newspaper, the *Evening Post*, for May of the same years and uncovered a very similar story: a slight, but unspectacular, rise in the interest in American topics since the 1950s; a heavy concentration on New Zealand subjects emerging first in the 1960s; and a clear decline, again most dramatically in the 1960s, in British topics discussed in the paper's editorials.[3] Neither were the editorial writers being untrue to the rest of their newspaper. Taking every story (except sports stories) for the second Thursday in May each decade, we find that whereas in 1947 about half of the stories concerned New Zealand, for the last twenty years about seven stories in every ten have concentrated on a New Zealand subject. During the same years the figures point to a steady decline in printed stories with a British byline until in 1987 the figure was little more than 5 percent of the total. Significantly, the number of stories from Australia and the United States did not change dramatically over the whole period.

Statistical tables are very blunt instruments indeed with which to analyze the orientation of the New Zealand consciousness over the past forty years. Yet they do tell a consistent story. Over that period the culture and news events of both the United States and Australia, the ANZUS partners, have occupied a largely unchanging place in the New Zealand mind. Among certain literary groups there appears to have been some rise in interest in things American in the 1960s and perhaps a slight increase in interest in things Australian more recently. But the changes are undramatic. The dramatic story is to be found by the clearcut loss of involvement in things British, whether news, television, films or books, and the equally remarkable rise in a self-confident national culture. What we see revealed is the emergence of New Zealand as a home in thought.

A NEW SOCIAL CLASS

What lay behind these changes? As British power became self-evidently weaker in the years after World War II, it was natural that New Zealanders would come to think of that country as a less automatic source of authority. But, interestingly, the British decline did not lead to a new overseas focus. The United States did not step in as a replacement to become a new emotional and intellectual center. Britain's retreat from our mental maps was filled by an interest in our own history and traditions. The reason for this was not a simple demographic one, a result of a growing proportion of New Zealand-born people; for in fact the relative numbers of native-born, as of British-born, has remained almost constant over the years since World War II: In both censuses of 1945 and 1986 the proportion of native-born was 84.5 percent (Department of Statistics 1946: 10; Department of Statistics 1987a: 13).

The explanation is that the country developed a population capable of generating its own norms. At the end of World War II New Zealand was a remarkably undeveloped economy and society. With an assured British market for well-established agricultural staples, our population did not need to be well educated and our towns were small service centers. Over the next forty years all this was transformed. Growth in the labor force came in the manufacturing and, even more, the service sectors. This growth increasingly depended on a highly educated work force (Franklin 1978; Hawke 1981: 369; Hawke 1985: 250–77). Expertise, specialization, and education became the entry requirements to this world. The best expression of this change was the growing importance of tertiary education. Up to World War II the total number of graduates of the University of New Zealand since university education began in Otago in 1869 was about 10,000 (University of New Zealand 1959). And of the small number who graduated each year, many of the most able left for richer intellectual sustenance overseas, particularly in Britain. In 1986, by contrast, over 8,000 degrees were awarded in one year, and the total number of people in society who have received some university education has risen from about 5,000 in 1945 to over 170,000 in the census of 1981 (Department of Statistics 1987b: 278). The figure must be over 200,000 today.

These people comprise a group achieving increasing social and economic status in the society. Some find wealth and power in the business and financial world; others fill influential positions in the service sector, working in the media, as expert consultants, as teachers, or as government servants. They are by no means a united group in terms of their opinions.

The capitalist elite, represented perhaps by Bob Jones and the New Zealand Party of 1984, espouse a free-enterprise philosophy. Those in the intellectual professions are more interested, as we shall see, in social issues. But both inhabit the city, share in its growing economic dominance of New Zealand and have access to those opinion-making institutions—from newspapers to theaters to activist political groups—that a city permits. So the new educationally based elite are able to win power for themselves. To take one very crude example, the Labour cabinet of Peter Fraser in 1949 contained only four members out of twenty-four with a university degree. The Labour cabinet of 1988 contained only four out of twenty without a degree.[4]

FROM TERRITORIAL OF EMPIRE TO NEW ZEALAND NATIONALISM

My argument, then, is that since World War II New Zealand has seen the emergence of a new social class, and this class has the self-confidence and intellectual training to start producing visions and goals for itself. This development is crucial to an understanding of the country's changed response to ANZUS. If we go back to the early 1950s when ANZUS was set up, New Zealanders still read British books and listened to the BBC news, and so understandably they continued to have a self-identity that was defined by their place in Britain's world. New Zealand's national self-image was essentially that of the loyal territorial of empire. This definition first emerged at the turn of the century during the Boer War, when the high numbers of men rejected from the British armed forces inspired fears that Britain's urban life style was leading to a physical, not to mention moral, degeneracy of the race. In this hour of imperial need the colonies could play a crucial role. They, and New Zealand in particular, had men toughened by frontier experiences who could fight honorably in the battles of empire, and could keep the British race competitive in the coming struggle for survival. In 1905 this self-image was confirmed by the triumphant tour of the New Zealand rugby team, the All Blacks, and New Zealanders basked in the showers of praise bestowed on their manhood by members of the English ruling class. Two world wars in which New Zealand lost respectively about 18,000 and then 11,000 men served to confirm these images of New Zealand as the "empire's finest son." The point is, however, that this self-image, which determined New Zealand's posture toward the world, was derived initially from British ruling-class sources and suited the needs of that ruling class (Phillips 1987b: 152–58).

Probably the best example of this attitude came during World War II at the conclusion of the North African campaign. New Zealand had entered the war in the spirit of Prime Minister Savage's famous phrase, "Where Britain goes we go . . . " and in 1943 we lived up to the promise. The Pacific was at that point under threat of complete Japanese domination, yet when Churchill asked the New Zealand government to send its men to Italy rather than bring them back home to defend their own part of the world, the New Zealanders, unlike the Australians, agreed. Churchill himself remained a hero in New Zealand, because he was a hero in Britain, despite the fact that in two world wars he had been responsible for sending New Zealand men to their deaths in ill-conceived southern fronts, first at Gallipoli and then in Greece and Crete. Again the contrast with Australia is striking.

In the early 1950s, then, we still thought of ourselves as the loyal territorial of empire. On the eve of the young Queen's coronation in 1953, we proved the strong and chivalrous quality of our Anglo-Saxon manhood when Ed Hillary climbed Mt. Everest. Several months later New Zealanders turned out in their thousands to welcome the Queen herself. This was the environment in which New Zealanders signed the ANZUS treaty. Though the recent report of the Defence Committee of Enquiry tries to interpret the treaty as "the most 'independent' act ever taken by New Zealand," this was only so in the sense that the treaty was signed with the United States rather than with Britain (Defence Committee 1986: 9–10). In every other respect it was an action within the traditional self-definition. The role was still that of a loyal servant of a larger empire. Although world Communism rather than Germany was perceived as the expected enemy, New Zealand continued to see itself as part of an alliance in which Britain played a central role. The treaty worked on the assumption that in the event of a world conflict, the United States would guarantee New Zealand's defense—"bolt New Zealand's backdoor" was the phrase—and so allow our men, as they had always done, to rush to Britain's aid. New Zealand was expected to fight once more, as in two previous world wars, in the Middle East. It would be the bars of Cairo once again.

I don't want to rehearse in detail the steps by which this vision of the world began to unravel. The Suez crisis of 1956 obviously ruled out those Cairo bars for a time and seriously dented images of Britain's power. Even more serious were the final withdrawal of British troops from East of Suez in 1974 and its entry into the EEC the previous year. Rather, I would like to focus on those moments when some New Zealanders—a small minority at first—began to generate for themselves a rather different self-image about their place in the world.

The Vietnam War was one such moment. For the first time New Zealand found itself called on to serve the territorial role in a conflict that did not involve Britain. The uncertainty this created even among the supporters of New Zealand's involvement can be seen in the pathetically few men who were sent to fight in the jungles of Southeast Asia. The commitment did not suggest that the country really believed its own welfare to be at stake. However, there came out of opposition to that war ideas that would help to create a new vision of New Zealand's identity. There was the attack on the "domino" theory and the slow realization that in fact New Zealand was an awful long way from creeping Communism; there was the sense of shame that New Zealand was but a pimple, indeed a purely symbolic pimple, on the tail of a very large eagle, and out of this feeling emerged an anti-bases movement that has worked steadily over the past fifteen years to disentangle New Zealand from the United States communications network.

In the early 1970s a conservation movement appeared which focused particularly on the campaign to save Lake Manapouri and eventually spawned a briefly successful political party, the Values Party. Although not directly concerned with foreign relations, these "greenies" did seek to redefine national goals and images. The movements proclaimed a highly nationalistic defense of the New Zealand ecology and attacked the view that New Zealand's bush should be replaced by exotic pines, or its lakes drowned to process overseas aluminum. Suddenly plant shops began to sprout large native sections. Contrasting images of virgin forest and multinational pollution appeared.

The Labour government raised two issues of importance in 1973. First, the nuclear and French presence in the Pacific received attention as Norman Kirk sent a frigate off to Mururoa Atoll. The feelings of national pride that this act tapped suggested that for some people a moral anti-nuclear stand promised an excitingly different identity.

The second issue was to be more divisive. Norman Kirk cancelled the 1973 rugby tour by the South African Springboks. This was not a new matter. Since 1949 there had been protests about aspects of sporting contact with South Africa, but in the ten years after 1973 the debate reached an intensity that was unusual. Much of that debate was really about New Zealand's self-image. At the heart of opposition to South African tours was a feeling that New Zealand should no longer identify itself with white dominance of the world. The racist underpinning of the old view—the sense of New Zealand as a "white" dominion and upholder of Anglo-Saxon values—came under attack; instead, opponents of South Africa sought to identify with black and indigenous people. Inevitably, as the movement reached a climax in the protests against the 1981 Tour, serious questions began to be asked about the place of the Maori people and Maori values in Aotearoa. The Maori themselves had already begun to pose the question with a series of powerful protests, beginning with the Land March of 1975 and reaching a more confrontational level with the Bastion Point occupation by the Ngati Whatua in 1978. After 1981 no Pakeha of liberal persuasion could afford to avoid the issue of whether New Zealand was really a "white man's country."

The other element of the campaign against the Springbok rugby tours was a resentment about the centrality of rugby itself to the New Zealand value system and to New Zealand nationalism. This feeling came through explicitly in a survey of 1981 anti-tour marchers that I and some students conducted; it was particularly forcefully expressed by women (King and Phillips 1982: 12). Increasing numbers of people began to believe that New Zealand should no longer be the male-dominated rugby-playing territorial of empire. For the first time in our history rugby was becoming a source of international embarrassment, not pride. In 1976 the African countries boycotted the Olympic Games because of New Zealand's rugby tour of South Africa; then in 1981 rugby brought violence and bitter social division to a land that thought of itself as a peaceful island of harmony. Inevitably, rugby began to lose its unquestioned place at the core of our national identity (Chapple 1984).

I have already mentioned the involvement of women in the anti-tour movement. No one surveying changing self-images in the last twenty years can possibly ignore the profound impact of the reawakened feminist movement in New Zealand. As a new generation of women started to demand rights in the areas of reproduction, education, the economy, and politics, their effectiveness was marked not only by a greater prominence of women in public life (where there was one woman MP in 1951, there are now thirteen), but even more by a questioning of a national identity that had been so heavily focused on male achievement. In particular, women were drawn into the peace movement in the belief that war was an expression of male culture and because a pride in its military tradition had been central to the identification of New Zealand as a "man's country" (Dann 1985).

If these movements served to question old identities and forge new definitions, one still has to ask why they should have had a more profound impact in New Zealand than elsewhere. For were there not antiwar, indeed antinuclear movements in other Western countries? As the build-up of nuclear forces around the world began to reach ludicrous and dangerous levels in the 1970s and 1980s, large numbers of people in Holland, Denmark, Germany, Britain, and even in the United States have called out for a halt. The New Zealand situation is only a difference of degree. And were there not in other places too conservation, antiracist, and antisexist movements? We must also concede that even in New Zealand these movements did not attract everyone in the society. Far from it, for they were all highly divisive issues. In 1981, it can be argued, Robert Muldoon partly won the election by campaigning against the Springbok tour protesters.

Yet there were two important factors in New Zealand's case. First, these movements were able to exploit a postcolonial yearning for a new nationalism. As Britain's retreat threw old certainties into doubt, these protests offered not merely piecemeal reforms; they were presented as offering new visions of what it meant to be a New Zealander.

Second, though the participants in these movements in New Zealand were a minority, they were a significant minority whom we have met before. Let us examine their sociological profile. Those who took part tended to be born in the 1940s or 1950s, having been brought up in the postwar years of relative affluence, welfare state security, and international peace. The centers of protest were the large cities. In the 1981 conflict over the Springbok tour, for example, there was a striking difference between the attitudes of the provincial towns and rural areas and those of the city (McKinnon 1982: 32). And within the city it tended to be the educationally based middle class, those who had been to university and were achieving growing social status, who gave support to these movements. They were the new opinion-makers. The leaders of the anti-Vietnam protests were university students; the areas that voted for the conservation-minded Values Party in 1972 were the affluent suburbs; and those who marched against the tour, so our survey showed, were often professional people. Over 50 percent in our survey had a university degree (King and Phillips 1982: 9). The recent poll of the Royal Commission into ANZUS also showed that those with a tertiary education were most likely to be hostile to ANZUS (Defence Committee of Enquiry 1986: 40). Of course, not all graduates were protesters. There tended to be a division between those in the financial or business world, whose ideology came from Ayn Rand and whose sympathies went with the Business Roundtable, and those in the "caring" professions of teaching, journalism, and social work, who, so our survey showed, were well represented in anti-tour marches. The one great exception to these sociological generalizations was the active participation of Maori people in these protests, but I want to come to their role a little later.

At this point it is important to realize that the young, urban, well-educated people who were sympathetic to these various social movements were the very people achieving growing power and influence in the society, and becoming a new generation of locally produced opinion-makers. From their ranks were recruited those who moved into the Labour Party in the late 1960s and early 1970s (James 1985). For some, like Helen Clark and Phil Goff, it was the Vietnam War that turned them to politics; for others, such as Margaret Shields, it was the women's movement; for David Lange it was Norman Kirk and the frigate to Mururoa. Over half of the 1987 Labour MPs had previously been teachers, lecturers, researchers, scientists, or broadcasters—people who were concerned with transmitting ideas. There were only nine with a trade union or blue-collar background. These people came to political power in 1984 with the youngest and best-educated cabinet in New Zealand's history; they replaced an administration that in its early years had contained seven people who fought in World War II. Muldoon indeed had been the quintessential representative of older values. A war veteran himself, he upheld the rights of rugby players over South African blacks, offered a frigate to Britain during the Falklands War, and once sold himself during an election as "a little bit the Churchill way."

DEFINING THE VISION: AOTEAROA AND UTOPIAN MORALISM

Having established that over the last twenty years New Zealand has developed both the social basis and the media possibilities to produce an identity for itself rather than having one imposed from outside, and having argued that in a series of movements the old definitions came under attack and new visions began to form, it is now important to explore what that new vision consists of, why it appeals, and why it has awakened a degree of response outside the rather small but powerful circles in which it originated. As we shall see, part of the new vision's appeal is that it is not entirely new, but in fact gives new meanings and a new context to older New Zealand traditions.

The first important element in the new identity is the image of New Zealand as a Maori country, as Aotearoa. There are precedents in this vision. In the 1890s there was a literary and cultural movement to present New Zealand as "Maoriland"; and in token gestures such as Maori motifs on stamps and coins or hakas before football matches, elements of this vision became institutionalized. But, as I have argued elsewhere, the 1890s movement was promulgated by the Pakeha for strictly Pakeha purposes. Resting on the comforting assurance that the Maori were a dying people whose land was now in "productive" white hands, "Maoriland culture" provided a settler people with an instant mythology and a romantic history. Maori culture was assimilated to a eurocentric vision. The Maori myths, safely bowdlerized, were seen as the equivalent of Norse or Greek legends; the Maoris' seafaring skills turned them into "the Vikings of the Pacific"; while their abilities to fight battles and compose poetry gave them qualities recognizably Anglo-Saxon. In other words, the Maori was presented as an "honorary white." Selective elements of the culture of "our Maoris" were seized upon to give white New Zealand a mythology and history just like Britain's. Maoriland culture served to make New Zealand more, not less like the motherland (Phillips 1983: 520–35).

The movement of the 1970s and 1980s has been very different. For a start it has been the Maori people themselves who have forced the pace. The political mobilization of the tribes in events such as the Land March, the protest at Bastion Point, and the series of confrontations at Waitangi have made the loss of Maori land, language, and identity central issues of New Zealand life. In cultural matters too it has been Maori art, preeminently with the Te Maori exhibition, and Maori writers like Patricia Grace, Witi Ihimaera, and Keri Hulme who have awakened the interest and tapped feelings of national pride in both Pakeha and Maori—a very different scenario from the 1890s, when the movement was expressed in romantic paintings and writings by European artists of Maori subjects. This Maori renaissance has inevitably led many New Zealanders—Maori and Pakeha—to be rather more questioning of European cultural dominance in this part of the world and rather more conscious of some of the costs of outside imperialism (Renwick 1987: 197–214; Walker 1987; Awatere 1984). At home there have been strenuous efforts to strengthen the Maori langauge with Te Kohanga Reo (preschool learning nests), bilingual schools, and increased Maori language on radio and television. The Waitangi Tribunal has given renewed pertinence to the promises contained in the Treaty of 1840. Abroad, the revival leads, for example, to immediate sympathy for the Kanak cause in New Caledonia.

A more assertive Maori presence, allied to the beginnings of a Pacific Island immigrant voice in New Zealand, has also strengthened a sense of New Zealand's South Pacific identity. In some respects an awakening to New Zealand's Pacific location had begun in the three decades after the fall of Singapore, but during that period the Pacific that New Zealand looked to was the Pacific rim and included Southeast Asia, Japan, and the United States. Within that Pacific world New Zealand identified with the upholding of Western economic and political interests. This was the point of view that led to New Zealand involvement in Korea, Malaya, Singapore, and Vietnam. The Colombo Plan was started, SEATO was joined. In the last ten years, partly as a result of Maori radicalism, New Zealand has located itself physically in the South Pacific. Events in Fiji, Vanuatu, Kanaky—not Southeast Asia—have become the focus of attention.

This South Pacific identification has had two important consequences. First, it has strengthened a self-perception of New Zealand as another island of surf and sun, a paradise that should be protected from outside pollution. Second, it has changed our perception of the threats to New Zealand. Communist China, Soviet Russia, and Communism in Southeast Asia do not seem like credible dangers. They are seen as inhabiting a very distant and different world. Instead, when we look out to the South Pacific we see the looming shadow of France exploding atomic bombs and suppressing the Kanak movement; we look upon American ships and bombs as dangerous and unnecessary interlopers in this part of the world.

New Zealand as Aotearoa, a Maori and South Pacific country, is the first element of our new nationalism. The second is a sense of New Zealand as a moral example to a corrupt old world. Once again this sense has precedents. Like most settler societies, New Zealand sought to attract immigrants from the old world and sought to give validity to its place in world history by presenting itself as a new world, a utopia, another Eden, God's own country. All this will be recognizable to Australian (another "God's own country") and American historians (the "city upon a hill"). In New Zealand's case, this utopian vision had in the past largely applied to domestic conditions. We were to be the "social laboratory of the world," although as always we had largely a British audience in mind. In the reforms of the 1890s and 1930s, part of the motivation was to guard ourselves from the industrial and urban evils of the old country.

In the years since World War II that identity has become, to say the least, somewhat tawdry. There has been a loss of confidence in the welfare state, especially among some sections of the urban middle class; few now believe that New Zealand has much to teach the world in terms of social policy. Roger Douglas, it is true, has tried half-heartedly to present his economic policy in utopian terms, but most people see his policy as following ten years behind Ronald Reagan and Margaret Thatcher rather than leading the world. Unable to see easy remedies at home and no longer interested in attracting immigrants from Britain, other New Zealanders have turned instead to New Zealand's foreign role and redirected the utopian thrust in that direction. Instead of a "social laboratory" we could be a moral example to the world. This view found early expression in the sending of a frigate to Mururoa Atoll in 1973 and it lay behind much of the opposition to the 1981 Springbok Tour. When in the second match of the tour a large group of protesters stormed onto the rugby pitch at Hamilton and forced the cancellation of the game, the chant that group latched on to was "The whole world is watching." The decision to refuse entry to nuclear ships was wholly in this spirit of utopian moralism.

This moral role has a number of attractions. It accepts the small size of New Zealand and argues that since we are too small to have an influence through the exercise of force or through a large economic leverage, our only possible impact on the world can come through example. The role also gives a positive content to New Zealand's acute sense of isolation. Instead of seeing our isolation as a cause for embarrassment, something that has to be compensated for by an enthusiasm to get involved in the "real world" overseas, New Zealanders can now see their isolation as giving them an Olympian detachment from the world and a special duty to nudge the world in a peaceful direction. Physical isolation also plays into the desire to keep old world diseases at bay. In the past, this framework of thinking was used to motivate domestic reform. Accepting old world judgments that England was being corrupted by its urban life style and its class inequalities, New Zealanders could strive to ward off these dangers at home. Now they can see themselves warding off the nuclear disease and keeping their South Pacific paradise pure. The nearest equivalent I can think of was the issuing of the Monroe Doctrine by the United States in 1824. Carried along by a tide of utopian nationalism and self-discovery, the United States argued that the American continent should not be corrupted by old world values. Colonialism was a European disease, and so the Europeans should stay away. It may not be too fanciful to see New Zealand's nuclear ship ban as its equivalent of the Monroe Doctrine.

It should now be obvious why the emerging national identity of New Zealand as a moral exemplar and as a Maori South Pacific people has something to do with the nuclear ships ban. Of course, I don't want to suggest that all New Zealanders now share this view of national identity. They clearly do not. Opposition is especially strong in rural and provincial New Zealand. There is still majority support for ANZUS, and the attempts to strengthen the Maori content of New Zealand life, particularly in the school system, have created an ugly backlash. As decisions of the Waitangi

Tribunal threaten economic interests on the land and at sea, that backlash threatens to become even uglier. Even Labour is not totally committed to a new identity. They have no intention of taking the Union Jack off the flag or changing the official name of the country to Aotearoa. They do not even want to withdraw from ANZUS. But the vision that I have outlined does, I believe, impel many of those well-educated opinion-makers who have achieved increased social and political power in the past few years. Because, in the case of nuclear ships, the vision has brought little obvious pain, and has been able to tap into older traditions, the rest of the country has happily gone along with it. And because it is a vision that is self-generated, rather than emerging from British judgments about ourselves, it is borne along with a tide of nationalism that is infectious. In my view the nuclear ships ban has little to do with New Zealanders' particular feelings toward the United States, and much to do with this emerging nationalism.

NEW ZEALAND AND AUSTRALIA

Let me end with a few comments about what all this has to do with the relations with Australia. In the older formulation of national identity, in which New Zealand was the empire's most loyal son, there was always a degree of jealousy and suspicion of Australia as the larrikin older brother, who was rather too boisterous, crude, and unreliable. Cricket controversies notwithstanding, there is some evidence from the Closer Economic Relations arrangement and recent defense talks, not to mention growing intellectual and tourist interchange, that relationships are approaching that of independent nations rather than being perceived through a competition for the mother country's affection. It is also clear that the focusing of New Zealand on the Pacific has strengthened the sense of a natural alliance with Australia for both trading and defense purposes, and all the indications are that these links will become ever more significant. Yet to the extent that the Pacific identity has heightened a Polynesian consciousness, there has been some suspicion that the Australians are not really a Pacific people, and of course there has been disappointment in some quarters about their continued loyalty to U.S. nuclear interests. To the extent, too, that we have seen a growing demand for national independence and dignity in New Zealand, the slightest suspicion of condescension by the Australians has been strongly resented.

A more fruitful question may well be to ask why Australia has not followed the same reevaluation of its national identity as New Zealand,

and why this has not produced similar diplomatic consequences. Although I speak from relative ignorance, I am sure that in Australia too the period since World War II has seen a strengthening in the position of the educationally based middle class and a reduction in the influence of British opinion-making. But the baseline situation was very different. By the 1940s, Australia was already a highly urban society, and possessed a greater degree of national self-confidence and deeper traditions of independent nationalism. In the 1890s there emerged an anti-British nationalism that never had an equivalent in New Zealand. In 1943 Australia did choose to bring its men back to the Pacific rather than leave them in Europe. There has been less of a need on Australia's part to assert its own independence and claim a sense of its own uniqueness.

A second important difference concerns the relative size of the two countries. As a small and isolated country, New Zealand was forced to accept the fact that its degree of political power and military influence would always be limited and therefore its only chance to play a role on the world stage was as a moral example. Australia, by contrast, possesses a consciousness of itself as a sizeable continent with the potential to be a powerful world actor. The country therefore is able to look on an alliance with the United States as a partnership of equals. Great-power aspirations are enhanced, not diminished by the relationship.

Finally, the geographical difference between the two countries is important. New Zealand, as we have seen, has increasingly looked out on the South Pacific as its area of prime concern, while Indonesia and Southeast Asia have been thought of as a long way over the horizon. This perception has been reinforced by South Pacific immigration and the Maori revival. In Australia immigration has come from Europe and increasingly from Asia; the numerical weakness of the aboriginal people has diminished the aboriginal role in national self-perceptions. More importantly, Australians have always looked northward to the huge populations of Indonesia and Asia and felt an insecurity about their own defenses. Australia involved itself in the Vietnam War with a degree of commitment entirely lacking in New Zealand. The difference in perceptions can be seen in two recent surveys that invited people in each country to name present military threats. While about a third of both publics (in Australia, 37 percent; New Zealand, 31 percent) shared a fear of Russia, thereafter perceptions differed markedly. In Australia the next highest threats came from Asian countries (Indonesia 15 percent, China 13 percent, Vietnam 7 percent, Japan 6 percent), but none of these places rated as much as 5 percent on the New Zealand poll. For New Zealanders, the most dangerous threats after Russia were considered to be the United States (14 percent) and France (13 percent). New Zealand's South Pacific, rather than Asian, orientation is therefore obvious (Defence Committee of Enquiry 1986: 40; Matthews and Ravenhill 1987: 163).

Thus the Australian comparison serves from my perspective to sharpen our sense of the factors unique to New Zealand. Coming out from under the British empire, the country has slowly become capable of defining a place in the world for itself. In seeking that identity New Zealand has turned to elements that make the country distinctive: its small size and isolation, which encourage a moral role in world affairs and feed the utopian vision of a place free from old world diseases; its Maori inhabitants, growing in numbers and influence, which help to shake confidence about the necessary dominance of Western interests; and its South Pacific location, which counterpoises romantic island dreams against superpower bombs. This awakening of Aotearoa to a new vision of itself has been the most challenging and exciting development of the last twenty years in New Zealand. It was the United States' misfortune to be on the receiving end.

NOTES

1. Of course, one immediate response might be that it is not New Zealand that has changed, since the government still wants to be a part of ANZUS, but the United States, which has come to require nuclear deterrence as a part of the package. This is true, but there can be little doubt that there is much less New Zealand enthusiasm for a defense arrangement with the United States today than there was a generation ago.

2. Of programs in the top twenty, 42.5 percent were from the United States, as compared with 39.7 percent, which was the figure for the proportion of American programs in all hours of transmission (Lealand 1988: pp. 40, 44).

3.

Editorials in the Evening Post (%)

Subject	N.Z.	U.S.A.	U.K.	Australia	Other
May 1947	46.4	21.4	17.9	7.1	7.1
May 1957	64.0	2.0	30.0	0	4.0
May 1967	87.5	4.2	8.3	0	0
May 1977	91.7	8.3	0	0	0
May 1987	81.8	9.1	4.6	0	4.6

4. The four with degrees in Peter Fraser's cabinet were Mason, McMillan, Nordmeyer, and McCombs; those in the cabinet of 1988 without a degree were Moore, Wetere, Moyle, and Rodger.

10

Peripheral International Relationships in a More Benign World: Reflections on American Orientations toward ANZUS

JAMES N. ROSENAU

Imagine that you hold in your hand three tables of data, one for each of the three major television networks in the United States. Suppose further that each table has eleven columns, one for each of the ten years between 1972 and 1981 and the eleventh for the sum of the entries in each row across the ten columns. Then picture some fifty rows, each of which lists a country in the order of the number of times it was mentioned in an international news story carried nightly by the network during each year of the decade. Now, with this eleven-by-fifty table of data fixed in your imagination, and drawing on your knowledge of ANZUS and its underlying dynamics, estimate where Australia and New Zealand ranked among the top fifty for each of the networks.

In fact, such compilations have been made (see Larson 1984: 182–87). They reveal that the United States had the most mentions across the decade for all three networks: a total of 1,355 by ABC, 1,446 by CBS, and 1,343 by NBC. The fiftieth country for ABC involved a tie between Nicaragua, Chile, Sweden, and East Germany, each with sixteen mentions for the ten years, while El Salvador and East Germany tied with eighteen mentions each in the CBS rankings, and Algeria was fiftieth with sixteen mentions in NBC's news coverage. With these parameters providing a more secure basis for making the estimate, draw again on your understanding of where the other members of ANZUS fit in the American sensitivities to the world.

The empirical answer serves as the basis for organizing this chapter. It could hardly be more clearcut: The other ANZUS countries are as far removed perceptually from the United States as they are geographically. In none of the three lists does either Australia or New Zealand appear!

IN SEARCH OF PERSPECTIVE

Given these findings, how does one write a paper about the U.S. domestic scene and how it may be related to the policies and politics of Australia and New Zealand? Do such findings not suggest the need to contrive, to make a non-topic seem like a cluster of urgent issues? Six responses to these questions seem plausible:

1. Dismiss the data on the grounds that they are out of date, that the subsequent breakdown of ANZUS raised the level of consciousness in the United States, and that comparable data for the 1980s would reveal New Zealand, at least, in the list of fifty most cited countries.
2. Dismiss the data on the grounds that they are woefully incomplete, that they describe a sensitivity only to current issues and do not depict patterns of trade, tourism, artistic exchange, and a host of other dynamics through which nations are linked to one another.
3. Interpret the data as affirming the solidity of the U.S.-New Zealand and U.S.-Australian relationships on the grounds that nightly news stories are descriptive of conflict and that the absence of them thus testifies to the underlying warmth of the links between the United States and its historic allies in the South Pacific.
4. Discount the data on the grounds that the television networks cater to mass audiences, whereas issues pertaining to ANZUS are of interest only to elites in the United States.
5. Treat the data as insufficient inasmuch as they do not identify possible indicators of peripheral political relationships.
6. Accept the data as highlighting the need to theorize afresh about international relationships that are peripheral to world politics and yet central to particular regions.

A good case could be made for all six of these orientations toward the South Pacific's lack of continuing salience in American politics. They are not mutually exclusive responses, and each points up a relevant dimension of the ANZUS relationships from an American perspective. In all probability the 1985 breakdown of ANZUS over the availability of harbors to ships with nuclear warheads did elevate Australia and New Zealand into the top fifty countries mentioned on network news for the 1980s. And surely it is the case that the second and third responses can also be readily justified: The data are incomplete in that international relationships do rest on much more elaborate predispositions and perceptions than the momentary conflicts that frame daily headlines. Trade, tourism, scientific and technological exchange, artistic and cultural communications, and a host of other nonpolitical interactions do persist among the ANZUS countries despite the 1985 breakdown of their treaty and, as indicated by the high positive association with New Zealand and Australia uncovered by interview surveys, they do form patterns that suggest the prevalence of warm and cordial relations.[1] More than that, such social and economic underpinnings also serve to define and shape reactions to political crises when they do arise. Favorable inclinations toward kangaroos, koala bears, blond golfers, and stunning opera houses can readily be relevant to the way in which threats to alliances are interpreted and handled.

Similarly, a cogent case can be made—and is made below—for viewing the politics of the South Pacific as primarily a concern of elites, as too distant to capture the attention of mass publics and the mass media that cater to their unsophisticated tastes through truncated treatments of the day's news. Considerable evidence can be accumulated to demonstrate that the media on which members of the mass public depend for their pictures of the world are very different from those on which attentive citizens and leaders rely.[2] This argument becomes suspect, however, when the coverage of these countries by an elite medium, *The New York Times*, is assessed. Such an assessment was accomplished through a comparison of the number of column inches in the index of that newspaper for each of the same ten years encompassed by the survey of network news, with the decadal totals for Australia and New Zealand being contrasted with comparable figures for four of the countries (Algeria, East Germany, Nicaragua, and Sweden) that were either fiftieth or tied for fiftieth in the ABC, CBS, and NBC rankings. The results can hardly be viewed as support for the fourth of the possible responses to the data for television news: The totals for both Australia and New Zealand (respectively, 206 and 41 column inches) were less than those for East Germany (355) and Nicaragua (357), and New Zealand's total was also less than those for Algeria (84) and Sweden (125). It follows that while the ensuing analysis is concerned with elite orientations, these must be interpreted cautiously insofar as their relevance to ANZUS is concerned. Under normal circumstances the South Pacific is, relatively speaking, of only peripheral concern to elites as well as mass publics in the United States.

As for the fifth of the foregoing responses—that while the ANZUS relationships may ordinarily be politically peripheral from an American standpoint, they are not so quiescent as to be irrelevant when conflicts arise in the South Pacific—the three countries have enough in common to sustain an alliance in the event circumstances activate their shared concerns. Issues of poverty, for example, do not divide them, and neither do population questions or race relations. The differences in language are minuscule, and those pertaining to culture are not so great as to be a source of contention. The politics of all three nations spring from the same Western traditions and there is no threat of one of them using nuclear weapons against the others. To be sure, they are competitively involved in global economic and financial processes, but such conflictful overlaps do not appear to be so pervasive as to justify claiming that the ANZUS countries are locked into active political antagonisms.

For all practical purposes, in short, it is an exaggeration to posit their ties as pervasively political. They are, rather, mostly economic, social, and cultural. To treat them as other than nonpolitical ties, as embracing urgent conflictful issues, is to elevate the exaggeration to a set of expectations that can hardly clarify the dynamics at work. Yet their shared language and culture do constitute indicators of peripheral international relationships, of a latent readiness to come together, or at least not be drawn apart, in the event the global agenda is marked by new political issues that span the geographic distances that separate them.

But how to probe peripheral international relationships? These are not core–periphery links in the Marxist sense of industrially rich countries in the West dominating poor countries in the Third World. They are, rather, relationships between industrial countries with common cultures, economic structures, and political institutions that are peripheral in the sense of being far apart. Under what circumstances, and in what ways, might such distant links become close-at-hand concerns? The question emphasizes the importance of the sixth of the foregoing responses—the need to search for an integrating perspective, one that neither contrives nor exaggerates the relevance of globally peripheral and regionally central international relationships.

Two prime components of such a perspective come immediately to mind. One is that it must be organized around elite orientations. Given the absence of widespread mass sensitivity in the United States about the normal, daily course of ANZUS relationships, the attitudes and actions of elites, and the structure of their decision-making processes, must perforce command a central place in any meaningful analytic scheme. To focus on mass opinion in the United States just because mass publics in Australia and New Zealand may be preoccupied with the United States would be both to contrive and to exaggerate the nature of the American contribution to the ANZUS relationships. The limited *New York Times* data noted above hardly depict a high degree of elite sensitivity to Australia and New Zealand, but surely elites are likely to predominate among those who do maintain a continuing involvement in ANZUS affairs.

The second component involves the need to focus on the future contexts rather than the present realities of the American contribution. If concern about the South Pacific presently lies at the periphery of elite orientations in the United States, and if nuclear-free zones constitute the only issue currently on the global agenda that may affect the dynamics of ANZUS, then analysis must probe the prevailing belief systems of elites for an understanding of their application to the South Pacific in the event of changes that may profoundly alter the structures of world politics, the role of superpowers, and the salience of peripheral relationships. In effect, an overall perspective is needed that allows for the derivation of the United States' likely orientations toward alliances in general and ANZUS in particular if developments transform the premises and procedures through which states and societies conduct their external affairs.

A DIVIDED LEADERSHIP COMMUNITY

The belief systems American leaders employ to infuse structure into world politics have undergone two major shocks in the last fifty years, one that fostered cohesion and consensus in their ranks, and a second that splintered them into several irreconcilable parts. The first of these shocks occurred with the Japanese attack on Pearl Harbor and the onset of World War II. Those events brought an end to the prewar cleavages that focused on whether the United States should retain its isolation in the world or undertake an active role in international affairs. From the 1940s through the mid-1960s a widespread consensus prevailed in which the policy of containment was deemed appropriate as the foundation of U.S. conduct abroad. It was a consensus stimulated by the wartime experience and an appreciation that only through strong international leadership, undertaken through a variety of activities in all parts of the world, could U.S. interests be protected and advanced. It was a consensus that clearly rejected isolationism as a viable posture. Senator Arthur Vandenberg serves as a prime exemplar. A Michigan Republican, Vandenberg was one of the country's leading isolationists prior to World War II, but the entry in his diary the day after Pearl Harbor read, in effect, "Isolationism is no longer tenable!" Subsequently he became one of the nation's leading internationalists and, as chairman of the Senate Foreign Relations Committee, led the fight that generated congressional support for the United Nations, the North Atlantic Treaty Organization, the Truman Doctrine, the Marshall Plan, and the many other instruments of innovative policy that marked the immediate postwar years.

Some might quarrel with the view that the two decades following World War II were a period of widespread consensus. But relative to the prior and subsequent decades such a characterization can be readily demonstrated. To be sure, Henry Wallace dissented from the containment policy and in the 1948 presidential election garnered some two million votes in support of the contention that a Cold War could be avoided through accommodation with the Soviet Union. And, admittedly, in the early years of the emergent consensus Herbert Hoover, Robert Taft, a few revisionist historians, and some other leaders of note voiced perspectives that ran counter to the themes of internationalism. On balance, however, the preponderance of the evidence points up the pervasiveness of the society's postwar commitment to the policies of containment. The Senate approved joining the United Nations by a vote of eighty-nine to two, the Marshal Plan by sixty-nine to seventeen, NATO by eighty-two to thirteen, aid to Greece and Turkey (the first expression of the Truman Doctrine) by sixty-seven to twenty-three—majorities that are in sharp contrast to the Senate's rejection of the League of Nations in an earlier era and the close, often reversed House votes on aid to the Nicaraguan rebels in a subsequent era. Similarly, in contrast to the opposition to the war in Vietnam reflected by the twenty-seven advertisements signed by 9,476 individuals in the "News of the Week in Review" section of the Sunday edition of *The New York Times* during the first year after the inception of American bombing raids on North Vietnam in February 1965, only two such advertisements, one without signatures and one signed by a single individual, appeared in the same newspaper for the entire three years of the Korean War (Rosenau 1974: 57). Such data are not, of course, the equivalent of systematic survey findings, but they are indicative of what a full historical account of the 1945–65 period would probably reveal insofar as the predominant orientations of the national leadership community were concerned.

The second shock was Vietnam. It not only shattered the consensus, but more importantly for present purposes, its consequences linger to this very moment.[3] Such, at least, is the major finding of the Foreign Policy Leadership Project (FPLP), which is founded on systematic data generated through mailed questionnaires to a broad sample of nearly 5,000 leaders of American life eight months before the presidential elections of 1976, 1980, 1984, and 1988.[4] While the results from the 1988 survey have yet to be fully analyzed, those from the three prior years are unambiguous and consistent in portraying the absence of consensus and a leadership community deeply divided over the nature of world politics and the proper role the United States should play in it. The divisions, however, are not amorphous and lacking in structure. Vietnam did not foster disarray and confusion among the elites of the society. Rather, the breakdown of the postwar consensus was followed by leaders adhering to any one of three (relatively) mutually exclusive and internally consistent belief systems about the country's role in international affairs. Labeled "Cold War internationalism," "post-Cold War internationalism," and "semi-isolationalism," the distribution of the three leadership samples among the three belief systems has been roughly 30, 55, and 15 percent respectively. Table 10.1 outlines the core perspectives comprising each belief system. By comparing across the rows one can discern the mutual exclusivity of the three systems, just as reading down the columns provides a measure of their internal consistency.

It is important to emphasize that this three-way division does not appear to be a temporary and transitional condition. The FPLP is designed to probe beneath the level of momentary opinions and immediate issues. Its methodology focuses on teasing out the presence and nature of belief systems, those underlying and primary syntheses of values, information, and experiences through which people organize their understandings of the course of events. Belief systems do not normally change because they are so all-encompassing as to be able to readily absorb any new developments that may unfold anywhere in the world. And, indeed, the durability of belief systems across time is so conspicuous in the 1976, 1980, and 1984 surveys as to suggest that it will take another trauma on the order of Pearl Harbor or Vietnam before the cleavages that mark the leadership community undergo change. The persistence of the three disparate belief systems through the Ford, Carter, and Reagan presidencies is clearly manifested in the distributions for each of the first three surveys. Neither the hostage crisis in Iran nor the Soviet invasion of Afghanistan nor any other event between 1976 and 1984 undermined either the structure of the belief systems or the commitments to them.

To be sure, the immediate circumstances surrounding the war in Vietnam may be fading as stimuli, but its larger lessons pertaining to the loci of

Table 10.1. Summary of Three Foreign-Policy Belief Systems Currently Held by American Leaders

	Cold War Internationalists	Post-Cold War Internationalists	Semi-Isolationists
Structure of the international system	bipolar	multipolar	multipolar
Loci of primary problems	East-West issues	North-South as well as East-West issues	within the United States
Sources of the main threats to the United States	the Soviet Union	poverty, inequitable distribution of resources, population pressures, and regional antagonisms in the Third World as well as the Soviet Union	decaying cities, inflation, unemployment, cultural decadence, environmental depredation, etc., at home
Nature of conflict	zero sum	non-zero sum	non-zero sum
View of the Soviet Union	powerful and aggressive	militarily powerful but not awesome as they otherwise resemble a developing country	powerful but beset with domestic problems and, thus, conservative
View of the U.S. role in the world	leader of the non-Communist world, protector of its integrity and values	selective leadership on key issues	U.S. capacity for leadership abroad highly limited and of doubtful desirability
Bases of U.S. foreign policy	keep up with the Soviets militarily and respond to their efforts to extend their influence in the Third World	promote a multiplicity of economic and political institutions to facilitate movement toward world order and away from confrontation	keep foreign involvements and commitments to a minimum (i.e., primarily to Western Europe, Japan and Israel)

problems abroad, the main threats they pose, the U.S. role in the world, and the conduct of foreign policy linger as bases for responding to world affairs. The second shock is symbolized by the reaction in September, 1983, of the commander of the U.S. Marine Corps, General P.X. Kelley, when he testified before Congress about the presence of the Marines in Lebanon: "The mission, the role, of the marines," he said, "who went into Vietnam . . . " The audience gasped. "I mean into Lebanon," he corrected himself, referring to the mistake as "a Freudian slip." Long after the last troops pulled out of Saigon in 1975, in short, Vietnam and its searing memories lurked not far below the level of the consciousness of many leaders.[5]

VACILLATION AS A STRUCTURAL NECESSITY

To grasp the significance of the three-way cleavages that divide the American leadership community, it is important to take note of the highly decentralized character of the United States' policymaking system. While the President may have prime constitutional responsibility for the conduct of foreign policy, empirically that responsibility is widely fragmented and distributed throughout the several branches of the federal government and the many agencies, subagencies, and sub-subagencies of the several branches. Literally hundreds and perhaps thousands of top executive and legislative officials share in the responsibility for what the United States does abroad. In the years since World War II, morever, the tendencies toward decentralization of the foreign-policymaking system have acquired an ever more rapid momentum. As technology renders the world more complex and interdependent, and as private organizations and political movements have become more numerous and demanding, so has a corresponding proliferation occurred in the policymaking system and so have specialized agencies and subcommittees of Congress become increasingly outspoken on behalf of their perceived responsibilities. Thus it is that the United States speaks and acts in the world through a multiplicity of voices.

The findings of the FPLP with respect to these multiple voices are highly pertinent. Most notably, when the data for the three surveys were probed for a socioeconomic profile of those who adhered to each of the three belief systems, the pattern was unmistakable: In every walk of American life—in both major parties, the military, both houses of Congress, the foreign service, the media, the business community, the universities, and so on—substantial numbers of adherents to all three belief systems can be found. It is not the case that military leaders are largely Cold War internationalists while academics are largely post-Cold War internationalists and labor leaders are largely semi-isolationists. Traces of such tendencies were uncovered (Holsti and Rosenau 1988: 40–41), but the extent of these correlations seems quite unimpressive when compared with the central finding of wide dispersion among all three belief systems.

Such an overlay of decentralized responsibility and diverse belief systems is a prescription for stalemate and vacillation, for transitory commitments and reversals of course, for government by trial balloons and clarifying statements. And that, of course, is precisely what stands out as the most salient feature of U.S. foreign policy over the last two decades. One can readily conclude that when the leadership community of a superpower is beset by deep cleavages over the country's proper role in a rapidly changing world, vacillation gets built into the structures through which it copes with crises and manages its far-flung commitments.[6]

THE STRUCTURE OF PERIPHERAL RELATIONSHIPS

It seems quite unlikely, however, that even the most wide-ranging vacillations of American foreign policy will encompass Australia and New Zealand. While no items about either country were included in the four quadrenniel questionnaires, it does not take much study of Table 10.1 to appreciate that issues pertinent to them are not likely to be salient in any of the three belief systems. Cold War internationalists tend to see the world along an East-West dimension that is essentially located in the northern hemisphere, and only if Soviet influence were to extend more fully into the South Pacific would the ANZUS countries be likely to be encompassed by their concerns. Although the post–Cold War internationalists are inclined to structure the world along a North-South as well as an East-West dimension, their preoccupations with the South are confined to the Third World, of which neither New Zealand nor Australia are perceived to be members. As for the semi-isolationists, their world is organized along a more domestic dimension that extends as little as possible from American shores and certainly does not reach the country whose largest western city, Perth, is the furthermost point from Washington, D.C., to which a U.S. foreign service officer can be assigned.

With the possible exception of a few strategic planners and a small number of persons engaged in foreign trade, then, no subset of leaders is drawn by fundamental predispositions to a preoccupation with the course of events in the South Pacific. There are just too many things going on in our ever more interdependent world to take note of those distant countries.

However, it is the very nature of belief systems that they are so thoroughgoing that their premises can be applied to any systemic situation, even those located on its distant boundaries, if events impinge on the consciousness of their adherents. How might this happen in the present case? Around which aspects of belief systems might the structure of peripherality focus? One aspect looms large in this regard: The readiness of the diverse segments of the leadership community to perceive U.S. obligations abroad as requiring it to maintain a reputation for being a

Table 10.2. Leadership Responses to Items on Three Foreign-Policy Goals, 1976–84 (percentages)

	Importance respondent believes should be attached to goal:			
Goals	very important	somewhat important	not important at all	not sure
"Defending our allies' security"				
1976	37	55	4	4
1980	44	52	3	1
1984	47	49	3	1
"Promoting and defending our own security"				
1976	85	13	1	1
1980	90	9	1	0
1984	83	16	0	0
"Securing adequate supplies of energy"				
1976	72	25	2	1
1980	78	21	1	0
1984	84	15	0	0

Note: Number of respondents in the sample was as follows: 1976—2,282, 1980—2,502, and 1984—2,515.

Source: Foreign Policy Leadership Project surveys.

reliable ally and, conversely, to demand that the country's allies maintain comparable degrees of reliability, constitutes a latent orientation that would be quickly evoked in the event of situations in the South Pacific that challenged the integrity of the ANZUS countries and their alliance. Put differently, while the underpinnings of ANZUS may have weakened since 1985, the fact that its members sustained a long-standing alliance suggests the presence of a latent structure that can usefully be explored through the orientations of American elites toward links to other allies—such as Israel, South Korea, and Taiwan—whose status and reliability are presently on the global agenda.

As measured by the three FPLP surveys, the inclination of American leaders to give high priority to alliance relationships is marked by some ambivalence. As a general proposition, coming to the defense of allies is consistently seen as a salient goal for the country: The first three rows of Table 10.2 reveal that a huge majority in each sample attached some degree of importance to this goal. On the other hand, the remainder of the table suggests that this majority tends to be less impressive when its differentiation between two degrees of importance ("very" and "somewhat") is taken into account in comparison with each sample's evaluation of the

Table 10.3. Leadership Responses to Items on Israel, South Korea, and Taiwan, 1976–84 (percentages)

Item	agree strongly	agree somewhat	disagree somewhat	disagree strongly	no opinion
"The U.S. has a moral obligation to prevent the destruction of the state of Israel"					
1976	33	36	18	11	2
1980	40	35	13	10	2
1984	39	36	15	10	1
"The U.S. should maintain its military commitment to South Korea"[a]					
1980	36	38	12	7	8
1984	32	44	13	7	5
"The U.S. has a moral obligation to prevent the military conquest of Taiwan"[b]					
1984	14	33	27	22	5

Note: Number of respondents in the sample was as follows: 1976—2,282, 1980—2,502, and 1984—2,515.

a. This item was not included in the 1976 survey.

b. This item was not included in the 1976 or 1980 surveys.

Source: Foreign Policy Leadership Project surveys.

importance of defending America's security interests and of securing adequate supplies of energy. Such a comparison suggests that the leadership community does not fully equate the United States' alliances with its security and well-being, that direct threats to national interests are likely to be viewed a bit more seriously than those that come indirectly through allies. Equally indicative, the readiness to come to the support of allies diminishes further when the question focuses on specific allies that are geographically distant. As can be seen in Table 10.3, the support for Israel, South Korea, and Taiwan is considerably less than would have been predicted on the basis of the data in Table 10.2.

In short, the majorities that make for reliability can be discerned in the data, but so can signs that such commitments are far from deep-seated and unquestioning. Indeed, the data in Tables 10.2 and 10.3, along with a host of others that reflect a disinclination to support military involvements abroad, suggest that geographically peripheral allies may find the United States hesitant about meeting its alliance commitments in the event they are under attack. Viewed in this way, the readiness of the United States to alter sharply its ties to New Zealand in response to the latter's 1985 position on the admissibility of nuclear-armed ships to its harbors is perhaps a measure of the peripherality of the ANZUS relationship in the consciousness of American elites. And even if the strong U.S. reaction was partly designed as a message to other allies, it is difficult to imagine the United States undertaking similar actions if NATO countries were to resist the message and emulate the New Zealanders.

It may well be, in other words, that the principles of political realism—which in the international realm dictate a readiness to form and abandon alliances as security threats wax and wane—may be especially attractive to the American leadership community insofar as the country's peripheral relationships are concerned. Or at least such a perspective may seem particularly compelling if, as argued below, the overall context of world politics begins to move in more benign directions. Indeed, if this is the case, if the amelioration or intensification of superpower confrontations is a key variable in the structure of peripheral relationships, the 1988 FPLP survey can be expected to reveal an expansion of the patterns depicted in Tables 10.2 and 10.3.

POTENTIAL FOR CHANGE

As noted at the outset, and as this identification of potential variability in alliance commitments suggests, elite orientations and divisions are not the only consideration on which to base a theoretically fresh approach that neither contrives nor exaggerates the relevance of peripheral international relationships. Account also needs to be taken of future contexts. Thus far the analysis has presumed that the prevailing structures and dynamics of world politics will remain essentially unchanged, that no equivalent of Pearl Harbor or Vietnam is on the horizon that might alter the belief systems of American leaders and the cleavages that divide them. There are reasons to wonder, however, whether this assumption continues to be warranted. Elsewhere (Rosenau 1990) I have outlined the case for viewing global politics as presently in a period of transition unlike any that it has passed through in 300 years, a period in which the dynamics of worldwide turbulence—driven by technological innovations, by an expansion of the number of transnational issues (such as currency crises, environmental degradation, terrorism, and the drug trade) on the global agenda, by a diminution of the effectiveness of states, by a transformation of the criteria used to comply with authority and assess legitimacy, by a pervasive subgroupism that is superseding nationalism, and by an enlargement in the analytic and cathectic skills of citizenries—has encompassed the prime parameters of global politics and fostered the emergence of new global structures and processes. Although these developments have evolved across a longer timespan than the abrupt shock of a Pearl Harbor or even the several-year shock of a Vietnam, they may well prove to be on the order of a comparable trauma insofar as the degree of consensus among elites and the central features of American foreign policy are concerned.

I employ the term "intensified pluralism" to describe the dynamics of turbulent change and "post-international politics" for the structural conditions fostered by intensified pluralism. Among the numerous consequences of intensified pluralism, and perhaps the prime characteristic of post-international politics, is a bifurcation of global structures into two worlds, one being the long-standing state-centric world and the other being an emergent multicentric world of diverse collective actors that are not states but that are sufficiently autonomous to conduct their affairs by a separate set of rules and procedures.[7] Figure 10.1 outlines the historic evolution of the two worlds of world politics and the dynamics that have given rise to the structural bifurcation.

Another central feature of this ever more pluralistic, interdependent, two-world universe of global politics is a diminution in the relative capacities of the superpowers and a decreasing utility of long-range nuclear weapons. Technological breakthroughs in all walks of life have rendered world affairs so complex that neither the United States nor the Soviet Union can control the course of events within their alliance systems, much less at home or elsewhere in the world, with the same degree of effectiveness as they did in the immediate postwar decades. Thus superpower rivalry has undergone a shift away from military competition in the strategic realm and a lessening of tactical confrontations in the Third World. In the sense that global war has become increasingly unlikely, post-international politics portends a more benign world even as the breakdown of authority structures, the mushrooming of subgroupism, and intensified pluralism portends a trend toward more numerous and pervasive low-intensity conflicts in every country and region of every continent.

It is here, in the prospects of a more benign world in which the major threats to security are likely to arise from internal rather than external sources, that a new trauma for elite belief systems may be presently cumulating in the United States. Under conditions of intensified pluralism, what will happen to the foreign-policy belief systems of Americans if it becomes increasingly clear that no foreign adversary threatens its security? After some fifty years of coping with a major adversary, first Germany and

Figure 10.1 The Two Worlds of World Politics

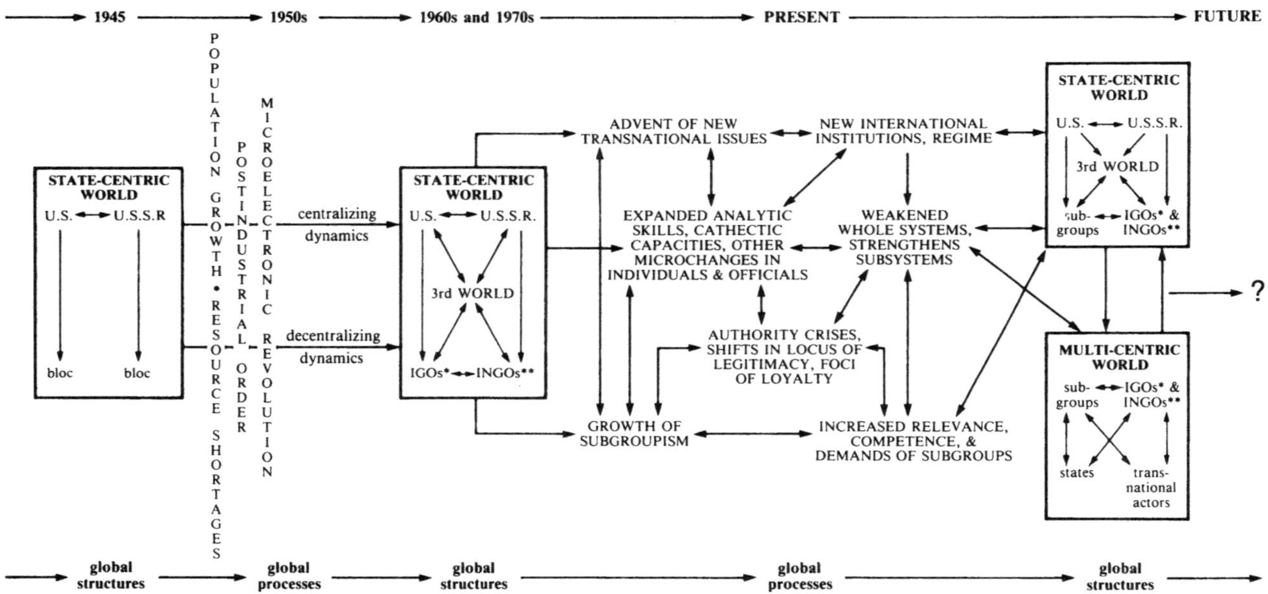

*IGOs — International Governmental Organizations
**INGOs — International Non-governmental Organizations

Source: Reproduced from James N. Rosenau, "Patterned Chaos in Global Life: Structure and Process in the Two Worlds of World Politics," *International Political Science Review,* Vol. 9 (October 1988), p. 338.

then the Soviet Union, will the onset of a benign period of world politics foster disarray and confusion about foreign policy? Or is it just possible that a prolonged period of nondramatic and moderate competition will serve to bridge the deep cleavages that have divided the American leadership community ever since the Vietnam War? Could it be that a nationwide consensus lies ahead if the profound changes at work in world politics increasingly persuade Americans that their physical security is not endangered and that the competition for markets, prestige, and democratic values has shifted from the military arena to the performance of economies and polities? And if so, what will be the consequences for the peripheral international relationships in which the United States is a partner?

I do not pretend to know the answers to such questions, but I am increasingly persuaded that they may not be as far-fetched as they seem at first glance, that dynamics are at work which may confront the people of the United States with circumstances that none of its living generations has ever faced. No American currently alive has ever known a complex, industrial world in which the affairs of his or her country have been closely intertwined with a continual flow of events abroad that are essentially free of immediate military threats to the nation's security. No living American has ever known a time in which a steady stream of changes in the Soviet Union point to a withering of ideological aggressiveness and a readiness to compete in terms of the conventional norms of diplomatic and capitalist rivalry. And no American under fifty years of age has ever known a time in which the horizons of world politics have not been clouded with the possibility of global war.

Some might quarrel with the premise that such circumstances are emerging on the current scene—surely it is possible that the changes at work in the Soviet Union may undergo major setbacks, even reversal, in the years immediately ahead. But the possibility of enduring change is great enough to justify pondering the foregoing questions. Curiously, while much is known about the way Americans respond to crises and military challenges, we know very little indeed about the range of possible responses that may be evoked by a prolonged period of low-level conflict and benign competition. The point here, however, is not to demonstrate that such changes are occurring; rather, it is to ponder what may follow if it is presumed that the changes are operative and that they will continue to unfold.

This focus has its genesis in a realization, at once so obvious and so startling, that our presumptions in the FPLP about the persistence of cleavage and the prospects for consensus among American leaders over issues of foreign policy have been one-sided. On the basis of the two modern situations that induced belief-system change in the ranks of the elite, Pearl Harbor and Vietnam, we focused on the idea that major crises involving large-scale military confict constitute the prime dynamics through which belief systems are likely to be undermined. The persistence of the three-way cleavage as the central finding in the first three administrations of the questionnaire reinforced the inference that the three belief systems are as empirically stable as theoretically they can be expected to be—since leaders tend to structure what happens in the world in terms of their preexistent belief system—and that the likelihood of a new consensus emerging in the foreseeable future was thus not very great. After all, we reasoned, if the Soviet invasion of Afghanistan and the crisis precipitated by the seizure of the U.S. embassy in Tehran had no noticeable consequences insofar as fostering a new national consensus was concerned, then surely the cleavages dividing the belief systems are stable and unlikely to be bridged by any developments other than severe national traumas on the order of a Pearl Harbor or a Vietnam.

In an era of post-international politics, however, this link between the large-scale military conflicts and belief-system change seems unduly one-sided. War and suffering are so arresting, so deeply reflective of mortality, that one can readily appreciate how the onset of war in a sneak attack or its repeated appearance on nightly television may conduce to pause and revision with respect to basic beliefs about the proper stance toward world politics. No less comprehensible is the opposite extreme to which violent conflict can lead tendencies toward nationwide consensus: Given the historic bases of political communities, we can easily grasp that a crippling surprise attack would evoke the shared values of a nation and bridge the gaps among its previously discrepant belief systems, just as our sense of the fragility of communities enables us to appreciate that a prolonged war depicted daily in the living rooms of their members can lead to an unraveling of its sense of shared values and an emergence of conflicting belief systems. While it is thus hardly surprising that our thinking about national consensus formation and breakdown has focused on violent conflict as a prime source of belief-system change, it is startling that we have not recognized the one-sidedness of this perspective and have ignored the ways in which the absence of a potential for violent conflict may undermine belief systems and the gaps between them. But given intensified pluralism and an amelioration of the U.S.-Soviet strategic rivalry and, even more, given the possibility of profound sociopolitical change in the Soviet world, the undermining of these gaps and the emergence of a new consensus is precisely what may be unfolding in the United States today. Viewed from this perspective, the similarity between the Senate's aforementioned foreign-policy majorities in the late 1940s and its vote (ninety-three to five) on the 1988 INF treaty may eventually prove to be the first signs of trauma-induced belief-system change.

The question to be pondered is not whether the belief systems of American leaders will be responsive to alterations in the U.S.-USSR relationship, but whether a less internationally aggressive, more domestically preoccupied Soviet Union that backs up its verbal retreats from long-standing positions with concrete actions will serve to diminish the mutual exclusivity of the belief systems to which American leaders subscribe and, in so doing, initiate counter-processes toward the restoration of a modicum of consensus among them. The question has two separate parts: Will the belief systems undergo transformation? And if so, will they be replaced by coherent and consensual perspectives or by inconsistent and contradictory orientation? Integrated belief systems are not bound to evolve. Even the most thoughtful and educated citizens are vulnerable to confusion and inconsistency. It is thus conceivable that the absence of severe threats to the nation's security could lead to a breakdown of the existing belief systems without a corresponding emergence of consensus. Conceivably, the three belief systems that are currently held in the American leadership community will give way to disarray, to people not knowing what to make of a world in which no adversary adheres to a threatening philosophy and maintains a military machine capable of implementing it.

And to the potential bewilderment inherent in a world free of military adversaries must be added the enormous perplexities that derive from the turbulent conditions through which national economies are being globalized and sociopolitical processes are becoming ever more interdependent on a worldwide scale. As noted, states are becoming less effective, claims of sovereignty less convincing, territoriality less meaningful, and authorities less respected as global markets and global television shrink distances and render long-standing values increasingly awkward. In the context of habitual approaches to international politics these are mind-boggling circumstances; as they sustain the restless, relentless movement of world affairs toward ever greater interdependence, they seem bound to be more conducive to confusion than consensus within the American leadership community.

Needless to say, students of such matters are no more equipped to anticipate the belief-system consequences of such developments than are the leaders whose beliefs are being challenged. Our knowledge of the dynamics of consensus formation is limited by our history of a one-sided approach to them, and our tendencies toward caution make it difficult to be rigorous about the problem until such time as the evidence of change in the Soviet Union is more durable and substantial. But two considerations do seem reasonable if we are playful and allow ourselves to ruminate on the implications of a world marked by the absence of an endlessly threatening military adversary. One is that in all probability the existing belief systems will not break down quickly. Second, and equally plausible, a new national consensus is unlikely to emerge unless a coherent belief system appropriate to a highly interdependent, adversary-free world is articulated by some element of the leadership community that comprehends the way that American interests can be well served in such a world.

The likelihood that belief systems will be slow to break down derives from the kind of habits that have to be undone. All three of the systems turned up by our FPLP data share a distrust of the Soviet Union. Such an orientation is felt more deeply by the Cold War internationalists, but they are not alone in this respect. The post-Cold War internationalists and semi-isolationists also have long been wary of the Soviet Union and skeptical of its capacity for genuine change. Thus, while a Vandenberg can feel that his beliefs collapsed on a particular day as a consequence of a particular event, a comparable collapse with respect to the advent of a more benign Soviet Union is extremely doubtful. Trust can disintegrate with a single devastating bombing, but distrust does not deteriorate on the basis of one accommodative action. It is rooted too deeply in suspicion, fear, and cynicism for a single development to matter, and thus years, even generations, may pass before trust begins to build, with the result that an INF treaty, a Soviet withdrawal from Afghanistan, a diminution of support for regimes in Nicaragua, Ethiopia, Vietnam, and Angola may not be enough to allay the fears of some leaders to the point of disrupting the consistency of their belief systems.

Hence a wrenching period of adjustment and learning lies immediately ahead if in fact such an adversary-free world comes into being and persists. This period will by marked by disbelief, reluctant acknowledgment, redirected hostilities, and a host of other mechanisms for clinging to existent belief systems. Doubtless, shrill voices will continue to warn of deception and the dangers of retreat from confrontational policies, just as equally shrill demands will surely continue to be made for swifter and less cautious steps toward accommodation and a nuclear-free world. Indeed, the cacophony of radical voices from all extremes on the political spectrum may well get increasingly shrill as the threats abate.

However, when paradigms begin to crumble, they can crumble very fast indeed. Trust may be slow to replace distrust, but doubts about the validity of a major component in a belief system can cast the whole system in question and thus lead to its swift collapse even if a new one does not immediately emerge to replace it. It is one thing to become convinced that changes in the Soviet Union are genuine and quite another to conclude that the Soviets are trustworthy.

Thus does it seem likely that the cleavages that have marked the American leadership community will initially give way to disarray in the event that hypothesized changes in the Soviet Union come to pass. And since some vestiges of the discarded belief systems will doubtless linger, the disarray seems bound to persist until such time as an effective and eloquent political leadership emerges with a compelling and integrated belief system that pieces the diverse and swiftly moving events of an adversary-free world into a coherent whole and is capable of then interpreting them in satisfying ways.

And even if the initial period of disarray were to yield to the reconstruction of new, or substantially revised, belief systems that presume a more benign world, it is difficult to imagine that in this context peripheral international relationships will become more salient in the perceptual worlds of American elites. Having already noted data (Tables 10.2 and 10.3) that indicate that the structures of such relationships may be variable in the context of superpower rivalry, it seems unlikely that a substantial redirection, if not a diminution, of this rivalry will redound to the benefit of peripheral relationships. Some, or even most, Cold War internationalists may warn of an extension of Soviet influence in the South Pacific, but in the emergent context of post-international politics such warnings are not likely to galvanize American politics to any noticeable extent. Rather, in such a context the realist value that attaches importance to the reliability of allies seems likely to attenuate as superpower confrontations lessen and as world affairs thus become less turbulent.

As a political-military alliance, in short, ANZUS may be in for a long period of benign neglect in the context of a more benign world. From a variety of perspectives, such a future may be highly desirable.

ACKNOWLEDGMENTS

I am grateful to Ole R. Holsti and William Tow for their reactions to an earlier draft of this chapter and to Brian Findley for his help in compiling data from *The New York Times*.

NOTES

1. See, for example, the data reported by William Watts in Chapter 7 of this volume.

2. Still one of the best discussions of these differences is Key (1961: Chapters 14 and 15).

3. This is not to imply, however, that Vietnam was the only dynamic that shattered the consensus. The 1960s were a special period marked by internal upheavals that also contributed to the breakdown of shared values over the United States' proper role in the world.

4. Launched by Ole R. Holsti and myself in 1975, the Foreign Policy Leadership Project surveyed leaders in all walks of American life as a means of probing how the country has adjusted to a changing world since the end of the war in Vietnam. Some of the more general findings and conclusions generated by the project are presented in Holsti and Rosenau (1984; 1988a: 33–44; 1988b).

5. Reported in *The New York Times*, October 2, 1983.

6. For an extended analysis of the structural tendencies toward vacillation in the policy-making process, see Holsti and Rosenau (1983).

7. Elsewhere I have differentiated these actors from states by referring to them as "sovereignty-free actors" and designating states as "sovereignty-bound actors" (Rosenau 1988: 357–94).

Comment

RICHARD W. BAKER

The chapters in this section clearly document both the distinctive current outlooks of the three nations and the varying historical paths that have led them to these positions. Their differing views of their importance to each other and their contrasting perspectives on security issues are only the most obvious examples of this diversity. Nevertheless, in reviewing these individual stories one cannot help but also be struck by a number of common strands in the problems each of the nations has confronted, the historical and other forces that have influenced them, and the dynamics through which their national self-images and role perceptions have evolved. In this note I want to highlight several of these common elements.

First, each of the three societies has been subject to the conflicting pulls of the desire for autonomy and the imperatives of dependence or interdependence. The ways in which the balance between these factors has been drawn have been quite different, as have the directions of change and the specific events that have triggered changes, but the underlying issues and dilemmas are the same.

For almost a century and a half, American international relationships were driven largely by a powerful impulse to avoid entanglement in the conflicts of the outside world, while concentrating on domestic expansion and development. The United States moved from this deeply ingrained isolationism to its current international role only as a result of the profound traumas of Pearl Harbor and World War II as described in Professor Rosenau's chapter. In the postwar period, the alliance structure has been a means of sharing the burdens—and relieving the loneliness—of the new international leadership responsibilities. It is indeed arguable that the very tenacity with which America's postwar leaders have worked to maintain the integrity of the alliance network is a direct result of the World War II experience (for many a personal experience) of the costs of previous U.S. isolationism, and a related determination to contain any developments that might trigger a resurgence of the isolationist impulse within the American body politic. (This mindset may also help explain the strength of the response of Reagan administration policymakers to what they saw as New Zealand's rejection of a central element of alliance policy.) The persistent fear of such a resurgence, and the frequency with which allusions to isolationism are heard in present-day debates over trade and other policy issues (as well as the growth of an identifiable new "semi-isolationist" group in the U.S. elite as documented by Rosenau) attest to the continuing influence of this historical experience on the American political psyche.

Australia and New Zealand approached the postwar era from almost the opposite starting point and have traveled a different road since, each at its own pace and to a distinctive current position. From insecure origins (both different in circumstances and of far more recent memory than the corresponding period of American history), in which their very existence depended on continued support from mother England, through the period of instinctive identification with British international interests as "loyal territorials of empire," they came to their membership in the ANZUS alliance conditioned in the assumption that the world (and their Asian-Pacific region) was a very threatening place in which their survival was largely dependent on having "great and powerful friends." In the postwar period, the United States essentially succeeded Britain as the greatest and most powerful friend, but did not in so doing eliminate the British tie. As Matthews/Ravenhill and Phillips note in their chapters, both countries at least initially viewed the ANZUS relationship as complementary to, rather than a substitute for, their previous dependency and alliance relationship with Britain.

It is appropriate to note in this connection that the New Zealand public never embraced the U.S. alliance as wholeheartedly or felt as much affinity generally with the United States as did the Australians. However, as pointed out by Jock Phillips, the alliance was nevertheless compatible with the relationship with Britain and was seen as reinforcing national security in the new conditions. For New Zealand too, the history of close ties and common action with Australia gave an additional logic to participation with Australia in ANZUS (as it does to continuation of bilateral security cooperation with Australia now).

In the four decades of the postwar period, both countries have moved toward more independent postures, placing progressively higher priority on what are seen as national rather than alliance interests. The processes of change were stimulated both by a rising tide of nationalism and self-consciousness at home and by the behavior of the great and powerful friends—as Britain moved out of Asia and into the European Community, and the United States proclaimed the Guam Doctrine and then proved unable to prevail in Vietnam. Australia started considerably earlier (the initial turn to the United States for partnership during World War II was a key watershed) and has moved by relatively gradual stages to reach something of a middle position, with a present outlook perhaps best described as "self-reliance within alliance." As described by Phillips, the changes in New Zealand crystallized later and have been both more thoroughgoing and arguably more enthusiastic than those in Australia, producing for many an almost triumphant sense of having now established an individual identity and charted an independent path. However, it also appears to be the case that the consensus in New Zealand around the new outlook is less broadly based at this point than that in Australia, and its future evolution is subject to correspondingly greater uncertainty.

There are ironies in these processes. As the traditionally isolationist America has sustained its belated conversion to internationalism, its erstwhile instinctively internationalist allies have moved toward increasingly national and inward-oriented, if not actually isolationist, postures. And given the overwhelming interdependence of the modern world, the attainment of any measure of genuine autonomy is clearly even more elusive in the present era than in earlier periods. American historians observe that the United States was able to proclaim its Monroe Doctrine only from safely behind the skirts of the British navy and the expanse of the Atlantic Ocean; the modern New Zealand equivalent evoked by Phillips is similarly made tenable by the U.S. fleet (or at least the international strategic standoff) and the Australian continental barrier. But no natural law dictates that the desire of a nation for control over its own destiny need be totally realistic or the resulting policies totally ingenuous, and the vicissitudes of life in a dependent or interdependent world can provide strong reinforcement for the longing for autonomy. No student of the history and politics of any of the three nations can have difficulty recognizing the forces at work in all three cases, or the powerful influence of these forces on the national consciousness of each country.

A related commonality among the three countries is the strain of national exceptionalism in their self-images, a concept that can readily be invoked in support of the autonomy impulse. Based in large part on their respective origins as settler communities building new nations out of wilderness, each of the societies has tended to view itself as a unique and extraordinary entity—a "city on the hill" or equivalent imagery. This common trait has colored both the way in which each society has viewed and interpreted its own changing circumstances, and also inevitably the ways in which each has dealt with the outside world. The utopianism of such views has imparted a tone of moralism and even fervor into the conception of the role that each society has played—whether as a place of refuge or of rehabilitation, as a site for the new order or a laboratory of social experiment and change, and ultimately, when the nations have become involved in European conflicts, as the new world coming to the rescue (and/or reform) of the old. Such self-perceptions can seriously complicate the conduct of external relations, and have done so in various ways for all three.

On another level, the perceptual changes that each society has undergone in the postwar years can be seen as part of a process by which each has been coming to terms with its own location and limitations. Australia and New Zealand have come to place increasing weight on their Asian and Pacific location in the formulation of their national policies. This shift is both reflected in and reinforced by the changes in their threat perceptions, with both publics attributing growing importance to problems closer to home (such as Indonesia for Australians, or the nuclear presence in the South Pacific for New Zealanders). At the same time, both nations have begun to address more explicitly the constraints imposed in such areas as defense capabilities by their limited resources and competing requirements. This has reinforced their turn away from a historic emphasis on broad international developments and often distant conflicts and toward more immediate regional concerns.

Throughout this period, the focus of American attention, both that of the general public and of the principal policymakers, has remained centered on the global issues related to the international security role and responsibilities of the United States. The changes and divisions in American threat perceptions described by Rosenau do encompass differences over the geographic locus of the threat (such as whether the Soviet Union or regional conflicts are the more serious), as well as questioning of the relative importance of any military threat by the new semi-isolationists. However, these trends do not show any marked shift toward a focus on any particular geographic subregion or regions. One consequence is that the Southwest Pacific region of increasing concern to

Australia and New Zealand continues to occupy at best a very secondary position in this American world view.

The United States too over this period has become more conscious of the limits of its national power, although there remain wide divergences of view over the seriousness of these limits and the policy consequences that should follow. As the United States is forced more clearly to acknowledge these constraints and define its own priorities in its international role, this process is most likely to mean still further relative shifts of attention and resources away from relationships, such as ANZUS, that are not central and where the partners are essentially able to sustain themselves. The 1969 Guam Doctrine was taken by Australia and New Zealand as signaling just such a shift, even though it was not consciously aimed at the ANZUS relationships by the American leadership of the time.

Again, as the three countries have come to grips with the constraints of geography and resources, a similar dynamic has led each of the three partners to rather different conclusions—or at least present positions.

A comment is also in order here on the ways in which the three societies view each other. Each of the country chapters, as well as Watts's survey, deals with aspects of this question. The major point to note is that these are essentially a very positive set of mutual images.

To be sure, there are significant national variations, as well as some problems. There is a remarkable ignorance and inattention on the part of Americans toward both Australia and New Zealand. Australians demonstrate the same proclivity with respect to New Zealand. Conversely, Australians show signs of frustration and diminishing confidence in their relations with America. Phillips and Matthews/Ravenhill point out that New Zealanders can be acutely sensitive over their treatment by the other two and tend to be somewhat more critical in their judgments of the others as well. And New Zealanders generally believe they have far less in common with America and Americans than do Australians.

But these imbalances and tensions notwithstanding, we are not dealing here with basically conflictual relationships. The fundamental cross-perceptions are strongly favorable, and would rank at the high end of the scale on most international comparisons. Americans react very positively to Australia and New Zealand (as Watts notes, favorable ratings of New Zealand have risen steadily following the ANZUS blowup, although the most likely explanation is that the dispute did not really register with most of the American public). Australians express similarly positive, if not very detailed, impressions of New Zealanders.

Although the Australian public attributes far less importance to New Zealand than the reverse, Matthews and Ravenhill point out that Australian elite surveys reveal a much higher consciousness of New Zealand's importance to Australia. In his examination of New Zealand-U.S. relations, Phillips stresses the U.S. connections of many of those who have shaped New Zealand's new world view, historical evidence supporting Prime Minister Lange's assertion that his government's policy on nuclear ships was not a manifestation of anti-Americanism. And as indicated in the polling data cited by Watts, the security relationship continues to receive high levels of public support in all three countries. If the problems and the changes in attitudes arouse concern (as they unquestionably do), it is not because they point in the direction of serious conflict between the countries but because they represent an erosion of relationships previously seen as fundamentally strong and harmonious.

A final point worth emphasizing is that both the national self-images and the world views of the three countries are presently in a state of flux. In none of the cases can a broad national consensus now be said to exist. Matthews and Ravenhill observe that Australians remain divided and ambivalent over how their nation can reconcile its European heritage with its Asia-Pacific location. Phillips notes that there is strong opposition and even backlash within New Zealand to the new vision being put forward of their country as a moral exemplar and a South Pacific nation. And Rosenau points to the strength and persistence of the cleavages between the three current American world views, including the new isolationist strain. Neither does it seem likely that new consensus views will coalesce in any of the three in the near future. Truly traumatic new events could, of course, change these pictures and crystallize new visions (whether common or disparate among the three). But such events cannot be rated as likely in the present international environment, and thus a period of gradual further change and continued diversity of world views seems in prospect for all three.

SECTION IV

Implications for Relationships

RICHARD W. BAKER

The preceding sections have considered and compared the changes in Australian, New Zealand, and American societies, politics, and national role perceptions over the four decades of the ANZUS alliance. This section examines the implications of these findings for the relationships among the three countries in the next decade.

Specifically, can we say whether the three societies are becoming more alike or more divergent? Does the basis for cooperation among them appear to be widening or narrowing? And can any lessons be drawn in terms of the ways in which the bilateral and trilateral relationships are managed?

The argument made in this section can be summarized as follows: The patterns of social and political change in the three countries over the post-World War II period and the set of major challenges that each is now facing are remarkably similar on many important dimensions. The network of contacts and interactions between the societies is also strong and essentially self-sustaining, regardless of tensions or conflicts in some areas. However, important if sometimes subtle differences in scale, institutional structure, political processes, and cultures complicate cooperation and inject a degree of emotional volatility into government-to-government relations among the three.

At the same time, although a good case can still be made for security cooperation among the three, the shared sense of external threat, which provided the original impetus for the establishment of the alliance relationship, has now considerably diminished in salience, particularly for the political elites. The new problems they all face in the economic, social, and other fields could provide a renewed stimulus and subject matter for cooperation, but these challenges have not to date been perceived or articulated in such terms. The domestic focus of many of these problems, and the directly competitive nature of some of them, further reduce the likelihood that these challenges will have a significant unifying impact.

Under these circumstances, the natural tendency will be for domestic political considerations in each country to dominate government decision-making on key issues affecting the relationships. For cooperative relationships to be sustained in the face of these pressures, the political and opinion leaders of each country will have to exert conscious efforts to control the centrifugal forces, resist temptations to play to nationalistic emotions at the expense of the others, and maintain broad public support for cooperation and the necessary mutual accommodations involved.

THE COUNTRY EXPERIENCES

The individual chapters have described the evolution of each of the countries during the four decades of the alliance. In each case, there have been changes in social structure and relations, in political issues and alignments, in levels of national prosperity and power, and in the way the society perceives itself and its place in the world. The processes of change have been dynamic and, at least in the latter half of the period, the pace extremely rapid. The result has been in many ways a stressful experience for all three. Further, there is uncertainty in each country as to whether and when a new equilibrium may be reached, and what form it may take.

Parallels

An intricate pattern of similarities, differences, and interrelationships can be traced between the three countries and their experiences over these decades.

The basic similarities have been referred to and remain obvious and visible. Their mutual English heritage is evident in their populations, language, and mainstream cultural traditions. They share strong democratic political systems and values, with institutions based on parliamentary models and common law. And they all have mature, developed economies combining market capitalist principles with superimposed government regulatory mechanisms and social welfare structures. Of the other nations of the Asia-Pacific region, only Canada possesses all these attributes to a similar degree.

A striking degree of parallelism can also be identified in many of the changes the countries have undergone during the postwar period, as well as the challenges they now face.

As *societies*, all three have been making a transition from heavy Anglo-Celtic male domination to a more significantly multicultural complexion with greater participation by both ethnic minorities and women. They have experienced common demographic trends of postwar baby booms followed by a progressive aging of their populations, urbanization/suburbanization, and rising education levels and requirements. They have seen periods of social activism and pressures for change, and associated adaptation and backlash reactions on the part of the mainstream populations. They have all faced issues related to changing sources and rates of immigration, and latterly the problems of dealing with emerging and increasingly locked-in economic/ethnic underclasses.

Politically, relatively long-standing internal alignments in all three have yielded to more fragmented systems of shifting interest-group coalitions and corresponding competition between political parties for the critical uncommitted portion of their electorates. A well-established "liberal" policy consensus focused on direct government action as the principal instrument of public welfare has eroded, giving way (to differing degrees in the three societies) to a greater emphasis on competition, the role of the private sector, and individual incentive and responsibility. In none of the countries is there now a real consensus about the successor concept, and contentious domestic policy debates on these issues continue in all three.

In *economics*, all have faced reduced international competitiveness and flat or even declining domestic standards of living, painful changes for societies accustomed to thinking of themselves as being at the top of the world economic ladder. They are all dealing with similar challenges of the loss of traditional industries and secure overseas markets, the need for major restructuring and reinvestment, and the increasing importance of intensely competitive and volatile service, high technology, and specialty industries. Straitened government finances have reinforced pressures on spending for social programs in all three.

Finally, the *international orientations* of the three countries have also evolved, from an overriding focus on ties with and events in Europe to increased consciousness of the Asia-Pacific region and their relationships with it. At the same time, they have had to adjust to the gradual change from a largely U.S.-dominated to a more multipolar international order at both the global and regional levels.

Distinctions

There are, however, also many significant—though in some cases subtle—differences between the makeup and experiences of the three which are equally important to the dynamics of their relationships. Given the potential to underrate differences in basically similar societies, these merit particularly careful attention.

The most fundamental set of contrasts between the three societies and polities is simply the dramatic differences in *scale* among them. Nations of 240, 16, and 3 million people have vastly different weights in the world and corresponding differences in their ranges of involvements and priorities. In a sense, the entire subject of the relationships among these three countries is pervaded by the asymmetrical nature of these relationships. One New Zealander phrased the point this way:

> The United States is a super-power with global strategic interests and a complicated network of alliances to be managed. Australia, with a population of 16 million in a large, mostly empty continent, has had historic anxieties about security to its north. New Zealand with a population of 3 million is by comparison very small, . . . three hours flying time from its nearest neighbours, . . . not much given to thinking about security issues.[1]

A direct corollary of these differences in scale is the different *salience* each country has for the others. The United States inevitably looms very large in the external world and the internal debates of both the other countries. The converse is clearly not the case; Australia and New Zealand rarely rise above the horizon of national political consciousness in the United States. What James Rosenau terms the "peripheral" nature of the relationship with the ANZUS allies for the United States is a recurring theme in the American chapters in this volume. As the Trevor Matthews/ John Ravenhill chapter demonstrates, a similar pattern applies between New Zealand and Australia. Australia is a major focus of attention for New Zealand. Yet despite their physical proximity, historic ties, and increasing interdependence on a variety of dimensions, New Zealand still occupies a relatively minor position in the pantheon of Australian national concerns.

The reason for these contrasts is clear enough. For Australia and New Zealand, U.S. actions impinge directly and more or less continuously on their worlds, for good or ill. From the prospects for global peace and international economic conditions to specific issues of regional policy or trade, they depend to one degree or another on U.S. decisions. In this situation, the United States is both an object of interest and efforts to exert influence, as well as something of a lightning rod for the emotions and frustrations of its partners. The reverse occurs at most only rarely and ephemerally. In William Watts's phrase, American "radar screens" are very crowded. A whole range of other urgent global, regional, and domestic issues virtually always claims higher priority on the American agenda, and it is difficult for Australia or New Zealand to command wide attention. Donald Stokes points out that this tends to be the case even when there are serious problems or conflicts. Relations with New Zealand figure more prominently in Australian policymaking, politics, and public (particularly elite) consciousness, but there is a similar asymmetry in the importance each country has for the other.

There are also significant differences in *political structures* among the three which again are highlighted in the country chapters. New Zealand's unitary state and single-house Parliament give to its national leadership a degree of control and dominance over the political decision-making processes not known in either of the other two. The U.S. federal and checks-and-balances system has virtually the opposite effect of imposing limits on executive power and a highly diffuse, even labyrinthine political decision-making process. As Hugh Collins points out, Australia's parliamentary/federal amalgam places it in a middle position between these two poles, with cross-cutting attributes of both.

These structural differences impose rather different imperatives on political processes and management—what can be done and how it gets done—in the three countries, and lead to a different set of vulnerabilities and weaknesses in each case. American politics combines the painstaking construction of bipartisan congressional coalitions on specific legislation with national election campaigns conducted at a very high level of generality and symbolism. Australian leaders must meet the demands both of increasingly media-dominated, presidential style national political competition and of hard-nosed factional negotiations within powerful party caucuses. In New Zealand's national village, political discourse can more easily be dominated by one or two forceful personalities, with the result that a well-presented program can be carried through with minimal compromise or even extensive debate.

There are also historical differences in the nature and orientation of the *political groupings* that compete within these different structures. The major political parties in Australia and New Zealand have traditionally had a far stronger ideological coloration than the rather eclectic coalitions represented in American parties. Most significantly for the relationships, both Australia and New Zealand have strong "socialist Left" political movements that are closely tied into both their powerful labor movements and major (Labor) political parties. This phenomenon is largely traceable to nineteenth-century British origins. The United States has had no real equivalent, and as a result the agenda and ideology of the left wing simply are not pertinent to mainstream political competition in America in the way that they are in Australia and New Zealand.

The political Left in Australia and New Zealand has the additional attribute of an ideologically based hostility to the United States. This injects a permanent anti-American factor into the political equation in both countries, and forces both the moderate wings of the respective labor parties and the conservative parties to take into account the inevitability of left-wing criticism when formulating their positions on issues relating to the United States and the alliance. Anti-Americanism has not played the determining role in major policy decisions, but it has had a persistent influence on the atmospherics and nuance of policymaking involving the United States in both countries.

Further, there are differences of ethos and values—that is, *culture*—among the three. These extend beyond the cosmetic paraphernalia of national identity (accents, dress, food, and a variety of other symbols) that can charm or confuse the short-term traveler. Longer-term visitors and students identify deeper differences in attitudes and behaviors which mark genuinely cross-cultural distinctions.

Some examples drawn from Australian and American experience illustrate this point. While both societies pride themselves on their egalitarianism, this feature takes different forms. In America, the emphasis is on equality of opportunity and particularly on individual ability to achieve material success, as exemplified in characteristic expressions like "upward mobility" and "rags to riches." Australian egalitarianism, while not demanding equality of outcomes, is more readily captured in phrases like "mateship," "Jack's as good as his master" and "cutting down the tall poppies," with their sense of status equality and a degree of leveling thrust. And despite ongoing changes in both societies, the Australian ethos still puts more emphasis on quality of life and on leisure than the American. The Australian tends to be iconoclastic toward the organization but deferential to peer groups, while the American stereotype is of the ambitious individual who is nevertheless generally respectful of organizational goals and pecking orders. The movie image of the picaresque Australian Crocodile Dundee, first-naming everyone and sitting up front with the taxi driver, while the proper Americans use formal address and sit in back, is a caricature, but a plausible one, of some of these distinctions. The net impact of such differences on the way societies operate and the goals they pursue can be substantial.

Such differences can also be identified between the Australian and New Zealand cultures, although the two are very similar in many respects and their differences are less marked than those between either of them and the American. (Indeed, it is in comparison with others that the two are most reminded of the extent of their similarities, so this is an area in which an outsider is well advised to tread lightly.) New Zealand's egalitarian spirit is if anything even more robust than that of Australia—"the Great New Zealand clobbering machine" is the forceful New Zealand idiom coined to describe the impact of the egalitarian/conformist ethos on those who would assert superiority. A more pervasive retention of a rural (and still strongly British) flavor and style in New Zealand are among the other distinctions noted by Australians and New Zealanders familiar with both societies.

The interplay of these various factors has also produced distinctions in *political style*. Perhaps the most directly relevant of these for the relationships is the more contentious and personalized nature of political debate in Australia and New Zealand. The parliamentary structure in these countries pits the national leaders against their opponents in virtually daily, face-to-face confrontations. This puts a premium on effective performance by Australian and New Zealand politicians in the cut and thrust of standup debate, and on the ability to both administer and withstand barbed criticism and direct personal attack. Despite a tradition in the United States of no-holds-barred electioneering, and the recent popularity of "negative advertising" techniques, modern American politicians for the most part are not similarly exposed to hand-to-hand verbal combat. There is also less routine need for cooperation and compromise on substantive policy issues between government and opposition in the parliamentary systems than in the looser American structure. Combined with the sharper ideological cleavages between the parties in Australia and New Zealand, these elements have made the use of hyperbolic partisan rhetoric a more prominent and accepted feature of Australian and New Zealand political life (and media commentary on these subjects) than is the case, at least at the national leadership level, in the modern American system.

A final, more speculative, factor differentiating the three societies that is mentioned in several of the chapters is the phenomenon of generational change. If common experiences tend to bind communities and nations, then it is pertinent that the most dramatic and affecting common experiences of Australia, New Zealand, and the United States occurred in the increasingly distant past. The generations in each country that were bonded by the shared perils and triumph of World War II (and the smaller-scale common endeavor in Korea) are now grandparents going on great-grandparents, and in the process of passing from positions of influence. Their children, who are now playing leadership roles in all three societies, absorbed much of the World War II ethos from the preceding generation but then experienced the far different mutual trauma and more mixed emotions of the Vietnam period. And the younger generations now completing their education and emerging into the national mainstream in each country's economic and political life, while inevitably influenced to a degree by the attitudes of the older groups, have had no personal involvement or even direct memory of any major common undertaking by the three countries. To the extent that the sense of British ties and heritage is diminishing among the more multicultural (or at least bicultural) younger generations in Australia and New Zealand, this element in the forging of the original ANZUS bond is also weakening. In terms of a sense of common interests and destiny, time alone is serving to blur this perception in the three countries. Poll evidence does not yet definitively establish generational differences in basic attitudes, but logic strongly suggests that this is likely to be the case.[2]

THE RELATIONSHIPS

Levels of Interaction

Regardless of the previously noted asymmetries in their relationships, there is a broad and intense network of linkages between these countries. As modern, advanced, open societies, they are linked on multiple levels—personal, professional, institutional, official, and even in intangible ways through exposure to common information and images. This applies across a vast range of fields from culture and sports to commerce and technology to education and research to law, government, and politics. Contacts take place within the private sector, between the governments and their various technical agencies, and between governments and non-governmental organizations. These interactions are so numerous and occur at so many different levels that it would be impossible to catalog them all.

The flows of interaction and influence within these various relationships would be still more difficult to map. The United States clearly has been for an extended period a major source of innovations that have been adopted (or adapted) by the other two, from the use of sophisticated polling and marketing techniques in politics to the various cultural influences enumerated by Jock Phillips. Again, this is importantly a reflection of the sheer differences in scale, and does not seem likely to change—despite the evidence noted by Watts of some resistance in Australia and New Zealand (as elsewhere) to American "cultural imperialism." However, like the linkages themselves, these influences run in all directions, and as the numbers of contacts and the ease of communication grow, the specific paths and patterns of influence increasingly defy prediction. Australian newspaper management, yacht design, and kiwi fruit are only particularly colorful instances of the variegated Antipodean influences on American life in recent years. These influences may not be as omnipresent as that of American culture on Australia and New Zealand, and in some cases the origin may not even be correctly identified by much of the American population, but the impact is nonetheless real.

It is also the fact that most of these interrelationships are formed and sustain themselves quite independently of one another—or, for the most part, of any conscious intervention by governments. Further, their compartmentalization is such that simultaneously there can be competition or frictions in some areas but cooperation and harmony in others. So it is actually a misnomer to speak of the relationships in any holistic sense, as though they were responsive to central direction or (mis)management. The totality of the relationships between these societies is broad, deeply rooted, and fundamentally strong. And it can be confidently predicted that these ties and interactions will continue and even further intensify over the coming years.

That having been said, and acknowledging Rosenau's observation that at bottom the relationships between these countries are not primarily or even pervasively political in nature, it is nevertheless also true that it is government-to-government relations that are most centrally identified by the national leaderships, media, and public opinion with the bilateral relationships as a whole. The general state and atmospherics of political relations also inevitably have some influence on the myriad other linkages between the societies, even if only in indirect ways. Therefore these relationships assume a perhaps disproportionate visibility, and for that reason merit particular attention. The rest of this discussion will accordingly be addressed largely to these official relationships.

The intergovernmental relationships themselves are quite varied and intense. Between Australia and New Zealand there is cooperation and consultation on economic relations within the framework of the Closer Economic Relations (CER) agreement, on defense matters under their continuing bilateral security ties, and on a wide variety of other subjects. In a unique international practice harking back to the period in which the Australian states and New Zealand were co-equal colonial entities, New Zealand ministers are full participants in regular consultative meetings of their counterparts from the Australian federal and state governments.

Australia and the United States have a whole series of bilateral security and foreign policy links and consultations, capped by annual Australian-U.S. ministerial talks, which after 1984 succeeded the tripartite ANZUS ministerial meetings. Australian-U.S. defense cooperation, through the placement of personnel in line positions in each other's defense establishments, mutual information-sharing, the joint defense facilities, as well as regular exercises and equipment procurement arrangements, represents as high a level of integration as either country has with any other. Other consultations and cooperative activities run the gamut from economics to science to law enforcement.

Although high-level U.S.-New Zealand contacts are now more limited than before the breach in their alliance ties, bilateral cooperation continues in many non-defense areas as well as on some security matters, including arms sales.

Contacts between parliamentarians of the three countries are on a less regular or organized basis, but occur both bilaterally and in a number of international organizations and other multilateral fora.

The three governments frequently take similar or coordinated approaches to a wide range of international matters, from arms control to trade, development assistance, environmental problems, and human rights questions. This collaboration is a product both of the similarity of their national interests on many of these subjects and of the habit of cooperation built up over four decades. And it can be anticipated that this pattern too will continue, despite disagreements that may arise over specific issues.

Political Psychology

The government-to-government relationships, and public perceptions of them, are particularly subject to the influences of a set of intangible political and emotional factors that can be termed the "political psychology" of asymmetrical relationships. This can be a remarkably volatile mix. It will be readily apparent that these problems are not unique to the ANZUS relationships (for example, much of this argument applies within the NATO alliance as well), but they are highly pertinent and in some respects even central to the Australian-New Zealand-U.S. relationships.

Fundamental to this psychology is ambivalence over the concept of alliance itself. In the preceding section we noted the inherent tension in all three countries between the competing demands of alliances and national autonomy. Both the publics and the political leaderships register high levels of support for the concept of alliance. The three publics all welcome the increased confidence in dealing with external threats brought by combining forces with others, and partly in recognition of these public attitudes the political leaderships in all three countries (even New Zealand after the break with the United States) characterize participation in ANZUS as one of the major elements of their foreign and security policies. Despite the existence of left-wing opposition to the U.S. alliance in both Australia and New Zealand, the basic electoral calculus in both countries has been such that in neither case has the anti-alliance position been adopted as government policy. The political leaders and government officials of all three countries are also aware of other, more tangible benefits that can be derived from alliance relationships—technology, supply, training, intelligence, air/sea access, use of facilities, and/or provisions for consultation on important issues—in differing combinations and priority orders for each partner.

At the same time, in each country there is resistance to the loss of national autonomy imposed by membership in an alliance. To varying degrees, Australians and New Zealanders feel a derogation of their sovereignty in a situation where fundamental decisions on their national security are in the hands of the government of another country in whose selection they have no say. (In the nuclear age this would be the case whether they were allied with the United States or not, but the alliance serves to give focus to the discomfort.) The hosting of foreign (even if "joint") military facilities, and other specific issues such as the possible presence of nuclear weapons on visiting warships can evoke the same emotions in even more pointed terms.

For the smaller partners, the differences in size and power only increase the sense of being vulnerable to domination and manipulation in the alliance relationship. With its global interests and crowded agenda, the United States inevitably appears preoccupied and insensitive from the perspective of its smaller partners. There is also the constant danger that the partners' interests will simply be overlooked and important decisions affecting them will be made without adequate—or any—consultation. Only small numbers of officials within the foreign policy and legislative institutions can be counted on regularly to be alert to their concerns. Direct, concentrated high-level attention to problems involving these relationships is relatively rare.[3] Inevitably, the fact that they are essentially peripheral considerations within the U.S. policy process communicates itself to the partners. The feeling of being ignored or, worse, forgotten can be the ultimate insult.

Although in a less focused way, Americans also find alliance relationships frustrating. Desiring approval and appreciation for what they generally view as an altruistic international role, Americans tend to be surprised and unsettled when such expressions are not forthcoming. And having taken on the leadership job, it has frequently been difficult for Americans to accept criticism and opposition from allies and friends to U.S. actions or policies seen through American eyes as being in the common interest. As other countries have become stronger in recent years and the domestic resource squeeze in the United States has become tighter, both relations with allies and the U.S. international role itself have increasingly become vulnerable to questioning and a degree of resentment within American society.

Between Australia and New Zealand an equally or perhaps even more complicated set of influences is at work. Economic interdependence and even integration is increasing rapidly, particularly under the influence of the Closer Economic Relations agreement. New Zealand's loss of defense ties with the United States has also meant in practice greater dependence on defense cooperation with Australia. However, as between the United States and Canada, the combination of physical proximity and interdependence serves to heighten the nationalistic sensitivities of the smaller partner. Elements of a little brother/big brother syndrome and other aspects of sibling rivalry readily suggest themselves in both of these relationships. The New Zealand public reacts even more strongly to suggestions of Australian efforts to exert influence than to similar charges against the United States. As the survey data indicate, New Zealanders readily acknowledge the importance of Australia to their country but at the same time resist suggestions for closer political integration, which they presumably regard as risking being absorbed by the larger country.[4] (Nationalistic rivalries are so much a part of the Australia-New Zealand relationship, and so easily sparked, that the family analogy is instructive here in another sense as well—as a reminder especially to third parties that both sides fundamentally accept the closeness of the relationship and the necessity to "get on with it" despite the antagonisms and occasional scraps. At least this has been the case to date.)

The net result is that in all three pairings, both the electorates at large and the political elites in the smaller partners are highly sensitive to perceived slights or pressure from the larger partner. Correspondingly, an independent or critical posture toward the larger country and its policies, couched in local nationalistic terms, can almost always be guaranteed to attract support from at least significant portions of the domestic constituency. On issues where there is a strong sense that national interests have been damaged, such positions can evoke an overwhelming popular response. When this dynamic is combined with the tradition of blunt rhetoric in the Australian and New Zealand political cultures, such episodes can also provoke angry reactions in the other country and trigger harsh bilateral exchanges.

Paradoxes

Two additional complexities in this equation are worth highlighting. First, the public opinion polls document an inverse—indeed almost perverse—correlation between the knowledge each of the publics has of the other countries and their feelings of affinity toward those countries. Australians know far less about New Zealand and New Zealanders than the reverse, yet identify very little about New Zealanders that they dislike. New Zealanders are far more knowledgeable about Australia and Australians but also find more to criticize.[5] Americans know vastly less about Australia or New Zealand than both other peoples know about America, yet Americans consistently rank the other two among the foreign countries that they view most positively and would be most willing to defend if necessary; at the same time, the confidence of the others that the United States would come to their defense has been declining, and statistically significant minorities in both the other countries have come to identify the United States as an actual threat to their nation's security.[6]

Thus a conundrum: Ignorance and insensitivity do not necessarily translate into ill will, and increasing knowledge and contact do not inevitably create more positive feelings and attitudes. It is true that, as Ravenhill and Matthews point out, much of the information about the other societies is acquired through the news and entertainment media, which can be a selective and distorting filter. More information acquired via these channels does not necessarily make for a more accurate picture. Relatively little is taught in the schools in any of the countries about the others' societies and political systems, so the base for real understanding may be equally low on all sides. But other screening processes are undoubtedly also involved in translating factual information into images and attitudes.

Second, there is the issue of "linkage" between various aspects of the relationships, particularly whether the existence of a security alliance should influence policy decisions by the member governments in other fields. There is conflicting evidence as to the attitudes of the leaders and publics in the three countries on this subject. When the question is put directly, there is a general tendency to resist linkage. U.S. policymakers insist that the security alliance is sufficiently important in its own right that it should be protected from the fall-out of divisive issues such as differences over trade policy. The leaders of the other two countries agree, with slight variations in the way they phrase the argument (see below). Public opinion polls also show support for the concept that the alliance relationship should stand on its own.[7]

However, in practice there is a tendency on all sides to treat the relationships in rather undifferentiated terms. When it suits their interest, all parties argue that the existence of a "special relationship" should carry over to other policy areas. The U.S. government regularly seeks the support of its allies for policies and actions—often decided unilaterally—in the name of alliance interests and solidarity. And as noted above, when allies are not cooperative on important issues the result can be public questioning of the U.S. contribution to its alliances. Linkage is also cited in domestic American debates regarding relations with allies. Prior to the break in security relations with New Zealand, for example, American executive branch officials successfully invoked the "special relationship" with New Zealand as an argument against congressional initiatives to restrict important New Zealand exports to the United States (the derivative milk product casein was a target of the competing American industry for many years).

In Australia, in 1986–87 when the United States refused to modify its agricultural export subsidy program to protect Australian market interests, both Australian government leaders and members of the normally strongly pro-alliance Australian farm community said this action called into question the value of the alliance to Australia. As tempers cooled, Australian officials elaborated a more sophisticated argument that there is inescapable indirect linkage between trade policy and security cooperation because an economically weakened Australia would be incapable of fulfilling its alliance responsibilities, and that Australian public perceptions of unfair economic treatment by the United States would inevitably erode support for the broader association between the two countries (Hawke 1988; Hayden 1988; Joint Communique 1988). Essentially as a result of the importance of economic and trade issues for Australia in its relationship with the United States, these subjects now consistently occupy an important position on both the agenda and the concluding joint statements of the ostensibly security-oriented annual Australian-U.S. ministerial talks.

In New Zealand, deep concerns were expressed in 1985–86 that the U.S. suspension of security cooperation over the nuclear ship issue would be followed by economic sanctions—or at least the withdrawal of benefits previously defended on the basis of the alliance relationship—either at executive or congressional initiative. Statements by two members of Congress along these lines gained wide play and ready credence in New Zealand. That trade sanctions were disavowed by the administration and were not forthcoming from Congress did not fully relieve this apprehension, and there was a renewed round of concern in early 1989 when one of the two congressmen who had spoken out on the subject became Secretary of Defense in the Bush administration. (Further illustrating the tacit assumption that linkage should operate in these relationships, on the other side of the Tasman, when trade sanctions were not imposed against New Zealand but the export subsidies that were so objectionable to Australia were continued, the Australian foreign minister complained publicly that, while the United States was declaring New Zealand "a friend, but not an ally," it was treating Australia as "an ally, but not a friend.")

Australia and New Zealand, with their enhanced bilateral defense cooperation and moves toward greater economic integration, are increasingly encountering similar problems of interconnections between the various aspects of their relationships. The 1988–89 negotiations and debates over the complex issue of New Zealand's participation in the construction of a new series of naval frigates provided a good example. In New Zealand, questions about the project included economic costs and utilization of scarce infrastructure as well as the military justification for the frigates and whether they were as appropriate for New Zealand's as for Australia's defense needs. On the Australian side, New Zealand participation in the project tended to be viewed as an indicator of New Zealand's general seriousness about contributing to joint security capabilities. These connections were not directly drawn in the formal negotiations, but all concerned were aware of their existence and the wider ramifications of the issue.

On balance, then, although the linkage between issues has no official status, and can more easily be a complicating than constructive influence on bilateral dealings, it is now an established political fact of life with which all the parties must deal.

Taken altogether, these factors make for a convoluted and sensitive set of relationships. The leaders on all sides regularly attest to the importance of the relationships and their value to all the parties. But when difficult issues arise, the emotions and rhetoric can easily escalate and the atmosphere can become quite strained. Whether the relationships are fragile as well as volatile depends on the strength of the underlying basis for cooperation, which in the case of the ANZUS states has also been changing.

DRIVING FORCES

Declining Threat-Perceptions

Of all the parallel changes in the circumstances of the three countries in recent years, the one that most directly affects their relationships has actually decreased the incentive for cooperation among them. This is the decline in perceptions of an external threat. External threats were a powerful unifying force first in making the original ANZUS alliance possible and then in maintaining its viability over four decades. The threat perceptions of the three partners were not identical (in 1951, the United States saw ANZUS essentially as part of the worldwide anti-Communist network, while for the Antipodean partners an important impetus was their desire for assurance of a continued guarantee against Japan after the peace treaty was signed), and the absolute level of threat may always have been exaggerated to a degree, but the common sense of threat gave tangible value to the alliance relationship and served to mobilize and sustain public support.

By the late 1980s, however, perceptions of external threats had changed markedly in all three countries. As the chapters in Section III indicate, the sense of the likelihood of a major or extra-regional threat had declined for the elites of both Australia and New Zealand, and the American elite consensus on the nature of the security threat also broke down during this period. With at least incremental success in the arms control process, new reform-oriented leadership in the Soviet Union (and earlier in China), the beginnings of progress on a number of long-standing regional conflicts and a perception that more progress is possible on all these fronts, the vision of a more benign world is becoming an increasingly potent and beguiling one for significant portions of the elites in all three countries.

This is not to say that the external environment has in fact become benign for the three partners, or that there is no longer a serious role for security cooperation. Even if the promising signs and first steps continue to be translated into formal agreements and major reductions in levels of armaments and tensions, a strong argument can still be made for continuing security cooperation in order to discourage miscalculation by existing or potential adversaries as well as to provide a mechanism for coordinated action in response to lower-level conflicts and other contingencies. As exemplified in current Australian defense policies, alliance cooperation can also play an important role in maintaining individual national security capabilities. Those with responsibilities for security policy in all three countries are particularly conscious of these aspects of continuing alliance relevance, and of the numerous regional issues that could lead to conflict or otherwise require the use of military forces. And, as we have noted, the poll data clearly demonstrate that the general publics in the three countries continue to support maintaining the alliance.

Nevertheless, it is clear that for the political elites of the three countries the salience of external security threats as a priority of national policy and therefore as a basis for bilateral or trilateral cooperation has declined. Despite some differences of emphasis between the two major political parties in both cases, the defense policies of both Australia and New Zealand presume that no serious external threats will materialize over a ten-year period. It can only be expected that if present international trends continue, the sense of threat will decline still further and this view will come to be more broadly shared by the publics as well as the elites. With this evolution, the base of public and political support for material, as opposed to rhetorical, investments in alliance cooperation will also decline.

New Common Challenges

Interestingly, although the traditional security rationale for trilateral cooperation may be declining, all three countries are now facing a remakably similar agenda of new problems and challenges. It is accepted that, if they fail to make successful adjustments to the new social, political, economic, and international circumstances they now face, the costs to all three in terms of social harmony, economic welfare, and long-term fundamental national security would be enormous. The question arises as to whether these challenges might provide a new or supplementary basis and rationale for mutual cooperation.

A number of factors argue in favor of a collaborative approach to the new challenges. The three countries have as much in common as any group of developed countries. None has yet found definitive solutions to the new problems, although each has launched efforts in this direction. The differences in scale between the three might actually yield benefits in this context, as the experience to date indicates that it has been easier for the smaller countries to try bolder experiments.

New Zealand has attempted the most radical and thoroughgoing series of changes of the three, in economic policy and government structure as well as in adjudicating the grievances of its Maori population. Australia has also been innovative in economic and industrial policy, and in social policy has pursued multiculturalism and taken steps toward developing a new relationship with its aboriginal peoples. The United States has been innovative in areas such as deregulation but has moved more slowly on the serious economic problems of budget deficits and international indebtedness as well as such social issues as the cycle of poverty among ethnic minorities.

It would clearly be premature to presume that New Zealand or Australia have succeeded in identifying viable programmatic solutions to their problems. Neither can there be any certainty that even successful lessons are transferrable from one country to another. Nevertheless, the variety of approaches being tried does suggest that at a minimum there would be value in a mutual comparison of approaches and results.

It is thus at least hypothetically possible that these issues could provide a new impetus for collaboration among the three. However, the fact is that the new agenda of problems has not to date been visualized—or articulated—in these terms. On many of these issues, such as the need for domestic economic policy changes and restructuring, it is not self-evident that there is a significant role for practical cooperation (beyond mutual study and sharing of experiences). There is already a good deal of consultation and cooperation among the three states on various international aspects of the new agenda. However, this tends not to be seen as being uniquely pertinent to the three countries; it is not generally carried out on a tripartite basis, and thus does not contribute to a sense of the three as a grouping.

Finally, a number of the new issues, particularly in the international economic area, involve direct conflicts among the three countries in areas of great domestic sensitivity. Competition over exports to third country markets is only the most obvious of these. In these areas, the new agenda of issues can actually be divisive rather than unifying.

The Uruguay Round of multilateral trade negotiations has well illustrated this mixture of cooperation and conflict on international issues. The three have generally agreed on fundamental objectives, and they have cooperated on many specific issues although usually via bilateral consultations or as part of larger groupings and not as a threesome. But on the major issue of agricultural trade, Australia and New Zealand have participated in their own negotiating group (the Cairns group) and, despite sharing long-term goals with the United States, have often been quite critical of the U.S. approach to this subject in the negotiations.

The Primacy of Domestic Politics

With the declining sense of external threat reducing the earlier impetus for alliance solidarity, and the new common challenges providing no equivalent unifying force, the domestic political processes of the three are inevitably giving increased priority to national rather than alliance interests. Recent examples from all three demonstrate this point.

In the New Zealand-U.S. dispute over nuclear-ship access policy, it now appears clear that the Lange government was not willing to take on the major and divisive campaign within the Labour Party that would have been required to modify policy sufficiently to preserve alliance cooperation with the United States. This was the case despite the government's stated desire to remain within the alliance as well as poll evidence (as noted in Watts's chapter) that, if forced to choose, the New Zealand public was at least ambivalent over whether it preferred the antinuclear policy or ANZUS ties, thus providing room for the government to maneuver. However, opinion within the party on the issue was unquestionably much stronger, particularly on the part of the left wing, which was also restive over the government's Thatcherite economic policies. The economic policies in turn were far more central to the government's program than defense policy. Thus, the nuclear-access policy became involved in a larger set of political calculations, at the cost of the ANZUS relationship with the United States. Domestic (in this case intra-party) rather than alliance considerations were ultimately the determining factor.

Although it did not lead to similar damage to alliance relations, the Australian government faced its own domestic controversy over defense cooperation with the United States just as the U.S.-New Zealand dispute over ship access came to a head. This was the controversy over cooperation in MX missile testing referred to by Hugh Collins. When a long-standing but closely held agreement for Australian facilitative assistance in the MX test program leaked in the Australian press on the eve of a visit by Prime Minister Hawke to Washington in February 1985, it provoked storms of outrage within the Labour Party, including members of Hawke's own faction angered over the lack of consultation. (Labour opposed the MX missile as a destabilizing development—one of the areas in which Labor demonstrated its independence of U.S. policy—but Hawke had agreed to support testing because the arrangement predated Labour's election to government.) With his advisers predicting a party revolt, while en route to Washington Hawke publicly signaled the probability that he would reverse his earlier agreement. During his Washington visit, the Americans withdrew the request for assistance, thus effectively defusing the issue. But Hawke's statements had left little doubt that his own approach to the issue was driven by his domestic political concerns.

In the United States, the executive and legislative decision-making surrounding the Export Enhancement Program (EEP) of agricultural export subsidies in 1985–86, mentioned by both Watts and Stokes, best illustrates the primacy of domestic over alliance politics. In terms of U.S. interests, the EEP program offered the twin advantages of immediate increases in overseas sales for American agriculture and leverage in negotiations with the Europeans for reductions in the very high European subsidy levels. As the 1986 U.S. elections approached, the program also became increasingly attractive to Republicans in the Senate as a means of bolstering their support in the beleaguered farm belt states and thereby possibly preserving their slim majority in the Senate.

The surprise announcement in July that the EEP was being extended to sales to the Soviet Union came as a major blow to Australia, whose significant share in the Soviet market seemed threatened by this U.S. move. However, Australian protests, including the sending of an emergency all-party parliamentary delegation to Washington, fell on deaf ears. Perhaps the most telling moment was the delegation's meeting with Republican Senate leader Dole, who not only was unapologetic for the U.S. action but presented the delegation (and then immediately released at a press conference) a letter supporting even further extension of the program. The somewhat ironic outcomes, that the Soviets made no purchases under the U.S. offer (having already satisfied their needs elsewhere, including from Australia) and that the Republicans lost control of the Senate in the November election anyway, did little to diminish the bitter taste of the experience for the Australian side.

Given the trends and forces now operating within and between the three countries, their relationships appear to face a period of increasingly diffuse, issue-by-issue decision making, with common interests continuing to be invoked in public declarations and official exchanges but individual domestic calculations more often dominant when it comes to a crunch.

MANAGING RELATIONS

Maturity

The trends in the relationships described above are hardly unnatural. In fact, a good case can be made that the suppression of real differences in individual national interests and views just for the sake of maintaining a united front internationally is an unnatural state of affairs, and that more open and active expression of differences over a broader range of issues is a healthier situation that reflects greater maturity in the relationships. To the degree that this tendency also reflects the development of more independent identities and authentic voices for all three partners and a corresponding lessening of the dependency syndrome and its associated negative psychology, this could be a quite positive development. Neither is the forceful expression of differing views among the three partners a new phenomenon—there have been a series of vigorous exchanges over the years.

Nevertheless, the level and number of differences have arguably been higher in recent years than in previous periods, and this inevitably affects both the tenor of the relationships and the difficulties of managing them to advance and protect the continuing common interests of the three. "Mature" relationships are not necessarily easy ones, and can be even more complicated in some respects than more dependent relationships. However, they should be better able to handle stresses and strains. How well the ANZUS relationships have been faring in this regard is open to some question.

Leadership and Public Opinion

The key to the successful management of the ANZUS relationships lies in the interaction between public attitudes and leadership.

The ambivalence of public attitudes toward the relationships has been mentioned. All three publics are quite positively oriented toward at least the concept of the alliance and toward the other two countries (although there are obvious differences of degree among the three). Yet there are also underlying resentments and sensitivities, and all the publics are ultimately more engaged with issues of immediate concern than with the interests of alliance cooperation. Ignorance and/or distorted images in each of the societies of the others add to the potential for misunderstandings.

At the leadership level, there is a high degree of acceptance of the importance of the relationships. The regular public declarations to this effect on all sides have a ring of more than purely ritualistic incantations. There also tends to be considerable confidence in the basic resilience of the relationships, presumably reflecting in part the natural confidence of leaders in their own ability to manage problems successfully as well as, perhaps, assumptions about the "maturity" of the relationships noted just above. Paradoxically, then, when leaders take strongly nationalistic positions on issues involving the other countries, they seem confident that the long-term interests of the relationships will not be affected. Where public emotions are aroused and opinion is volatile, however, this can be an erroneous assumption.

For example, in the context of the ship visit dispute, New Zealand political and opinion leaders commonly portrayed the United States as a bully using excessive strong-arm pressure tactics on a small, relatively powerless ally. This rhetoric clearly was effective in rallying support from a domestic electorate predisposed to feeling somewhat vulnerable to the larger power. But at the same time, the tactic may very well have both enlarged and hardened the views of the 14 percent of the New Zealand electorate whose confidence in the United States is already so low that it identifies that country as an actual security threat. The growth of this view within the New Zealand public can only have a broadly corrosive long-term effect on relations between the two countries.

Similarly, assertions by Australian leaders and opinion-makers from a variety of points on the political spectrum that the U.S. export subsidy program could undermine support for the alliance in Australia had a tendency to become self-fulfilling prophecies, by stimulating or reinforcing precisely that reaction on the part of public opinion, at least in the most directly affected groups.

In both of the above cases, instances of domestic grandstanding on the issues in the United States invariably attracted wide publicity in the other countries and further compounded the problems.

Parallel examples can be cited in Australia-New Zealand relations. New Zealand leaders blamed the breakdown of negotiations with the United

States on the nuclear ship issue in part on a December 1984 letter from Hawke to Lange supporting continued access, which quickly leaked to the New Zealand press; the letter was pointed to as an effort to pressure New Zealand, which only made finding a solution more difficult. The criticism of the Australian action had undoubted appeal to New Zealand nationalist sentiments, but hardly served the cause of good bilateral relations at either the official or public levels. A later public jibe by the Australian foreign minister likening the New Zealand prime minister to a "one-eyed javelin thrower" (who can't win medals but keeps the audience on its toes) presumably had similar reciprocal impact.

There is survey data and other evidence supporting the tendency of public opinion to follow official positions (and consequently indicating the ability of national leadership to influence public attitudes) on issues regarding the relationships. In New Zealand, Watts describes two polls in 1985 and 1986 that reported that, if forced to choose between defense ties with the United States and the policy banning nuclear ship visits, by rather small margins of 48 to 44 percent and 52 to 44 percent the public would have chosen ties with the United States; when this question was asked again in a New Zealand public opinion poll (Heylen) in mid-1989, the outcome was reversed, with a clear majority of 52 percent to 40 percent now preferring to ban nuclear ships even if it was at the expense of defense ties with the United States. In effect, over the three-year period between these polls public opinion had solidified behind the course taken and defended by the government.

Watts also cites poll data indicating that between 1985 and 1986 Australian opinion swung from a narrow plurality (37 percent) to a clear majority (56 percent) supporting the view that Australia should remain neutral in the U.S.-New Zealand dispute over nuclear ship visits; this had been the stated position of the Australian government on the issue from the start. The same surveys registered increased support on the part of the general public for nuclear ship visits to Australia, again consistent with Australian government policy and opposed (as was the Australian government) to the New Zealand position. Finally, there is also at least anecdotal evidence that over this time Australian elite opinion (which, as noted by Matthews and Ravenhill, tends to be closer to official thinking than is general public opinion) has become more critical of New Zealand, especially over these defense policy issues.

Matthews and Ravenhill argue that public opinion more often acts as a constraint on government policy than as a determinant of policy. In the instances just cited, government policy seems to have had some influence on the direction of public opinion. Presumably these attitudes in turn are taken as confirming the correctness of government policy. Through this process leaders can actually harden their own positions on such issues. But this does not mean that they could not mobilize support for different or revised positions if they chose.

Possibilities

An alternative approach has been successfully adopted on some issues in the ANZUS relationships in recent years. Perhaps the most striking was the process by which the Hawke government overcame deep-seated and long-standing suspicions within the Labor Party of the Australian-U.S. joint defense facilities, which many in the party viewed as inherently inconsistent with Australian national integrity. Through a four-year effort involving internal policy studies, negotiations with the United States, public explanations and education, and head-on debate with critics within the party, Hawke and his colleagues (particularly Defense Minister Kim Beazley) obtained a general endorsement in the party platform of the positive contribution of the facilities to deterrence and peace as well as specific approval for up to ten-year extensions of the facilities agreements, which were subsequently negotiated with the United States and announced in late 1988. This was a clear case of leadership efforts influencing the atmosphere of domestic political opinion and producing policy change.

Alternative approaches might also be applied to the management of the bilateral dialogues. A particular question in this regard is how the smaller partners can effectively gain and hold the attention of the preoccupied, larger parties. Shouting is clearly one time-tested technique, but as we have noted it can also be counterproductive, raising emotions more than consciousness. This is particularly true on the most delicate issues in the relationships, those that engage important domestic interests on one or both sides.

This problem needs to be addressed with some sophistication. For the smaller partners, there is no substitute for detailed understanding of the decision-making processes and leverage points in the larger systems. Only an efficient early-warning and lobbying network is likely to keep the smaller party informed of developments that may affect its interests on a sufficiently timely basis to be able to ensure that its interests and views are taken into account before decisions are effectively set on course. Experience shows that, even with the best will in the world, the larger party simply cannot be counted on to perform this function consistently for the smaller one. Interestingly, largely in response to its experience with trade issues in recent years, the Australian government has undertaken precisely such an effort in the United States, allocating greater personnel resources for this purpose.

However, the larger partners also have responsibilities in this regard, because their interests are at stake too. In the case of the United States, which has a wide range of such relationships, there is a clear need to find ways to be more continuously attentive and sensitive to the impact of its actions on perceptions in the other countries. The fact that America's radar screens are crowded and these relationships are peripheral is just not an acceptable excuse for inattention or insensitivity. If the United States treats its important secondary relationships as peripheral, it may very well end up having to do without the assistance or support of these partners at other moments when it greatly needs their cooperation. In an era of declining relative U.S. power in the world, the wisdom of paying more careful attention to the interests of partners should be self-evident.

In fact, the United States has demonstrated sensitivity to alliance relationships and concerns. In the case of the issue of MX testing, the Reagan administration found a way to accommodate the Australian government, and this is well remembered within the Australian leadership. The United States could do better on other issues, even those, such as agricultural trade, which are more complicated in domestic terms. This is not to suggest that every such issue should or can only be resolved through unilateral concessions by the United States. But greater attentiveness could certainly reduce both the number and the level of the differences that do arise.

Similar arguments can be made for greater attention on the part of the Australian leadership to trans-Tasman relations. Australian leaders often acknowledge a lack of detailed understanding of—even travel to—New Zealand. If, as the polls indicate, Australians are in fact interested in closer political ties with New Zealand, and/or if, as many say is the case, Australian leaders are concerned lest New Zealand drift toward pacifism or neutralism, there is a corresponding obligation to act to join the bilateral dialogue on these subjects more than has been the case to date. The detailed and even intense government-to-government negotiations in recent years over such specific issues as CER, the mechanics of bilateral security cooperation following the New Zealand-U.S. breach or the frigate deal do not really substitute for a broader dialogue on basic outlooks and policies. The evident sensitivity of New Zealanders to any suggestion of Australian condescension or pressure complicates this task but does not negate the desirability or possibility of the effort.

In all these areas, the major burden and responsibility for handling the relationships clearly lie with the political and opinion leaders in each country. It is these leaders who are identified by Matthews and Ravenhill, Phillips, and Rosenau as central to the development of the respective national self-images and world views in each case, and who are responsible for the articulation of new visions for each nation's future. Only these relatively small groups in the elites of each nation pay detailed attention to the relationships between them or to the need for mutual understanding and thus are both equipped and in a position to exert influence.

The specific fields in which increased efforts could profitably be invested are so numerous and for the most part obvious that a detailed enumeration is hardly necessary for the basic argument being made here. Key examples would be education and other information flows, exchanges particularly among the leadership groups, and the building of stronger bi-national associations and other continuing institutional links between the countries. On the intergovernmental level, channels of communication between Australia and the United States and between Australia and New Zealand are relatively strong, although as indicated there is room for broadening the subject matter and changing the style of this communication in both cases; between the United States and New Zealand there is now no bilateral counterpart (even on non-security issues) to the regular consultations that previously took place in the annual ANZUS Council meetings. As previously argued, there are numerous opportunities for increased collaboration among scholars and policymakers alike on the new agenda of issues facing all of them. Without suggesting that such increased interchange would eliminate differences among the three countries, it could at a minimum help expand the basis of positive understanding, clarify the differences that do exist, and prevent distortion and magnification of these issues at both the official and popular levels.

Prospects

The sustaining and improving of cooperative relationships among the three countries is a long-term undertaking, the most significant benefits of which will accrue only cumulatively and over some time. As Harvey Franklin notes in his chapter, political systems with two- or three- or even four-year electoral cycles inevitably give priority to more short-term considerations. It may simply be too much to expect that the leadership of the three countries will be willing to make significant investments in such a long-term project, or to pass up the more immediate satisfactions of venting emotions in shouting matches—the time-honored Australian tradition of a good "blue"—for the sake of protecting the relationships. If this is so, then barring some new major external crisis (certainly in itself undesirable) that forces the three together again, the centrifugal political forces in the relationships are likely to dominate, and the atmospherics of the relationships to continue on their roller-coaster course of recent years. At the same time, the broad base of public confidence in the United States within Australia and New Zealand will continue its slow erosion, and the underlying sense of community between Australia and New Zealand may be strained as well.

The continuation of these trends would not mean the end of official cooperation, much less of the myriad unofficial links between the societies. But it would signal a new and less "special" set of relationships among the three governments, and both practical and potential benefits to all sides may be lost in this process.

ACKNOWLEDGMENTS

The analysis and ideas put forward in this section draw heavily on contributions by the chapter authors and other participants in the August 1988 conference in Honolulu. Numerous thoughtful comments on a preliminary draft were also received from participants and others. These included: project senior advisers Henry Albinski, Noel Lough, and Sir Wallace Rowling; Ambassador Rawdon Dalrymple, Richard Smith, and John Trotter of the Australian Foreign Service and James Nockels of the Australian Department of Defense; Peter Adams, John McKinnon, and Priscilla Williams of the New Zealand Foreign Service; and Frank Bennett, John Dorrance, and Alan Romberg of the U.S. Foreign Service as well as Gordon Tubbs of the U.S. Information Agency; Senator Fred Chaney of Australia, Professor John Higley of the University of Texas at Austin, and Sir Ewan Jamieson of New Zealand. While the author alone is responsible for the formulations contained here, he gratefully acknowledges his large debt to all these individuals.

NOTES

1. Remarks at the August 1988 Honolulu conference by William L. Renwick, former director general, New Zealand Department of Education.

2. As indicated by William Watts in Chapter 7 and Trevor Matthews and John Ravenhill in Chapter 8, survey data on Australian public attitudes toward the alliance do

show a number of differences between the younger and older age groups, but it cannot yet be demonstrated that these differences will remain as the younger generation ages.

3. For example, it was pointed out at the Honolulu conference that the ANZUS Council meeting in Wellington in 1984, immediately following the election of the Lange Labour government, was a fortuitous, rare occasion on which most of the authoritative U.S. officials on ANZUS matters were together under circumstances where they could focus singlemindedly over several days on ANZUS issues. The basic U.S. approach to the ship visit issue decided on among these officials at that time guided American policy throughout the subsequent period. A similar coincidence affected the MX testing issue with Australia in 1985 discussed later in this section; Hawke's Washington visit ensured early high-level attention on the American side and clearly contributed to the prompt, smooth resolution of that issue.

4. The 1984 McNair poll commissioned by the Australia New Zealand Foundation (*A Report* 1985) found that while New Zealanders ranked Australia as the most important country to New Zealand in the future, they opposed closer political relations by a margin of 50 to 39 percent. By contrast, Australians ranked New Zealand well behind the United States, Japan, and Britain in importance to Australia, but overwhelmingly supported the idea of closer political relations with New Zealand, with 70 percent in favor and only 16 percent opposed. A 1988 poll conducted by the *New Zealand Herald* and the National Research Bureau found that over the period 1979–88 support in New Zealand for an Australia-New Zealand common market had grown from 39 to 44 percent, while support for political union between the two countries had dropped from 15 percent to 14 percent (see Radio Australia South Pacific news summary, July 28, 1988).

5. The 1984 McNair poll reported that 53 percent of New Zealanders but only 27 percent of Australians considered that they knew "a fair amount" about the other country; when asked about likes and dislikes, only 36 percent of Australians but 71 percent of New Zealanders said there was something they disliked about the other (*A Report* 1985).

6. As noted by William Watts in Chapter 7, Australians' confidence that the United States would come to their country's defense, though still high in absolute terms, declined by over 10 percent during the decade of the 1980s, from 79 percent to 68 percent. Poll data from the middle of the decade cited in Watts's and Jock Phillips's chapters indicated that 14 percent of the New Zealand public and 4–6 percent of Australians claimed to see the United States as a threat to their country. Note also Matthews and Ravenhill's comment in Chapter 8 that this threat perception more likely reflects fears that the United States might provoke a conflict that would affect their country than a fear of direct U.S. attack.

7. A United States Information Agency survey of Australian public attitudes toward the United States in October 1988 found that a majority of Australians (58 to 31 percent) believed that questions of security ties with the United States should be kept separate from differences over trade issues (USIA 1988).

Bibliography

AUSTRALIA

Babbage, R. *Rethinking Australia's Defence*. St. Lucia: University of Queensland Press, 1980.

Ball, Desmond. *A Suitable Piece of Real Estate: American Installations in Australia*. Sydney: Hale & Iremonger, 1980.

———. "The Security Relationship between Australia and New Zealand." In D. Ball, ed., *The ANZAC Connection*. Sydney: George Allen and Unwin, 1985.

Beazley, Kim. "After ANZUS: Australia's Future Security Arrangements" (speech to the New South Wales Branch of the Australian Institute of International Affairs, July 17, 1985). *Australian Foreign Affairs Record*, 56, no. 7 (1985): 604–10.

Bell, Coral. "Australia in a World of Powers." In P. J. Boyce and J. R. Angel, eds., *Independence and Alliance: Australia in World Affairs 1976–80*. Sydney: George Allen & Unwin and the Australian Institute of International Affairs, 1983.

———. *Dependent Ally*. Melbourne: Oxford University Press, 1988.

Bell, R. J. *Unequal Allies: Australian-American Relations and the Pacific War*. Melbourne: Melbourne University Press, 1977.

Camilleri, J. A. *An Introduction to Australian Foreign Policy* (4th ed). Milton, Queensland: Jacaranda Press, 1979.

Campbell, David. *Ideology, Social Theory, and Foreign Policy: An Australian and New Zealand Case Study*. B.A. (Honours) thesis, Department of Political Science, University of Melbourne. Melbourne: 1985.

———. *Australian Public Opinion on National Security Issues*. Working Paper no. 1, Peace Research Centre, Australian National University. Canberra: April 1986.

———. *The Domestic Sources of New Zealand Security Policy in Comparative Perspective*. Working Paper no. 15, Peace Research Centre, Australian National University. Canberra: 1987.

———. "The Social Basis of Australian and New Zealand Security Policy." Department of International Relations, Australian National University (mimeo). Canberra: 1988.

Chapman, Bruce, and Paul Miller. "An Appraisal of Immigrants' Labour Market Performance in Australia." In M. Poole, P. de Lacey, and B. Randhawa, eds., *Australia in Transition*. Sydney: Harcourt Brace Jovanovich, 1985.

Cole, D. " 'The Crimson Thread of Kinship': Ethnic Ideas in Australia, 1870–1914." *Historical Studies*, 14 (1970): 511–25.

Collins, Jock. "The Political Economy of Post-War Immigration." In E. Wheelwright and K. Buckley, eds., *Essays in the Political Economy of Australian Capitalism*, vol. 1. Sydney: ANZ Book Co., 1975.

Department of Defence. *The Defence of Australia 1987*. Canberra: Australian Government Publishing Service, 1987.

Dibb, Paul. *Review of Australia's Defence Capabilities*. Canberra: Australian Government Publishing Service, 1986.

Edwards, P. G. "1941: A Turning Point in Foreign Policy." *Teaching History* 9 (August 1975): 18–26.

Goot, M., and P. King. "ANZUS Reconsidered: The Domestic Politics of an Alliance." In J. Bercovitch, ed., *ANZUS in Crisis*. London: Macmillan, 1988.

Goot, M., and R. Tiffen. "Public Opinion and the Politics of the Polls." In P. King, ed., *Australia's Vietnam*. Sydney: George Allen and Unwin, 1983.

Grant, Bruce. *The Boat People*. New York: Penguin, 1979.

———. *The Australian Dilemma*. Sydney: MacDonald Futura Australia, 1983.

Hancock, W. K. *Australia*. London: Ernest Benn, 1930.

Harries Report. *Australia and the Third World: Report of the Committee on Australia's Relations with the Third World*. Canberra: Australian Government Publishing Service, 1979.

Hawke, R. J. Speech to a joint meeting of the U.S. Congress, June 23, 1988. *Australian Foreign Affairs Record*, 59, no. 6 (June 1988): 223–26.

Hayden, Bill. "Australia and the Asian Region." *Australian Foreign Affairs Record*, 54, no. 10 (1983): 580–88.

———. "The ANZUS Treaty: Its Value and Relevance" (speech to Victorian Fabian Society Conference, May 5, 1985). *Australian Foreign Affairs Record*, 56, no. 5 (1985): 389–96.

———. "Australia and the United States" (speech to luncheon organized by the NSW Branch of the Australian Labor Party, in Sydney, July 2, 1987). *Australian Foreign Affairs Record*, 58, no. 7 (1987): 355–56.

———. "Leadership in the Asia-Pacific Region" (speech at the East-West Center, Hawaii, June 6, 1988). *Australian Foreign Affairs Record*, 59, no. 6 (June 1988): 237–42.

Higgott, Richard. "Australia and Africa." In P. J. Boyce and J. R. Angel, eds., *Independence and Alliance, Australia in World Affairs 1976–80*. Sydney: George Allen & Unwin and Australian Institute of International Affairs, 1983.

Higley, J., D. Deacon, and D. Smart. *Elites in Australia*. London: Routledge and Kegan Paul, 1979.

"Joint Communique of the Australian-U.S. Ministerial Talks," June 29, 1988. *Australian Foreign Affairs Record*, 59, no. 7 (July 1988): 285.

Katter Report. *Threats to Australia's Security: Their Nature and Probability*. Canberra: Australian Government Publishing Service, 1981.

Lloyd, Clem J., and G. Reid. *Out of the Wilderness*. North Melbourne, Victoria: Cassell Australia, 1974.

Mack, Andrew. "Gathering of the Doves." *The Bulletin*, September 6, 1988, pp. 63–64.

———. "Australian Defence Policy and the ANZUS Alliance." In J. Ravenhill, ed., *No Longer an American Lake? Alliance Problems in the South Pacific*. Berkeley: Institute of International Studies; Sydney and London: Allen and Unwin, 1989.

Matthews, Trevor, and John Ravenhill. "ANZUS, the American Alliance and External Threats: Australian Elite Attitudes." *Australian Outlook*, 41 (1987): 161–72.

———. "Bipartisanship in the Australian Foreign Policy Elite." *Australian Outlook*, 42, (1988): 9–20.

Meaney, N. *The Search for Security in the Pacific 1901–14*. Sydney: Sydney University Press, 1976.

———. *Australia and the World: A Documentary History from the 1870s to the 1970s*. Melbourne: Longman Cheshire, 1985.

Meaney, N., T. Matthews, and S. Encel. *The Japanese Connection: A Survey of Australian Leaders' Attitudes Towards Japan and the Australia-Japan Relationship*. Melbourne: Longman Cheshire, 1988.

Menzies, R. G. *The Measure of the Years*. London: Cassel, 1970.

Millar, T. B. *Australia in Peace and War: External Relations 1788–1977*. Canberra: Australian National University Press, 1978.

Miller, W. G. T. "Australia's Relationships with Western Pacific Countries in the 1980s." *Australian Foreign Affairs Record*, 55, no. 10 (1984): 1058–65.

Murdoch, W. *Alfred Deakin: A Sketch*. London: Constable, 1923.

"Our Elusive Soul." *Time*, July 21, 1986, pp. 48–55.

Overton, D., and B. McKenzie. "International Newsflow: An Australian Case Study." *Regional Journal of Social Issues*, 10 (May 1982): 20–30.

Pemberton, Gregory. *All The Way: Australia's Road to Vietnam*. Sydney: George Allen and Unwin, 1987.

Phillips, Donald J., and Jim Houston, eds. *Australian Multicultural Society: Identity, Communication, Decision Making*. Drummond, 1984.

Reese, T. R. *Australia, New Zealand and the United States: A Survey of International Relations 1941–1968*. London: Oxford University Press, 1969.

Renouf, Alan. *The Frightened Country*. Melbourne: Macmillan, 1979.

———. *Let Justice Be Done: The Foreign Policy of Dr. H.V. Evatt*. Brisbane: University of Queensland Press, 1983.

A Report on a Study Investigating Trans-Tasman Attitudes (prepared for the Australia New Zealand Foundation). Auckland: McNair Surveys New Zealand Limited; Sydney: McNair Anderson Associates, January 1985.

Richelson, Jeffrey, and Desmond Ball. *The Ties That Bind: Intelligence Cooperation Between the UKUSA Countries, The United Kingdom, The United States of America, Canada, Australia and New Zealand*. Boston: Allen & Unwin, 1985.

Sexton, Michael. *War for the Asking: Australia's Vietnam Secrets*. Ringwood, Australia: Penguin, 1981.

Shipton Report. *The ANZUS Alliance*. Canberra: Australian Government Publishing Service, 1982.

"Strategic Basis Papers." *National Times*, March 30–April 5, 1984.

Street, A. A. "Australia's Role as a Middle Power." *Australian Foreign Affairs Record*, 53, no. 5 (1982): 306–11.

United States Information Agency (USIA). "Australian Attitudes Toward Security and Economic Issues with the U.S." Research Report R-28-78. Washington, D.C.: International Communications Agency, 1978.

———. "Australians Have Favorable Opinion of U.S., Interested in American Science, Technology, Society, and Sports." Washington, D.C.: United States Information Agency, April 29, 1986.

———. "Australian 'Successor Generation' Attitudes Toward the U.S. and ANZUS." Washington, D.C.: United States Information Agency, December 23, 1987.

———. "Australian Views of the U.S., the U.S. Alliance, and U.S. Agricultural Policies." Research Memorandum. Washington, D.C.: United States Information Agency, December 15, 1988.

Viviani, Nancy. *The Long Journey: Vietnamese Migration and Settlement in Australia.* Carlton, Victoria: Melbourne University Press, 1984.

Wheelwright, Edward L., and Gregory J. Crough. *Australia: A Client State.* Ringwood, Victoria: Penguin, 1982.

Whitlam, E. G. Opening address to the 39th Summer School of the Australian Institute of Political Science. In G. McCarthy, ed., *Foreign Policy for Australia: Choices for the Seventies.* Sydney: Angus and Robertson, 1973.

———. *The Whitlam Government 1972–1975.* Ringwood, Victoria: Viking, 1985.

NEW ZEALAND

Alley, R. "ANZUS and the Nuclear Issue." In J. Boston and M. Holland, eds., *The Fourth Labour Government: Radical Politics in New Zealand.* Auckland: Oxford University Press, 1987.

Awatere, Donna. *Maori Sovereignty.* Broadsheet, 1984.

Boston, J., and M. Holland. "The Fourth Labour Government: Transforming the Political Agenda." In J. Boston and M. Holland, eds., *The Fourth Labour Government: Radical Politics in New Zealand.* Auckland: Oxford University Press, 1987.

Brooking, T. *Milestones: Turning Points in New Zealand History.* Lower Hutt: Mills Publications, 1988.

Brown, B. *The Rise of New Zealand Labour.* Wellington: Price Milburn, 1962.

Calleo, David P. *The Imperious Economy.* Cambridge: Harvard University Press, 1982.

Chapman, Robert. "From Labour to National." In W. H. Oliver, ed., *The Oxford History of New Zealand.* Auckland: Oxford University Press, 1981.

Chapple, Geoff. *1981: The Tour.* Wellington: Reed, 1984.

Clements, K. "The Defence Committee of Enquiry: A Unique Opportunity for Public Opinion." In J. Boston and M. Holland, eds., *The Fourth Labour Government: Radical Politics in New Zealand.* Auckland: Oxford University Press, 1987.

Cleveland, Les. *The Anatomy of Influence: Pressure Groups and Politics in New Zealand.* Wellington: Hicks Smith, 1972.

Collins, Simon. *Rogernomics: Is There a Better Way?* Wellington and Auckland: Pitman, 1987.

Dann, Christine. *Up From Under.* Wellington: Allen and Unwin, 1985.

Defence Committee of Enquiry. *Defence and Security: What New Zealanders Want.* Wellington: Government Printer, 1986.

Department of Statistics (New Zealand). *New Zealand Population Census, 1945.* Wellington: Government Printer, 1946.

———. *Report on the Social Indicators Survey 1980–81.* Wellington: Government Printer, 1984.

———. *Trends and Patterns in NZ Fertility 1912–1983*. Wellington: Government Printer, 1986.

———. *Demographic Trends 1987*. Wellington: Government Printer, 1987.

———. *New Zealand Census of Population and Dwellings: National Summary, 1986*. Wellington: Government Printer, 1987.

———. *New Zealand Official Yearbook, 1987–88*. Wellington: Government Printer, 1987.

Easton, Brian. *Income Distribution in New Zealand*. Research Paper 28. Wellington: New Zealand Institute of Economic Research, 1983.

Elkind, J. B. "The Bill of Rights." In J. Boston and M. Holland, eds., *The Fourth Labour Government: Radical Politics in New Zealand*. Auckland: Oxford University Press, 1987.

Franklin, S. Harvey. *Trade, Growth and Anxiety—New Zealand Beyond the Welfare State*. Wellington: Methuen, 1978.

———. *Cul de Sac—The Question of New Zealand's Future*. Wellington: Unwin Paperbacks, 1985.

Garnier, T., and S. Levine. *Election '81: An End to Muldoonism?* Auckland: Methuen Publications, 1981.

Gould, J. *The Rake's Progress?—The New Zealand Economy Since 1945*. Auckland: Hodder and Stoughton, 1982.

Gustafson, B. *From the Cradle to the Grave: A Biography of Michael Joseph Savage*. Auckland: Reed Methuen, 1986.

Hawke, Gary R. "The Growth of the Economy." In W. H. Oliver, ed., *The Oxford History of New Zealand*. Auckland: Oxford University Press, 1981.

———. *The Making of New Zealand—An Economic History*. Cambridge: Cambridge University Press, 1985.

Hunn, J. K. *Report on Department of Maori Affairs*. Wellington: Government Printer, 1960.

Interdepartmental Committee on Population Questions. *Population Policy Guidelines*. Wellington: Department of Statistics, 1975.

James, Colin. *The Quiet Revolution: Turbulence and Transition in Contemporary New Zealand*. Wellington: Allen and Unwin/Port Nicholson Press, 1986.

Jesson, B. *Behind the Mirror Glass: The Growth of Wealth and Power in New Zealand in the Eighties*. Auckland: Penguin, 1987.

Jones, R. "Optimism—and Issues." *North and South*, November 1987.

Kennaway, R. "Foreign Policy." In R. Goldstein, ed., *Labour in Power: Promise and Performance*. Wellington: Price Milburn for New Zealand University Press, 1975.

King, Peter, and Jock Phillips. "A Social Analysis of the Springbok Tour Protestors." In *Counting the Cost*. Occasional Paper no. 1, Victoria University History Department. Wellington: 1982.

Lange, D. "Foreword." In J. Boston and M. Holland, eds., *The Fourth Labour Government: Radical Politics in New Zealand*. Auckland: Oxford University Press, 1987.

Lealand, Geoff. *A Foreign Egg in Our Nest? American Popular Culture in New Zealand*. Victoria: Victoria University Press, 1988.

Legat, N. *Into the Pacific: Auckland at the Cross Roads*. Auckland: Metro, 1988.

Lipson, Leslie. *The Politics of Equality: New Zealand's Adventures in Democracy*. Chicago: University of Chicago Press, 1948.

McCraw, D. "Reluctant Ally: New Zealand's Entry into the Vietnam War." *New Zealand Journal of History*, 1981.

McKinnon, Malcolm. "Resolution and Apprehension: The Parliamentary National Party and the 1981 Springbok Tour." In *Counting the Cost*. Occasional Paper no. 1, Victoria University History Department. Wellington: 1982.

———. "The Richest Prize?" *New Zealand International Review*, 1986.

Metin, A. *Le Socialisme Sans Doctrines*. Paris: Alcan, 1910.

Mitchell, Austin. *People and Politics in New Zealand*. Christchurch: Whitcombe and Tombs, 1969.

———. *The Half-Gallon Quarter Acre Pavlova Paradise*. Christchurch: Whitcombe and Tombs, 1972.

Mulgan, Richard G. *Democracy and Power in New Zealand: A Study of New Zealand Politics*. Auckland: Oxford University Press, 1984.

Nash, Walter. *New Zealand—A Working Democracy*. New York: Duell, Sloan & Pearce, 1943.

Neville, R. J. W., and C. J. O'Neill. *The Population of New Zealand—Interdisciplinary Perspectives*. Auckland: Longman Paul, 1979.

Oliver, W. H. "The Awakening Imagination." In W. H. Oliver, ed., *The Oxford History of New Zealand*. Auckland: Oxford University Press, 1981.

Olssen, E. *John A. Lee*. Dunedin: University of Otago Press, 1977.

Ovenden, K. "Social Welfare and Public Ideology." In P. Davis, ed., *New Zealand Labour Perspectives: 1. The Challenge of the Third Depression*. Auckland: Peter Davis/ROSS, 1981.

Pearson, Bill. "Real Danger in Films." *Here and Now*, June 1953.

Phillips, Jock. "Musings in Maoriland—Or Was There a Bulletin School in New Zealand?" *Historical Studies*, 20, no. 81 (1983): 520–35.

———. "The Influence of American Culture on New Zealand Since the Second World War." In Ann Trotter, ed., *New Zealand, Canada and the United States*. Dunedin: University of Otago, 1987a.

———. *A Man's Country? The Image of the Pakeha Male—A History*. Auckland: Penguin, 1987b.

Planning Council. *The New Zealand Population: Change, Composition and Policy Implications*. Population Monitoring Group Report no 4. Wellington: New Zealand Planning Council, 1986.

———. *Tracking Down the Deficit*. Economic Monitoring Group Report no. 8. Wellington: New Zealand Planning Council, 1987.

Pomare, E. W., and G. M. de Boer. *Hauora-Maori Standards of Health 1970–1984*. Special Report Series 78. Wellington: Department of Health.

Pool, I., and N. Pole. *The Maori Population to 2011: Demographic Change and its Implications*. New Zealand Demographic Society Technical Paper no. 1. Wellington: New Zealand Demographic Society, 1987.

Poot, J., et al. *International Migration and the New Zealand Economy*. Wellington: Victoria University Press, 1988.

Renwick, William L. "Show Us These Islands and Ourselves . . . Give Us a Home in Thought." *New Zealand Journal of History*, 21, no. 2 (1987): 197–214.

"The Rich 100." *Personal Investment*. Auckland: August 1987.

Roberts, J. "Ministers, the Cabinet and Public Servants." In J. Boston and M. Holland, eds., *The Fourth Labour Government: Radical Politics in New Zealand*. Auckland: Oxford University Press, 1987.

Royal Commission on Social Policy. *The April Report*, 4 vols. Wellington: Government Printer, 1988.
Sinclair, Keith. *Walter Nash*. Auckland: Auckland University Press/Oxford University Press, 1976.
Skene, G. "Parliamentary Reform." In J. Boston and M. Holland, eds., *The Fourth Labour Government: Radical Politics in New Zealand*. Auckland: Oxford University Press, 1987.
Snively, Susan. *The 1981/82 Government Budget and Household Income Distribution*. Wellington: New Zealand Planning Council, 1987.
Sutch, W. B. *The Quest For Security in New Zealand 1840 to 1966*. Wellington: Oxford University Press, 1966.
Thurow, L. C. *Generating Inequality*. London: Macmillan, 1976.
Treasury (New Zealand). *Government Management. Vol. 2. Education Issues*. Wellington: Government Printer, 1987.
United Nations. *Population of New Zealand*, 2 vols. Country Monograph Series no. 12. New York: Economic and Social Commission for Asia and the Pacific, 1985.
University of New Zealand. *Alphabetical Roll of Graduates*. Christchurch: Whitcombe and Tombs, 1959.
Universities Review Committee (Watts Report). *New Zealand's Universities: Partners in National Development*. Wellington: New Zealand Vice Chancellor's Committee, 1987.
Vowles, Jack. "The Fourth Labour Government: Ends, Means and for Whom?" In J. Boston and M. Holland, eds., *The Fourth Labour Government: Radical Politics in New Zealand*. Auckland: Oxford University Press, 1987a.
———. "Liberal Democracy: Pakeha Political Ideology." *New Zealand Journal of History*, 21, no. 2 (1987b): 215–27.
Walker, Ranginui. *Nga tau tohe tohe: Years of Anger*. Auckland: Penguin, 1987.
"What Does David Lange Really Believe about Education?" *North and South*, April 1988.

UNITED STATES

Anderson, Karen. *Wartime Women*. Westport, CT: Greenwood Press, 1981.
Auletta, Ken. *The Underclass*. New York: Doubleday, 1981.
Banner, Lois. *Women in Modern America*. New York: Harcourt, Brace and Jovanovich, 1975.
Bell, Daniel. "The Measurement of Knowledge and Technology." In Eleanor Sheldon and Wilbert Moore, eds., *Indicators of Social Change*. New York: Russell Sage Foundation, 1968.
Blum, John. *V Was For Victory*. New York: W.W. Norton, 1975.
Caro, Robert. *The Path to Power*. New York: W.W. Norton, 1982.
Chafe, William H. *The American Woman*. New York: Oxford University Press, 1972.
———. *Women and Equality*. New York: Oxford University Press, 1977.
———. *Civilities and Civil Rights: Greensboro, N.C. and the Black Struggle for Freedom*. New York: Oxford University Press, 1980.
———. *The Unfinished Journey: America Since World War II*. New York: Oxford University Press, 1986.
Donaldson, Scott. *The Suburban Myth*. New York: Columbia University Press, 1969.

Dugger, Ronnie. *The Politician*. New York: Harper, 1984.
Evans, Sara. *Personal Politics*. New York: Alfred Knopf, 1978.
Forman, James. *The Making of Black Revolutionaries*. New York: Macmillan, 1975.
Freeman, Jo. *The Politics of Women's Liberation*. New York: David McKay, 1975.
Galbraith, J. Kenneth. *The Affluent Society*. Boston: Houghton Mifflin, 1958.
Gans, Herbert. *The Levittowners*. New York: Random House, 1957.
Glazer, Nathan, ed. *Clamor at the Gates*. San Francisco: Institute for Contemporary Studies, 1985.
Hamby, Alonzo. *Liberalism and Its Challengers*. New York: Oxford University Press, 1984.
Hartmann, Susan. *The Homefront and Beyond*. Boston: Allyn and Bacon, 1980.
Herring, George. *America's Longest War*. New York: Wiley and Sons, 1981.
Hodgson, Godfrey. *America In Our Time*. New York: Random House, 1975.
Holsti, Ole R., and James N. Rosenau. "American Leadership in a Shrinking World: The Breakdown of Consensus and the Emergence of Conflicting Belief Systems." *World Politics*, 35 (April 1983).
———. *American Leadership in World Affairs*. Winthrop, MA.: George Allen and Unwin, 1984.
———. "A Leadership Divided: The Foreign Policy Beliefs of American Leaders, 1976–1984." In Charles W. Kegley, Jr., and Eugene R. Wittkopf, eds., *The Domestic Sources of American Foreign Policy*. New York: St. Martin's Press, 1988a.
———. "The Domestic and Foreign Policy Beliefs of American Leaders." *Journal of Conflict Resolution*, 32, no. 2 (June 1988b).
Jackson, Kenneth. *The Crabgrass Frontier*. New York: Oxford University Press, 1984.
Kearns, Doris. *Lyndon Johnson and the American Dream*. New York: Random House, 1977.
Key, V. O. *Public Opinion and American Democracy*. New York: Alfred Knopf, 1961.
Kluger, Richard. *Simple Justice*. New York: Alfred Knopf, 1976.
Larson, James F. *Television Window on the World: International Affairs Coverage on the U.S. Networks*. Norwood, NJ: Ablex Publishing Corporation, 1984.
Leuchtenburg, William E. *A Troubled Feast*. Boston: Little Brown, 1983.
Marable, Manning. *Race, Reform and Rebellion: The Second Reconstruction in Black America*. New York: Random House, 1984.
McGinnis, Joe. *The Selling of the President*. New York: Macmillan, 1969.
Muller, Thomas, et al. *The Fourth Wave*. Washington, DC: The Urban Institute Press, 1985.
Phillips, Kevin. *The Emerging Republican Majority*. New York: Random House, 1969.
Rosenau, James N. *Citizenship Between Elections: An Inquiry into the Mobilizable American*. New York: Free Press, 1974.
———. "Patterned Chaos in Global Life: Structure and Process in the Two Worlds of World Politics." *International Political Science Review*, 9 (October 1988): 327–64.
———. *Turbulence in World Politics*. Princeton: Princeton University Press, 1990.
Sitkoff, Harvard. "Race Relations: Progress and Prospects." In James Patterson, ed., *Paths to the Present*. Minneapolis: Burgess Publishing Company, 1975.
———. *The Struggle for Black Equality*. New York: Hill and Wang, 1983.
Whyte, William. *The Organization Man*. New York: Random House, 1959.

Wills, Garry. *Reagan's America*. New York: Simon and Schuster, 1984.
Witcover, Jules. *Eighty-Five Days: The Last Campaign of Robert F. Kennedy*. New York: Doubleday, 1970.
Yankelovich, Daniel. *New Rules: Searching for Self-Fulfillment in a World Turned Upside Down*. New York: Harper and Row, 1982.

Index

About the Editor and Contributors

RICHARD W. BAKER is a research associate in the East-West Center's International Relations Program. He holds a master's degree in public affairs from the Woodrow Wilson School, Princeton University. From 1967 to 1987, Mr. Baker was a career officer in the U.S. Foreign Service, serving in Singapore, Indonesia, and Australia as well as the Department of State in Washington. In 1978–79 he was a Congressional Fellow, and he spent the academic year of 1983–84 at the East-West Center as a diplomat-in-residence. From 1984 to 1987 he served as head of the Political Section at the U.S. embassy in Canberra. His areas of interest and specialization include Southeast Asia, Australia/New Zealand, and the Pacific Islands as well as Asia-Pacific regionalism.

ROBERT CATLEY is the member of the Australian House of Representatives for Adelaide. He was formerly a senior lecturer in Politics at the University of Adelaide and chairman of the Department of Politics at that university (1984–85). He holds a Ph.D. from The Australian National University in International Relations. Dr. Catley has served as consultant to the Australian minister for Immigration and Ethnic Affairs (1985–87) and to the minister for Community Services (1987), and was private secretary to the Australian minister for Defence (1987–88). He is a member of the Australian Labor Party's national External Affairs Committee. Dr. Catley's publications include *Australia and Asia: Towards New Horizons*, proceedings of the 1984 Australian Institute of International Affairs National Conference. He spent 1982 as a visiting professor at the University of Delaware.

WILLIAM H. CHAFE is professor of History at Duke University, and founder and director of the Duke University/University of North Carolina Women's Studies Research Center. A historian specializing in American social history, Dr. Chafe's most recent book is *The Unfinished Journey: America Since World War II*. Dr. Chafe's teaching and research interests include women's studies and the civil rights movement. He received his doctorate from Columbia University, and was formerly co-director of the Duke University Center for the Study of Civil Rights and Race Relations. Dr. Chafe is a member of Duke University's Executive Committee of the Academic Council, and has lectured extensively in the United States and abroad on American society.

HUGH N. COLLINS is professor of Government and Politics at Murdoch University. He has a doctorate from Harvard University. His teaching and research interests include international relations theory, Australian foreign and domestic policies, and U.S. foreign policy. Formerly head of the Department of Political Science at The Australian National University, Dr. Collins is the author of various writings on Australian political ideology and foreign affairs. He served as academic-in-residence at the Australian Department of Foreign Affairs in Canberra (1974–75).

S. HARVEY FRANKLIN is professor of Geography at Victoria University of Wellington. He holds a doctorate from the University of Birmingham, and he was a fellow of the Rockefeller Foundation in 1959, a Simon Fellow at the University of Manchester in 1966, and a Fulbright Fellow during the 1983–84 academic year. Professor Franklin's principal fields of interest have been rural and social affairs. His writings include *Rural Societies, New Zealand: Trade, Growth and Anxiety—New Zealand Beyond the Welfare State*, which was awarded the New Zealand Non-Fiction Book Award in 1979, and *Cul de Sac: The Question of New Zealand's Future*.

GARY R. HAWKE is professor of Economic History at Victoria University of Wellington, and was seconded from the beginning of 1987 to be director of the Institute of Policy Studies for three to five years. He has written on the economic history of both New Zealand and the United States, and is an editorial adviser to the *Australian Economic History Review*. He has been a member of the Economic Monitoring Group of the New Zealand Planning Council since 1980, a member the Council since 1985, and was appointed its chairperson in 1986. He received his doctorate at Balliol and Nuffield Colleges in Oxford, England, and has been a visiting fellow at Stanford University, All Souls' College, and The Australian National University.

TREVOR V. MATTHEWS is associate professor in the Department of Government and Public Administration at the University of Sydney, and in 1989–91 a visiting fellow in the Research School of the Social Sciences at The Australian National University. Dr. Matthews has written extensively on government, pressure groups, and the political process in Australia as well as on Australia-Japan relations. He is co-author of *The Japanese Connection: Australian Leaders' Attitudes towards Japan and the Australia-Japan Relationship*. From 1978–80 he lectured at the University of Tokyo on Australian Studies. Dr. Matthews also served as a senior adviser in the Australian government's Department of the Prime Minister and Cabinet (1976–77). He earned his bachelor's and doctorate degrees from the University of Sydney.

CHARLES E. MORRISON is a special assistant to the president of the East-West Center and coordinator of the International Relations Program. Concurrently he serves as a research associate at the Japan Center for International Exchange in Tokyo. Dr. Morrison received his Ph.D. from the School of Advanced International Studies (SAIS) at Johns Hopkins University specializing in Southeast Asian international relations. From 1972–80 he worked as a legislative assistant to Senator William V. Roth, Jr., and has also taught Southeast Asian politics and international relations at SAIS. Dr. Morrison has authored or edited numerous books, his most recent being *Presence and Perception: The Underpinnings of ASEAN-Japan Relations* (1986), and *Political and Security Cooperation: A New Dimension in ASEAN-Japan Relations?* (1987). He is the editor of the East-West Center's *Asia-Pacific Report* series.

JOCK PHILLIPS is chief historian in the New Zealand Department of Internal Affairs. He was formerly reader in History and director of the Stout Research Centre for the Study of New Zealand Society, History and Culture at Victoria University of Wellington. Educated at Victoria and Harvard (where he received his doctorate), he has lectured on American and New Zealand history at Victoria since 1973. Dr. Phillips has written articles on American intellectual history and New Zealand social and cultural history. He was editor of *Te Whenua, Te Iwi—The Land and the*

People, and wrote *A Man's Country?—The Pakeha Male Stereotype: A History*, and *The Sorrow and the Pride: New Zealand War Memorials*.

ROBERTO G. RABEL is lecturer in History at the University of Otago in Dunedin, New Zealand. Educated at Victoria University of Wellington and Duke University (where he received a Ph.D.), Dr. Rabel is the author of *Between East and West: Trieste, the United States and the Cold War, 1941–1954*. He has also published articles on New Zealand foreign policy in the Cold War period, with particular emphasis on the United States. He was appointed official historian of New Zealand's involvement in the Vietnam War in 1989 and is currently preparing a book covering the diplomatic, political, and social aspects of that involvement.

JOHN RAVENHILL is senior fellow in International Relations, Research School of Pacific Studies, The Australian National University. He holds a Ph.D. from the University of California, Berkeley, and has taught at the University of Virginia and the University of Sydney. He has written five books, including *Collective Clientelism: The Lomé Conventions and North-South Relations*, and *Africa in Economic Crisis*, both published by Columbia University Press. His most recent book is an edited collection, *No Longer an American Lake? Alliance Problems in the South Pacific*, co-published in the United States by the Institute of International Studies at the University of California, Berkeley, and in Sydney and London by Allen and Unwin. He is the current editor of *The Australian Journal of International Affairs*.

JAMES N. ROSENAU is professor of Political Science and International Relations and director of the Institute for Transnational Studies at the University of Southern California. He is also Senior Fellow at the Center for International and Strategic Affairs at the University of California, Los Angeles. Educated at the School of Advanced International Studies of Johns Hopkins University (M.A.) and Princeton University (Ph.D.), Dr. Rosenau has held positions at Ohio State University, Rutgers University, and Princeton. He was visiting Fulbright Lecturer at Jawaharlal Nehru University, Colegio de Mexico, and the University of Belgrade. Dr. Rosenau has written extensively on world politics, international relations, and American politics. His most recent book is *Turbulence in World Politics: A Theory of Change and Continuity* (Princeton University Press, 1990).

DONALD E. STOKES is dean of the Woodrow Wilson School of Public and International Affairs and professor of Politics and Public Affairs at Princeton University. He received his Ph.D. in political science at Yale, and taught at that university as well as at Oxford, Michigan, the University of the West Indies, and The Australian National University. While at Michigan, Dr. Stokes also held the posts of program director of the Institute for Social Research; chairman of the Department of Political Science; and dean of the Graduate School. An early interest in voting and representative government in the United States led to books and numerous articles on the electoral process. Dr. Stokes's recent research has dealt with science policy in the United States, Western Europe, and Japan.

WILLIAM WATTS is president of Potomac Associates, a public policy research and issues analysis organization, and lecturer at the Johns Hopkins School of Advanced International Studies. He also acts as a consultant to the Gallup Organization. Mr. Watts earned his master's degree in Russian Studies from Harvard University, and served as a Foreign Service Officer for the State Department in South Korea, the Soviet Union, as well as in Washington, D.C. From 1969 to 1970 he was staff secretary and senior staff member of the National Security Council in the White House. He is the author of numerous books and articles on U.S. foreign and domestic policies. His most recent writings have focused on U.S.-Asian relations.

Sponsoring Organizations

The East-West Center is a public, non-profit educational institution located in Honolulu, Hawaii, with an international board of governors and staff. It engages in cooperative study, training, and research on major issues related to population, resources, development, the environment, culture, communication, and international relations in Asia, the Pacific, and the United States. The Center was established in 1960 by the United States Congress, which provides principal funding. Support also comes from more than twenty Asian and Pacific governments, as well as private agencies and corporations.

The Australian Institute of International Affairs is an independent, non-profit body established in 1933. Its purpose is to stimulate interest in and understanding of international affairs among its members and the general public. It has branches throughout Australia, and a national headquarters in Canberra. Funding comes from membership dues as well as grants from public and private sources.

The Institute of Policy Studies was established by Victoria University of Wellington in 1983. Its purpose is to promote the study, research, and discussion of current issues of public policy, both foreign and domestic, important to New Zealand, and to strengthen links between academics, the public service, and the business community. It is funded by the university and by grants and other support from the public and private sectors.

www.ingramcontent.com/pod-product-compliance
Ingram Content Group UK Ltd.
Pitfield, Milton Keynes, MK11 3LW, UK
UKHW020244290926
15470UKWH00002B/723